NOT WRITTEN
IN STONE

ALSO BY KYLE WARD

History in the Making: An Absorbing Look at How American History Has Changed in the Telling over the Last 200 Years

History Lessons: How Textbooks from Around the World Portray U.S. History (with Dana Lindaman)

In the Shadow of Glory: The Thirteenth Minnesota in the Spanish-American and Philippine-American Wars, 1898–1899

The Pacific War and History Textbooks: How Historians, Educational Research and Government Policies Have Influenced What Students Have Read and Learned About This Event

NOT WRITTEN

Learning and Unlearning American History
Through 200 Years of Textbooks

IN STONE

Kyle Ward

THE NEW PRESS

NEW YORK
LONDON

Requests for permission to reproduce selections from this book should be mailed to:
Permissions Department, The New Press, 38 Greene Street, New York, NY 10013.

Published in the United States by The New Press, New York, 2010
Distributed by Perseus Distribution

LIBRARY OF CONGRESS CATALOGING-IN-PUBLICATION DATA

Ward, Kyle Roy, 1969–
Not written in stone : learning and unlearning American history
through 200 years of textbooks / Kyle Ward.
p. cm.
Includes bibliographical references and index.
ISBN 978-1-59558-144-0 (pbk. : alk. paper)
1. United States—History—Textbooks.   2. United States—History—Textbooks—
Evaluation.   3. United States—Historiography.   I. Title.
E175.85.W373   2010
973—dc22   2009052770

The New Press was established in 1990 as a not-for-profit alternative to the large, commercial
publishing houses currently dominating the book publishing industry. The New Press operates
in the public interest rather than for private gain, and is committed to publishing, in innovative
ways, works of educational, cultural, and community value that are often deemed insufficiently
profitable.

www.thenewpress.com

Composition by dix!
This book was set in Minister Light

Printed in the United States of America

2   4   6   8   10   9   7   5   3   1

To Annika and Grace—with all my love

CONTENTS

ACKNOWLEDGMENTS

I would like to thank the following people who helped me finish this book by checking my manuscript or doing research on historical topics: Jenni Roman, Jenna Summers, Prof. Michael Hersrud, Adam Stock, Dr. Randy Baker, Connor Burns, Jack Schnettler, and Christopher Schnettler. I also need to thank Marc Favreau of The New Press for his patience and willingness to work on this project.

And finally a very special thanks to Dr. David Vancil and Mr. Dennis Vetrovec at the Indiana State University Library, Special Collections Department. These two men and their department were invaluable to this research to say the least. The ISU Special Collections Department currently houses thirteen major collections, two of which hold international importance: the Eugene V. Debs Collection and the Cordell Collection of Dictionaries. Other collections have a more regional or national focus, such as the Cunningham, Floyd Family, and Walker Collections. The Cunningham Collection contains early or important works in American education on practice and theory, while the Floyd Family and Walker Collections contain more than 2,500 cataloged textbooks. While these collections cover all subject areas, the largest number of books are in the fields of history and English.

A NOTE FOR TEACHERS

This book tries to show that the portrayal of historical events in U.S. history textbooks has changed over the years, owing to the powerful influences—whether political, social, cultural, or economic—at work when a given book was produced. Professional students of history take this for granted, though such an insight may by no means seem obvious to most readers of history. There is a technical term for this approach to history, which is called historiography. Historiography refers to the process by which one examines historical writing and historical methods, all the while understanding that how the historian writes and researches is affected by personal bias, perspective, and interpretation.

The astute student will want to know how this can happen. How can a historical story, which many believe is supposed to be based on fact, be told differently to different generations of students? The answer is simple: it's all about historiography. History has to be understood by looking at it as if it had layers. Once students learn that history needs to be studied in layers they are introduced to the world of historical research and methodology, and after that, how they perceive history will never be the same again. Gone is the memorization of names and dates and in their place comes critical, engaged thinking.

What is meant by understanding history in layers? To begin with, it is vital to understand that actual historical events involve real people—with all of the complexities, differences, and differences of opinion we take for granted in the present. Next, they need to know that ever since the moment this historical event happened, there likely have been people researching, writing, and analyzing it—often for generations. The final layer that students need to discover is that every person involved in a historical event, from the original actors to the historians who have written about it, has been influenced by their own society/culture, no matter what era they wrote and did their research in. History itself, that is, has a history!

For example, a textbook author writing in the 1850s would have all but ignored the institution of slavery, mentioning it only in passing as a vital economic institution. In the 1890s, a textbook author very likely would have portrayed slavery in a positive light, invoking the mythology of the "happy slave"; such was the state of race relations in the late nineteenth century and the widespread acceptance of racial inferiority. Not until much later—in the wake of the civil rights movement—would textbook authors look critically at slavery, influenced by the movements for racial justice that swirled around mid-twentieth-century America. One historical "event," three authors, three very different stories.

The same is true for almost every other story found in history textbooks, and that is what this book is all about. By taking a close look at history textbooks from the 1800s to the 2000s, I have laid out in chronological order how U.S. history textbooks have examined the exact same stories across the generations, but often in very different ways.

Unfortunately, those of you who have come to this book looking for answers, or the "real facts" about what actually happened, will be greatly disappointed. Those who are familiar with my last two books (*History Lessons* and *History in the Making*) will notice that in this book I did not write brief introductions to each section, which in the past I used to help guide the reader to issues or topics that I found of importance. Rather than try to add another layer of my own personal biases, perspective, and interpretations onto these events (which one could make a strong argument that I have already done just by choosing or not choosing particular events for this book), this time I prefer to let this book act, as I call it, as a "gateway," meaning that it should lead students to do more research beyond just answering questions found at the end of each section. As someone who

teaches future history educators, I am constantly reminding my pre-
service teachers that the best way to get a student hooked on history is to
allow him or her to become a junior historian. Let students try to re-create
what happened, let them look at primary and secondary documents
related to this event, and finally let them try to understand what biases,
perspectives, and interpretations successive authors/historians had that
impacted their research.

Once students become active learners, they are given the opportunity
to actually engage in an intellectual dialogue with the people and events
they are studying. Teachers who are willing to leave their lecture notes will
find that chief among the many rewards of teaching in this manner is that
their students will have a better understanding of history and its impact on
their everyday lives.

One way of doing this is to have students begin to deconstruct their
history textbooks. To deconstruct a textbook a student needs to analyze
written words in order to understand any biases, flaws, or inconsistencies
found within the text. By doing so students will begin to see how the stories found in history textbooks has changed over the years, and they can
begin to formulate answers based on their research, on how and why these
stories have changed over time.

In order to aid junior historians in their quest for historical knowledge,
in each section I have added a number of questions. These questions ask
students to go beyond the texts included in this book, in search of historical context—whether from books in the library or from sources on the Internet. My hope is that this process will further encourage the comparison
of historical perspectives, and thus the process of critical inquiry.

This book does not give concrete answers about the past. Instead, it
should spur questions—and provide the basis for a great deal more research and discussion among students. The study of history should, in the
end, open students' eyes, make them question what they know, and create
a path to open dialogue among people and groups with differing views.
This, in my view, is the only true future for the study of the past.

A NOTE ON
U.S. HISTORY TEXTBOOKS

Over the past five years I have published three books that look at what students learn from high school U.S. history textbooks. Again and again, I have found that textbooks have played a crucial role in what students learn about history.

In this case, I have taken a broader sample of textbooks, including those that would have been read by elementary and middle school students. The reason for this is quite simple: for much of American history, most students never received more than what we would identify as an eighth-grade education. What's more, until the twentieth century, in many places, students of various ages were assembled together into the same classroom. This work is a broad sampling of the kind of texts American students would have encountered over the past two hundred years.

While it is common today for social studies teachers in the upper grades to dominate the teaching of history, up until the early to mid-1900s the teaching of history was often done by primary school teachers (typically in the fourth through sixth grades). Students who went on would once again receive some history courses, but for the vast majority of America's youth their knowledge of American history came from their grammar school teachers, or, more accurately, their grammar school history textbooks.

For many Colonial Americans the Protestant Bible was usually the "textbook" of choice for those who were doing the teaching. It wasn't until after the American colonists won their freedom from the British crown that Noah Webster began to demand, and in some instances create, new textbooks for students. He wanted to do this in order to get rid of the old British textbooks and to help create a national history that would unify the new nation. Later, reform-minded individuals such as Horace Mann helped bring more textbooks into the schools by demanding that students be given better materials and that these schools be funded through tax dollars, therefore guaranteeing a more even playing field for all students.

Although both of these men, and various other educational reformers, tried to get better textbooks into the hands of students, it wasn't until after the Civil War that the concept of a public school U.S. history textbook really started. Although there was a smattering of grammar-school U.S. history textbooks to be found before the 1870s, they were not uniform nor mass-produced, as we think of textbooks being today. In this book the pre–Civil War textbooks are really only represented by Noah Webster's *History of the United States* (1832), William D. Swan's *First Lessons in the History of the United States* (1856), and Benson John Lossing's *A Primary History of the United States* (1860). The rest of the textbooks were printed after the 1860s, when the mass-marketing of history textbooks became a more realistic and profitable endeavor.

This lack of U.S. history textbooks does not mean that there was a lack of history being taught in the schools. Rather, it reveals how few people overall attended school in those early years as well as how expensive curricular materials were. History was usually considered a staple subject in public schools throughout the United States—even if teachers may have only had a couple of textbooks to go around.

Over the next century one could find a number of publishing firms all printing their versions of elementary and junior high U.S. history textbooks.[1] Often, these textbooks were written with the young reader in mind, telling narrative historical stories. This is a far cry from today's visually appealing history textbooks, which resemble small historical encyclopedias—and tend to be rather bland to read.

NOT WRITTEN
IN STONE

PART I

Discovery and Colonization

I

Images of Native Americans

Native Americans have occupied a unique position in U.S. history textbooks. Starting with history textbooks published in the late 1700s, up until the early 1900s, Native Americans were usually seen as being brutal savages who blocked the progress of white settlers. In the late 1800s to the mid-1900s, textbooks began to refer to Native Americans as "noble savages"—uncivilized people who were part of nature. This story stayed the same until the civil rights movement, and the American Indian Movement in the 1970s, when Native Americans began to demand a more historically accurate version of their ancestors' history.

1832

Noah Webster, *History of the United States: To Which is Prefixed a Brief Historical Account of our* [English] *Ancestors, from the dispersal at Babel, to their Migration to America, and of the Conquest of South America by the Spaniards*

Habitations and Furniture

The dwellings of the savages were huts called wigwams, made with poles fixed in the ground, bent together, fastened at the top, and covered with mats of bulrushes. Their fire was in the middle of the hut, and an opening was left at the top for the smoke to escape. Their beds were mats or skins spread on boards a little raised, for cooking they used pots made of clay; their dishes and spoons were of wood, hollowed and made very smooth. Pails were formed of birch bark, made square, and furnished with a handle. Baskets were made of the same material, or of rushes, bents, husks of the maize, silk grass, or wild hemp, curiously wrought and ornamented.

Dress

The natives of the northern parts of America had no clothing, when the English first came among them, except the skins of wild beasts, and a few mantles made of feathers curiously interwoven. But all the natives of this country were very fond of beads and trinkets, for ornaments; fasten them to their arms, legs, nose and ears. When the Europeans began to trade with them, they exchanged their skins for blankets, and other cloths, and these are their principal dress to this day: all savage nations are very fond of feathers.

Virtues and Vices

The good and bad qualities of Indians are few, or confined to a few objects. In general, a savage is governed by his passions, without much restraint from the authority of his chiefs. He is remarkably hospitable to strangers, offering them the best accommodations he has, and always serving them first. He never forgets a favor or an injury; but will make a grateful return for a favor, and revenge an injury whenever an opportunity offers, as long as he lives; and the remembrance is hereditary for the child and grandchild have the same passions, and will repay a kindness, or revenge wrong done to their ancestor.

Government and Religion

The tribes of Indians were under a government somewhat like a monarchy, with a mixture of aristocracy. Their chiefs, called sagamores, sachems, or cazekes, possessed the powers of government; but they usually consulted the old men of the tribe, on all important questions.

Their religion was idolatry, for they worshiped the sun, the moon, the earth, fire, images and the like. They had an idea of the Supreme Being, whom they called the Great Spirit; and they believed in an evil spirit. They had priests, called powwows, who pretended to arts of conjuration, and who acted as their physicians.[1]

1860

Benson J. Lossing, *A Primary History of the United States*

The Indians were tall and straight. They had straight black hair, fine teeth, and black eyes. They were seldom sick, because they had plenty of exercise and ate simple food. They lived in a sort of huts or tents, made of poles covered with the bark of trees or the skins of wild beasts. These were called wigwams.

The men went to war, hunted and fished; and the women planted corn and other things, and did all the hard work. They did not have good tools to work with, for these were made of stones, shells, and bones. Their food was the flesh of the deer, buffalo, and bear, roasted or boiled, with beans, peas, potatoes, and melons.

The Indians had money, but it was not like ours. It was made of shells in the shape of long beads which they strung on threads or fastened upon belts. So many of these pieces were worth a penny, and so many more were worth a shilling or a dollar. This money they called wampum.

The Indians had no schools, and the little children never had pleasant picture books to read. Their mothers taught them to make wampum, mats, skin and feather-clothing, and shell and bone ornaments. But I dare say they did not work much, but played nearly all day in the woods and by the pleasant brooks. They went to bed when the birds did, at sunset, and were up before the sun, and so they kept their eyes bright.

The Indian men loved to fight, for they sometimes felt like tigers. Forty or more of one nation would go and fight those of another nation; and sometimes there would be hundreds on both sides. They fought with bows and arrows, war clubs, scalping-knives, and tomahawks.

When the men were tired of fighting, they would sometimes become good friends, as we white people do. Then they would build a great fire in the woods, and the head men of both nations would meet around it and smoke a pipe which was handed from one to the other. This was called a calumet, or pipe of peace.

The Indian men played ball, fired at the mark, danced, leaped, played games, and had other amusements, but they would never let the women join them. They were not at all polite to the women. I am sure that no right-minded boy, when he gets to be a man, will let his mother, or sister, or wife, do all the hard work, while he hunts, or fishes, or plays; and then not let them have any of the fun.

The Indians did not always bury their dead in the ground. When they did, they wrapped them in skins, and want to use them in the spirit land. They often folded the body in skins, and laid it upon a high scaffold, where wild beasts could not get at it.

The Indians had no churches, yet they believed in God, prayed to Him, and worshiped Him. They called Him the Good Spirit; and they believed in an Evil Spirit. Instead of churches and meeting-houses, they had the sky for a roof; and the wind and the thunder, the singing of birds, and the roar of the storm, was their music. Then they would look up to the sun, the moon, and the stars, and believe that they saw God, for they knew of nothing greater. The Indians knew nothing of the Bible, and the religion of Jesus. They all had one belief, never quarreled about it, and were happy.

The Indians were governed by sachems, and chiefs. The sachems were general rulers; the chiefs were the commanders of the Indian armies. Only wise men were made sachems, and only brave men were made chiefs. These could not govern nor lead if they were not wise and brave.

Such, my young friend, were the copper-colored people who lived in this country hundreds of years ago, and some of whom live here yet. Unless you live beyond the Mississippi river, you seldom see any of them now. They are nearly all beyond that river, and are becoming fewer every year.

The time will come when there will not be an Indian on the earth. You may live to see that time, because they are passing rapidly away. The white man, from the beginning, has used the poor Indians badly. He has cheated and oppressed them, given them rum to take away their senses, and with swords and guns has driven them far into the wilderness.

God, in his wise providence, has permitted the white man to take the Indian's land away from him. The Indian would not cut down the trees and raise grain, except here and there a little patch; but the white man, as the Bible says, has made "the wilderness to blossom as the rose."[2]

1 8 8 5

Thomas Wentworth Higginson, *Young Folks' History of the United States*

The Indians had great courage, self-control, and patience. They were grave and dignified in their manners, on important occasions, in their councils they were courteous to one another, and discussed all important questions at great length. They were often kind and generous, and sometimes even forgiving; but they generally thought that sternness was a virtue, and forgiveness a weakness. They were especially cruel to captives, putting them to death with all manner of tortures, in which women took an active part. It was the custom among them for women to do most of the hard work, in order that the bodies of the men might be kept supple and active for the pursuits of the chase and war.

When employed on these pursuits, the Indian men seemed incapable of fatigue; but in the camp, or in traveling, the women carried the burdens, and, when a hunter had carried a slain deer on his shoulders for a long distance, he would throw it down within sight of the village, that his squaw might go and bring it in.

Most of the Indian tribes lived in a state of constant warfare with one another. When there was a quarrel between tribes, and war seemed ready to break out, strange ceremonies were used. Some leading chief would paint his body black from head to foot, and would hide himself in the woods or in a cavern. There he would fast and pray, and call upon the Great Spirit; and would observe his dreams, to see if they promised good or evil. If he dreamed of a great war-eagle hovering before him, it was a sign of triumph.

After a time he would come forth from the woods and return among his people. Then he would address them, summon them to war, and tell them that the Great Spirit was on their side. Then he would bid the warriors to a feast at his wigwam. There they would find him no longer painted in black, but in bright and gaudy colors, called "war-paint." The guests would be also dressed in paint and feathers, and would seat themselves in a circle. Then wooden trenchers containing the flesh of dogs would be placed before them; while the chief would sit smoking his pipe, and would not eat anything.

After the feast, the war-dance would follow, perhaps at night, amid the blaze of fires and lighted pine-knots. A painted post would be driven into the ground, and the crowd would form a wide circle round it. The war-chief would leap into the open space, brandishing his hatchet, and would chant his own deeds and those of his fathers, acting out all that he described, and striking at the post as if it were an enemy. Warrior after warrior would follow, till at last the whole band would be dancing, shouting, and brandishing their weapons, striking and stabbing at the air, and filling the forest with their yells.

Much of the night would pass in this way. In the morning the warriors would leave the camp in single file, still decorated with paint and feathers and ornaments; and, as they entered the woods, the chief would fire his gun, and each in turn would do the same.

Then they would halt near the village, would take off their ornaments and their finery, and would give all these things to the women, who had followed them for this purpose. Then the warriors would go silently and stealthily through the forest to the appointed place of attack. Much of their skill consisted in these silent approaches, and in surprises and stratagems, and long and patient watchings. They attached no shame to killing an unarmed enemy, or to private deceit and treachery, though to their public treaties they were always faithful. They were desperately brave, and yet they saw no disgrace in running away when there was no chance of success. Their weapons were at first, the bow and arrow, and a sort of hatchet called a "tomahawk"; and they had shields of bison-hide, and sometimes breastplates of twigs interwoven with cord. Afterwards they learned the use of fire-arms from the whites, and became skilful with these weapons, losing much of their skill with the bow and arrow. Some tribes built strong forts, with timber walls, palisades, banks, and ditches. In these forts they had magazines of stones to hurl down upon those who attacked them; and there were gutters by which to pour down streams of water, should the fort be set on fire.

When first visited by Europeans, the Indians along the coast were already diminishing in number, through war and pestilence; and they have diminished ever since, in the older parts of the country, till many tribes have wholly disappeared. At first they were disposed to be friendly with the white men; but quarrels soon arose, each side being partly to blame. The savages often burned villages, carried away captives, and laid whole regions waste. In return, their villages and forts were destroyed, and their tribes were driven westward, or reduced to a mere handful. Some of these wars will be described farther on in this history; and to this day some of the western settlements of the United States live in constant fear of attack from Indians. But the wilder tribes are passing away; and in another century there will hardly be a roving Indian within the limits of the United States. Only those tribes will survive which have adopted, in part, the habits of civilization.

Of the Indians now within the limits of the United States, more than 150,000 are wholly or partly civilized. About half of these live on what are called "reservations," in the Indian Territory; while the rest are scattered through various Territories and States. Many of those in the Indian Territory, especially the Cherokees, Choctaws, and Creeks, are quite prosperous, having good farms, herds of cattle, and graded schools. Many boys and girls from the wilder tribes are being educated in schools at Hampton, Va., and Carlisle, Pa.[3]

1906

Oscar Gerson, *History Primer*

Troubles with the Indians

The Indians who lived on this land were at first friendly with the white people. But they became angry when they found the white men were driving them from their hunting grounds. Before very long there were bloody wars between the Indians and the whites.

What the Indians Looked Like. How they Dressed

The Indians were large and strong. They had copper-colored skin and straight, black hair. The women wore their hair long. The men shaved their heads but left a little tuft on top. They called this the scalp lock. Their clothes were made of the skins of deer and other animals. They wore a kind of shoe made of buckskin. They called them moccasins. They were good for hunting. The Indians could sneak through the woods very quietly in them. In winter the Indians fastened broad, flat snow shoes on their feet. With these shoes they could walk upon the snow without sinking in too deep.

Indian Warfare

The Indians were good fighters. They painted their bodies and faces so as to make themselves look as fierce as possible. When they killed a man in battle they tore off his scalp. The Indian who had taken the largest number of scalps was thought to be the greatest warrior.

The Indians were brave but cruel. They thought men should be able to stand great pain without crying out. When they captured an enemy they would cut or burn him, or torture him in other cruel ways. If he cried out they would make fun of him and call him a "woman" or "squaw."

How the Indians Lived

The Indians got most of their food by hunting and fishing. Some of the tribes planted and raised corn. They also grew tobacco. The Indians taught the white men how to raise corn. They also taught them to smoke tobacco.

The Indian men did the hunting and fighting, but the farming and all the other hard work was done by the women. When all Indian villages moved to another place, it was the women who took down the wigwams and carried them and all their other goods to the new camping ground. The women then set up the wigwams again while the men sat by idly watching them. This seemed strange to the white men who would have been ashamed to allow women to do this kind of work.[4]

1913

Wilbur F. Gordy, *Stories of Early American History*

The Indian Brave and the Squaw

You may sometimes hear it said that the squaw had to do all the work. People who say this believe that the Indian brave was lazy, and wished to make a slave of his wife.

But this is not true, for the man had his own work just as the woman had hers. Hunting and fishing were his share; and any tribe whose men did not keep themselves trained for fighting and on the watch for foes would soon have been killed or made slaves of by some other tribe.

The Indian brave was quite willing to make arrows, bows, canoes, and other tools which he might need. But he felt too proud to do what he thought was a squaw's work. The squaw kept busy about the home. She cooked the food and made the clothing. She tended the patches of corn, melons, beans, squashes, and pumpkins. In doing this she scratched the ground with simple tools like pointed sticks, or stone spades, or hoes. She also gathered wood, made fires, and, set up the wigwam.

But the squaw's first duty was to care for the children. She had a queer-looking cradle, or cradleboard, for her little papoose; as she called her child, and used it till the baby was two years old or so.

The cradle was some two feet long, and nearly a foot wide. It was covered with skins, the outer one forming a pocket which was lined with grass and moss, making a soft little nest where the baby snuggled. She carried it on her back when walking. But when at work she stood it against a bush or rock or hung it on a low bough. Perhaps you have heard your mother sing to the baby:

> "Rock-a-bye baby upon the tree-top,
> When the wind blows, the cradle will rock;
> When the bough breaks, the cradle will fall
> Down down comes rock-a-bye baby and all."

This song came from the Indian mother's habit of hanging the cradle on a tree. The Indian boy did not go to a school like yours. His lessons were learned out of doors, and his books were the woods and the lakes and the running streams about him. By watching, and listening, and trying, he learned to swim like a fish, to dive like a beaver, to climb trees like a squirrel, and to run like a deer.

As soon as he could hold a bow and arrow, he was taught to shoot at a mark and to throw the tomahawk. He had also to learn how to set traps for wild animals and how to hunt them. He learned to make the calls of wild birds and beasts. For if he could howl like a wolf, quack like a duck, and gobble like a turkey, he could get nearer his game when on the hunt.

He had to learn how to track his enemies and how to conceal his own tracks when he wished to get away from his enemies. He had to become a brave, strong warrior, and be able to kill his foe and prevent his foe from killing him.

For, after all, the most important part of his work when he grew up was to fight the enemies of his tribe. If he did not make war upon them, they would think he was weak and would attack him. So whether he wished or not, he had to fight. Most boys like to "play Indian" and surprise those who they pretend are enemies. The real Indians were very fond of this kind of fighting by ambush. They would hide in the woods and then suddenly rush out upon their foes as they passed or shoot them down.

They learned to keep so perfectly still and so completely out of sight behind the trees or in the bushes and tall grass that the enemy would not suspect there was anybody near. Thus many of the enemy would be killed or captured while they themselves lost very few men.

On returning home, the war party would often bring back captives. Some of these they might adopt into their own tribe, for often their numbers became much thinned by war. But sometimes the captives were tortured and put to death. Does it not seem strange that any one could enjoy seeing people suffer?

The Indian's way of traveling from place to place was very simple. When he was looking for fresh hunting-grounds or new streams or lakes for fishing, or when he was with a war party, as a rule he went on foot. Sometimes he took a forest path or trail, but it was much easier to travel by water. Then he found his light bark canoe very useful. Two men could easily carry it, and even one could carry it alone over his shoulder.

The Indians and the Whites

Before the white men came, most Indians lived very simple lives as hunters, fishermen, and warriors. They had dogs, but there were no native animals which they could tame to give them milk like our cows, or to draw their loads like our oxen and mules, or to carry them like our horses.

The Indians were at first very much afraid of horses, but afterward used them with much skill in making war upon other tribes and upon the white man. Before the white man came, the Indian had never seen a sword, a gun, an iron axe, nor a knife made of metal. But he soon learned how to use all these. They made life much easier for him. For a wooden bow, a stone tomahawk or hatchet, or an arrow tipped with bone or stone killed fewer animals and got him much less food than guns and sharp iron tools.

You can see, then, that the coming of the white man greatly changed the red man's life. But the Indian also changed the life of the white man. For when the early settler went out into the woods to live, he found it best to live much as the Indians did.

He had to learn how to track his foe, and how to conceal his own trail through the forest. He even dressed like the Indian. He lived in simple houses like the "long houses" of the Iroquois, only smaller. He ate such food as the Indians were likely to find in the forest, and like them, he many times suffered for want of food.

Let us not forget, too, that more than once when food was scarce for all, the hungry settlers were kept from starving by the food which friendly Indians shared with them.[5]

1930

William Backus Guitteau, *Our United States: A History for Upper Grammar Grades and Junior High School*

The Natives of North America

When Columbus discovered the Bahama Islands, he also discovered a race of men unknown to the world before his time. Later explorers found the Indians, as Columbus named the natives, inhabiting the continent and islands of both North and South America. The Indians were usually tall in stature; they had high cheek bones, small, deep set eyes, and long

black hair; their skin was brown or copper colored, so that they are sometimes incorrectly called "Red Men." They did not lead a nomadic life, but
occupied fairly definite areas; such migrations as occurred were usually
due to the pressure of stronger tribes, or to the desire to find better hunting grounds. When Columbus first landed, about five hundred thousand
Indians were living on the North American continent, one half of whom
dwelt east of the Mississippi River.

Origin of the Indian Race

Many attempts have been made to explain how a race separate and
distinct from any other in the world came to be found in America. Because extensive mounds and earthworks were found in the Mississippi
and Ohio River valleys, it was once thought that an earlier people called
the "Mound Builders" used to inhabit the continent. These mounds were
sometimes raised embankments, sometimes square or circular inclosures
[sic], and sometimes earthwork made to resemble an animal that was held
in special veneration. We know today that the Mound Builders were not a
distinct race of people, but were the ancestors of the Indians themselves.
At some very early period, North America was probably peopled from
Asia, with which our continent was once connected. So our Indians may
be descended from men whose earlier home was in Asia.

The Indians of Northeastern America

There were three great families of Indians in the region between the
Mississippi River and the Atlantic Ocean. First, the Algonquin family,
which occupied most of the country north of Kentucky including all of
New England and a large part of Canada. Second, the Iroquois, who lived
south and east of lakes Erie and Ontario, in the present states of New
York, Pennsylvania, and northern Ohio. Third, the Southern or Muskogee
Indians, between the Tennessee River and the Gulf of Mexico.

Each of these large groups or families of Indians spoke a common language; each family included numerous tribes, and the tribes were in turn
divided into separate clans. The basis of clan unity was kinship, or descent
from the same female ancestor. Each clan had its totem, usually some animal by whose name it was known, as Wolf, Bear, Fox, or Turtle. Some

clans believed that they were descended from this totem, which thus became an object of worship. The clan had two kinds of leaders, a peace ruler or sachem elected by its members, and war chiefs who were chosen because of their individual prowess. There was also a council which included all the adult members of the clan, both men and women. In the same way, the tribe was governed by a tribal council, composed of all the sachems and chiefs within the clan; while some tribes had a head chief, usually one of the sachems who had shown special gifts of leadership.

Indian Warfare

Every Indian boy was trained to become a warrior, for there was almost constant fighting among the different tribes. The child's toys were miniature weapons, and the Indian youth soon became skilled in the use of bow and arrow, and in the hurling of the short spear or javelin. The hatchet or tomahawk was another favorite weapon, being especially useful in the hand-to-hand fighting of forest warfare. Among all the tribes, the military virtues of bravery, strength, and skill were held in the highest esteem; to die in battle was glorious, while the warrior who showed fear was the object of universal contempt. Among many tribes, the warrior's reputation rested upon the number of deeds of special prowess which stood to his credit. The acts which entitled him to distinction were killing and scalping an enemy, being the first to touch an enemy in combat, rescuing a wounded companion, and stealing a horse from the enemy's camp.

The Indians usually aimed to surprise their foe; they often made their attacks in the dead of night, for to take one's enemy at a disadvantage was regarded as the most skillful kind of campaigning. Their warfare was cruel almost beyond belief; the warrior scalped his dead foe, and wore the scalp as a trophy and proof of his prowess; the more scalps he could show at his belt, the greater his skill as a warrior. Captives were tortured with every cruelty that human ingenuity could devise in the hope that they would display some sign of fear. In the end they were usually killed with the tomahawk or burned at the stake, although sometimes prisoners were enslaved, or adopted as members of the tribe.

Indian Intellect and Character

Although a simple and unpractical race, the Indian was by no means lacking in intellect. He used a language of his own, filled with glowing phrases and figures of speech; and in simple, unstudied eloquence, he sometimes equaled the greatest orators of any race. The Indians of the plains used a series of gestures which formed an intelligible sign language. The more advanced tribes were able to express their ideas by means of pictures, sometimes painted on skins, sometimes carved on the rocks, or woven in wampum. The Indian was quick to learn the use of firearms, and became an expert marksman. He had a remarkable genius for military tactics and strategy; he was brave in battle, but he stalked his enemy like wild game, and never fought in the open if he could attack from ambush. A cruel and vindictive foe, the Indian was also a generous and hospitable friend. He had a rude sense of honor, and usually kept faith when fairly dealt with. As a scout he was loyal to a trust in the face of hardship or death itself. Washington was guided through the wilderness to Fort Duquesne by a nameless Indian; while Braddock's army was routed because he would not listen to the advice of his native scouts.

The Indians and the White Settlers

The white men who first came in contact with the Indians were treated with the utmost reverence. But when the natives learned that they could expect only harsh treatment in return, they became the foes of the settlers. The lands occupied by the different tribes were owned as common property, and the chiefs readily gave up the tribal hunting grounds in exchange for a few trinkets. They thought that the colonists would occupy the land for a short time, after which it would be given back to them. When it was seen that the hunting grounds were being permanently held, the inevitable struggle began. In this conflict, the white men won because they were the stronger race, and because the different tribes were constantly fighting among themselves. But in many cases, friendly Indians saved the settlements from attack, and brought supplies of corn to the starving settlers.[6]

1946

George Earl Freeland and James Truslow Adams, *America's Progress in Civilization*

Women in nearly all the North American tribes had to obey the wishes of their husbands. However, they had some specific rights. They were in complete control of household matters. In some tribes they were allowed to own property except weapons and horses, which had been brought to America by the Spaniards. They had charge of the children, until these became full members of the tribe. In some Eastern tribes the women had a right to speak in council. Iroquois women had more power than those of other groups. For example, the right of the women of the Iroquois to adopt a captive, and thus save his life, was commonly recognized.

Everywhere, the Indian woman did the heaviest work. Dangerous undertakings fell to the lot of the man. He did most of the hunting and fishing. The women skinned the game, made the pemmican, kept camp, prepared the food, and carried heavy burdens when on the march. Polygamy (several wives to one husband) was practiced among most of the tribes.

The most warlike Indians were those of the plains and those east of the Mississippi. The Indians of California and the Pueblos of the Southwest were the least warlike. Among the Indians of the plains and those of the Eastern forests, bravery in war and deeds of heroism were very important.

The Indian could either go to war or stay at home as he wished. The authority of the leader rested upon the wish of his followers to obey. This explains why it was often so difficult for the English, who had aroused the Indians to fight against the colonists during the War for Independence, to count upon their Indians. In the middle of a battle, the Indians might leave. Some superstition might cause them to think it best to withdraw and to fight another day.

If we remember that absolute authority by the chief was unknown, we shall have a better understanding of Indian life everywhere. The American Indian was a very independent person. Sometimes a strong chief gained a large following, but his followers obeyed him only as long as they wished, and he could not pass his leadership on to his sons.

The Indian had a great deal of free time. Both the men and the women seemed to enjoy life. They had athletic contests, played games, danced, held feasts, told stories, and some of them were great orators. Ball-playing was one of the chief delights. This game was especially prominent among the tribes east of the Mississippi and along the Pacific Coast. In the usual games, the ball was handled with netted sticks somewhat like tennis rackets. From this game arose the lacrosse and racquet of Canada and Louisiana. Many other athletic games were known to them. Foot-racing was common among the farming tribes, as was horse racing on the plains. Hiding games, dice games, and gambling were common everywhere.

Indian women also had their games. Among the women of the plains, "shinny" and football were popular. Singing and dancing were often engaged in by the players. Social dances of many kinds followed feasting.

Most of the Indians were very religious. They thought that every animal, plant, tree, or stone, had a spirit. This simple type of religion is called animism. It is common among primitive peoples throughout the world. Some of the spirits were thought to be more powerful than others. To some Indians the sun was all-powerful. Some worshipped fire; others, water. To the Plains Indians, the buffalo and cottonwood were especially powerful. By some groups the spirit of the eagle was worshipped; to others the rattlesnake was sacred; to the farming Indians corn and tobacco had magical powers. Among the California Indians the coyote played an important part. To many of the Indians the number "four" (the four directions, north, south, east, west) was highly important.

The Indian's Bad Qualities

The Eastern Indian's thoughtlessness for the future led the white man to scorn every kind of Indian planning. The latter had no idea of producing an abundance of anything for what the white man called "a rainy day." He could not be shown that he should save. Although many white people suffer from this trait, the most thoughtless white man was probably as careful as the most thrifty Indian in looking out for the future. The Indian did grow a few crops, especially corn. Dried meat prepared by him was also an important food. In both cases, he did this work because he enjoyed eating these things rather than from any thought for the future. What especially pained the white man was that the Indian felt his shiftless traits to be noble. He disliked the white man for his thrift even more than the white man despised the Indian for his apparent thoughtlessness and laziness.

As to the Indian's taste for liquor, it must be admitted that this curse was brought to him by the white man. In those days, it was a matter of pride among the whites who drank heavily not to get drunk. One who could drink a great deal of liquor without showing its effect upon him was regarded in some quarters as being superior. But the biggest, strongest, and most capable Indians were overcome by only small amounts of alcohol.

Neither could the white man understand the Indian's taste for liquor. The Indian knew just what it would do to him; yet he often went about preparing to get drunk. A band of Indians in possession of liquor often required certain of their number to keep sober. Those who were going to drink would put their weapons in charge of those who were to remain sober. Frequently upon such occasions, the fights that followed resulted in many persons being injured or killed. The drunken Indians yelled and jumped about and made weird motions until they were overcome. Any one who tried to interfere with them might be killed. Some of the greatest Indian massacres resulted from the fact that the red men discovered stores of liquor kept by the white men. White traders always carried liquor with them, and it finally became the custom for Indians not to trade with any white man who would not bring them whiskey.

The cruelty of the Indian was a most serious matter to the colonists and frontiersmen. It became a greater problem because here again the Indian regarded his cruelty as a virtue. You can understand the Indian's cruelty if you recall what was said of the education of Indian boys. They were taught that it was disgraceful to show any signs of pain when undergoing torture or hardship. This training resulted in making the Indian indifferent not only to his own feelings but to the feelings of others. It affected his treatment of his domestic animals to which he was most cruel. One Northern explorer, Stefansson, noted this in the Eskimo's treatment of his dogs. The Eskimo mistreated the dogs even though they made it possible for him to live.

Theodore Roosevelt noted this Indian cruelty to animals. He reported the children taking great delight in torturing little animals. He stated that he was sickened by the Indian's love of cruelty for cruelty's sake. He felt that children, trained in the cruel practices which he had observed, could only grow into adults who would find the keenest pleasure in causing pain in its worst physical forms to others. When we think how the Indians in their wartime raids must have murdered and mistreated white women and children, we can more easily understand the saying of the pioneers, "The only good Indian is the dead Indian."[7]

1977

JoAnne Buggey, *America! America!*

The rest of the culture areas in North America are descended from the Eastern Archaic tradition. These are the peoples of the Great Plains, the Southeast, and the Eastern Woodlands. They inhabited the area from the Rocky Mountains east to the Atlantic Ocean.

In the Southeast culture area farming became very important. Among the tribes in this area were the Cherokees, the Creeks, the Seminoles, the Choctaws, and the Chickasaws. These tribes depended heavily on farming, built permanent homes, and lived in villages. The Creeks had towns with open squares in the center. The Cherokees had large farms. Because their culture was most like that of Europeans, the white settlers who later came to America called these tribes "The Five Civilized Tribes." These southeastern tribes had loose governments that usually acted only in case of an outside attack.

The Indians of the Eastern Woodlands included the Massachusetts, the Delawares, the Mohawk, Seneca, Oneida, Cayuga, Onondaga, Hurons, Sauk, and Fox. Some Eastern Woodland tribes lived in wigwams. These were usually shaped like a dome. They were made of frames of long poles covered with animal hides and bark from birch trees. In the north, the Iroquois built larger buildings called "longhouses." Sometimes 10 or more families would live in one longhouse.

There was usually enough food, but the Woodland Indians had to work hard. After the fields had been cleared, the women usually took care of the crops, gathered firewood, cooked, skinned animals and made clothing, built the houses, and took care of the children. The men would clear the land for planting, hunt, fish, and fight in local wars. They hunted and fished mostly in the fall and winter after the crops were harvested. Often they had a great deal of free time the rest of the year. Much of this time was spent sitting in groups, talking, and sometimes smoking tobacco in pipes.

Boys and girls both helped the women and played. When they were about twelve years old, the boys would begin to help with tool making and go hunting with the men. Both girls and boys went through special ceremonies at about this age. Then they were considered adults.[8]

1991

Clarence L. Ver Steeg and Carol Ann Skinner, *Exploring America's Heritage*

Like a family today, an Indian family of long ago was made up of parents and children living together in the same home. Often other relatives, such as grandparents, also lived in the family home. Uncles, aunts, and cousins lived with or near their relatives. So close were the family bonds in some groups that the same word was used for "father" and "uncle."

Families worked together to do everything that was needed for the life of the family, the group, and the tribe. Many different tasks had to be done to provide food, clothing, shelter, and care for everyone.

In Indian groups, everyone had to work to meet the group's needs. Many Indian groups divided the work among family members. Men usually did the hunting and sometimes the farming. They made the tools needed for both tasks. In some Indian families, men also wove cloth for clothing and made pottery and baskets for food gathering. Indian men were also the warriors.

Women often built and cared for the homes. They also farmed, gathered wild plants, and prepared foods. They made baskets, bowls, pots, clothing, and other household goods. Women cared for the children. With the help of medicine men and women, or shamans, women also cared for the sick.

Groups of families often did tasks for the whole village. One group of families might take care of a community garden. Another group of families might prepare a feast for the whole tribe. In these ways, the people sometimes viewed the whole village as part of their family.

Learning might be different for boys and girls in Indian groups because, as you have read, adult work was divided up between the men and women in the family. For the most part, boys were taught what men had to know for adult life. Girls learned what women had to know.

Like children all over the world, Indian children learned from their families. The children learned the skills that would help them become responsible adults. They learned how to do the work their parents did to help the family survive. They learned about an adult's duties to the family, the village, and the tribe.

In almost every group, children learned without school buildings, books, or hired teachers. Parents, grandparents, and elders were the teachers. The world was the classroom. The subjects were how to survive on the land and how to live as a respected member of the tribe. A third likeness among Indian groups was in their beliefs about nature, humans, and gods. Most Indians, in all parts of the Americas, had a deep respect for nature. Their respect was so strong that they did not believe people could own land. They felt that people—like air, land, and water—were part of nature. The Indians felt that everyone must use the gifts of nature with care and honor.

Most Indian groups believed in nature spirits. Each animal, plant, and tree had a living spirit, or god. Gods also controlled soil, wind, rain, and fire—all of the earth and all of the sky. Some groups believed in one spirit that ruled over all of these nature gods. This spirit was often seen as a powerful creator who had made the world, all the animals and plants, and the people.[9]

DISCUSSION QUESTIONS

1. Give examples of how some of these textbooks described Native Americans in negative ways. What impact do you think these stories would have had on students reading these textbooks during the specific times they were published and used in schools across America?
2. Describe what was happening in the United States between the 1830s and the 1890s and describe the impact that U.S.–Native American relations may have played in how textbooks discussed Native Americans.
3. Many of these textbook selections focus on the bravery, savagery, and great endurance of the Native American men. Explain why a textbook author during that particular time would have been comfortable writing about Native Americans this way.
4. Analyze the role of Native American women in these textbook selections. Do you feel that the authors believed that Native American

men held a positive or negative view of their female counterparts? Compare the roles of white women during these periods to those perceived roles of Native American women. Do you find a lot of similarities or differences?

5. Many of the authors of these textbooks spend time discussing Native American religious beliefs. Research the religious beliefs of some specific tribes mentioned and discuss how close these textbooks were to describing their true belief system.

6. There is a shift in the story of Native Americans around the turn of the twentieth century in which they went from being cruel savages to noble savages. Research what was happening during this period that might explain why there was a shift in the perception of these people.

7. The 1860 textbook calmly discusses the extermination of Native Americans. According to the author of this textbook, what was the opinion of the Christian Bible regarding this genocide? Explain why you think this was an acceptable story for many textbook authors.

8. These textbook selections often compared the life of a Native American boy or girl to that of the white students who were reading these textbooks. Explain why you think authors/publishers added this part of the story to their textbook. Were the Native American children usually compared in a positive or negative light? Explain.

9. Research the American Indian Movement (AIM) and explain what, if any, impact this organization and its issues may have had on history textbooks' coverage of Native Americans.

It is interesting to note that throughout much of the nineteenth century white students could have been reading these textbooks with Native Americans living within very close proximity to them.

2

Columbus's First Voyage

"In 1492 Columbus sailed the ocean blue." Even though this easily remembered little rhyme tells elementary students what Columbus did, it does not tell students why he made the voyage. Why did some people help him out when others refused to do so? Here is the classic case of a seemingly ironclad story that is shot through with myths—and open to question by students. This section reveals that textbooks have offered various reasons for Columbus's voyage, reasons that are viewed as highly debatable by most historians.

It is also interesting to note that the celebration of Columbus Day is not as old as we might think. The day was first recognized in 1892, when President Benjamin Harrison wanted to commemorate the four hundredth anniversary of Columbus's landing in the New World. After 1892, Italian Americans continued to push to make this a national holiday, yet it was not made official until 1971, under President Richard Nixon.

1832

Noah Webster, *History of the United States: To Which is Prefixed a Brief Historical Account of our [English] Ancestors, from the dispersal at Babel, to their Migration to America, and of the Conquest of South America by the Spaniards of Columbus*

Christopher Columbus, the first European who discovered the western continent, was a native of Genoa, and was bred to navigation. By his knowledge of the form of the earth, and of geography and astronomy, and by some pieces of carved wood and a canoe, driven on shore by westerly winds, he was led to believe that there must be a continent on the west of the Atlantic to balance the vast tract of land on the east; and he imagined that by sailing westward, he might find a shorter course to China and the East Indies, than by traveling eastward. He therefore applied to the government of Genoa for assistance to enable him to undertake a voyage of discovery. He did not succeed. He then applied to Portugal, but with no better success. He was thought, as men of genius are often thought, a visionary projector.

Columbus's Application to Spain

Columbus then made application to Ferdinand, king of Spain, for ships and men to proceed on a voyage westward; but for some years, he did not obtain his request. Finally, by the influence of the queen, Isabella, he obtained three ships and ninety men. He also obtained a commission, dated April 30, 1492, constituting him admiral, viceroy, and governor, of all the isles and countries which he should discover and subdue, with full powers civil and criminal. With this authority, he sailed from Palos, in Spain, in August, 1492.[1]

1869

G.P. Quackenbos, *Elementary History of the United States*

Columbus was born at Genoa, in Italy, a country of Europe. His parents were poor, but had him well instructed. At an early age he went to sea, and visited various countries. On one occasion, the ship on which he served took fire, and he had to throw himself into the sea and swim for his life.

After making many voyages, Columbus became convinced that the Earth was round, and that by sailing west he would finally reach land. If you mark an orange, and place your finger on the opposite side, you will reach the mark whichever way you carry your finger round. So Columbus thought that by sailing west he would arrive at Asia, just as certainly as he would by going east. He knew nothing of the Western Continent; but he supposed that Asia extended much farther east than it does, and he determined to try to reach it by launching out on the unexplored ocean.

The Azores, as we have said, were the most westerly land known at that day. Now, after a violent west wind, trees torn up by the roots were sometimes washed on these islands. The bodies of two men, very different in appearance from the people of Europe and Africa, had also been thrown there. These facts confirmed Columbus in his belief, and made him still more anxious to set out on a voyage of discovery.

But where was he to get the means? He was poor, and had no ships of his own. He could only lay his plans before the different powers of Europe, and implore their aid. First he tried his countrymen, the Genoese, but without success. Then he went to Portugal. The King of this country listened to his arguments; but, wishing to have the honor of the discovery all to himself, he basely deceived Columbus, and sent out a vessel on the proposed course under another commander. The expedition, however, failed, as it deserved to do.

Columbus next turned to Spain, which was then ruled by the famous Ferdinand and his wife Isabella. He had by this time become so poor that on his way to the court he had to beg for food for himself and his little son. On his arrival, he found the King and Queen engaged in a great war with the Moors. They had no time to listen to a poor sailor whom every one laughed at. Still Columbus would not give up. Full of his great idea, he waited for a more favorable time, supporting himself by making maps and charts.

At last he obtained the ear of Ferdinand, and pleaded his cause so earnestly that he almost convinced the King. But the long war had exhausted the royal treasury, and money was too scarce to be risked on an uncertainty. So Ferdinand resolved to take the advice of the wise men of his kingdom. Columbus appeared before them at Salamanca, to unfold his cherished plan.

But the wise men of Spain could not believe that a poor sailor knew more than they did. How, they asked, could, the Earth be round? If it were, then on the opposite side the rain would fill upward; trees would grow with their branches down, and every thing would be topsy-turvy. Objects on its surface would certainly fall off the opposite side; and, if a ship by sailing west got around there, it would never be able to climb up the side of the Earth and get back again. How could a ship sail up hill?

Such was the reasoning of the wise men. By their advice, the King refused to furnish Columbus the ships he wanted. Who can describe his disappointment, after waiting so many years? There was yet one chance. Perhaps Queen Isabella would listen to him with more favor. He obtained an interview with her. Alas! She too was persuaded to refuse him.

Almost in despair, Columbus was on the point of quitting Spain forever, when a message from Isabella recalled him to court, with the glad tidings that the Queen had changed her mind. She had determined to fit out three vessels for the enterprise, even if she had to pledge her jewels to raise the necessary money.[2]

1885

Thomas Wentworth Higginson, *Young Folks' History of the United States*

There was born at Genoa, in Italy, about 1435, a boy named "Cristoforo Colombo," or, in English, "Christopher Columbus." His father was a weaver of cloth, but his ancestors had been sailors; and the little Columbus was sent to school at ten years old to learn navigation. At fourteen he went to sea; and from that time, so long as he lived, he was either making voyages or else drawing charts. He lived in Portugal, then in Spain, these being the great seafaring nations at that day; and he sailed to almost all the ports then known. Most of his voyages, however, were in the Mediterranean Sea. In these there was almost as much fighting as sailing; for that sea was full of pirates. On one occasion his ship was burnt, and he swam six miles to shore with the aid of a spar. And throughout all these adventures he was gradually forming the plan of sailing farther west upon the Atlantic than anyone had yet dared to sail.

But it must be remembered that the people of Europe, in those days, did not know the real shape of the earth, as it is now known. Most persons did not suppose it to be a sphere. They thought it was a flat surface, with the ocean, like a great river, lying round about its edges. What was on the other side of this river, they hardly dared to guess. Yet some scientific men had got beyond this ignorant view; and they supposed the earth to be a sphere, but thought it much smaller than it really was. They did not dream that there could be room on it for two wide oceans and for two great bodies of land. They thought that there was but one continent on the globe, and one great ocean, and that, by sailing across the Atlantic, you would come, after a time, to India and Tartary and Cathay (as they called China) and Cipango (as they called Japan). Many beautiful things were brought from those countries overland, gold and pearls and beautiful silks; and so the kings of Europe would have been very glad to find a short way thither.

Columbus became more and more convinced that, if he could only cross the unknown ocean, he would find India on the other side. Things often happened to confirm him in this opinion. Sailors from the Canary Islands told him of seeing land far in the west. His brother-in-law had seen a piece of curiously-carved wood that had been washed on shore in Portugal, after a westerly gale. An old pilot had picked up a carved paddle at sea, a thousand miles west of the European coast. At Madeira, Columbus heard of pine trees that had been washed up; and at the Azores they had found tropical cane stalks on the beach; and once the bodies of two men, of foreign dress and aspect, had been cast on shore. Then it is supposed that Columbus went to Iceland; and there he may have heard legends of the early expeditions to Vinland.

For ten years he endeavored to persuade some European government to send him on a voyage of discovery across the Atlantic Ocean. First he tried the republic of Genoa, then the republic of Venice, and then the court of Portugal. For seven years he tried to interest the two sovereigns of Spain, Ferdinand and Isabella. At last they gave him an audience, and liked his plans very much; but the Archbishop of Granada, who was present, thought that Columbus asked for too much power over the lands he expected to discover, so the archbishop objected. Columbus refused to lower his claims, and left the court. He had gone two leagues (six miles), when the queen sent for him to return; and, when he had done so, the king and queen signed an agreement with him on his own terms. Isabella decided to fit out the expedition at the expense of her own kingdom of Castile, the chief of the kingdoms of which Spain was composed.

In three months the expedition was ready to sail. But sailors were unwilling to go; and Columbus had to drive some of them by force into the service, as he had authority to do. There were three ships, the "Santa Maria," the "Pinta," and the "Nina." The "Santa Maria" was a good-sized vessel, ninety feet long, and carrying sixty-six seamen. It was decked all over, and had four masts, two with square sails, and two with lateen-sails. The other vessels were smaller, and without decks and they were all provisioned for a year. There were, in all, one hundred and twenty persons on this bold expedition.[3]

1913

Wilbur F. Gordy, *Stories of Early American History*

When Portugal had found her route by sailing south, Spain dared not sail over it herself for fear of trouble with Portugal. So she had to find another way. The man who showed her how was Christopher Columbus. He was not a Spaniard. Let us see how it came about that Spain was the country to send him out and get the glory for what he did.

Columbus was born in Genoa. His father was a poor man, who earned his living by making wool ready for the spinners. We do not know much about the boy Christopher, but we can well believe that he was fond of playing on the wharves near his home. Here he could see hundreds of vessels coming and going. We may be sure that he spent many hours watching their white sails. Most likely he was fond of the water and learned while he was quite young to swim and to sail boats.

But he did not play all the time. He had work to do like other boys. He learned his father's trade, and he also went to school, where he learned reading, writing, arithmetic, geography, and map-drawing. All these were of great use in his later life.

He must have heard older people talk a great deal about the loss of the Eastern trade after the Turks had shut up the Black Sea route, and about the need of finding a new route over the ocean.

Many years later, when he had become a grown-up man, he went to live in Lisbon, which, you know, is the capital of Portugal. Here lived one of his brothers, and here, as in Genoa, lived many sailors. Here again he must have heard much talk about finding a water route to India.

Columbus listened earnestly to sailors' stories; he studied maps and charts; he thought a great deal.

It seemed to him that the earth must be round like a globe, instead of flat as many others supposed. He tried to get all the proofs he could of this. He also took many voyages himself.

After many long years of study, he felt sure that he could get to India by sailing straight across the Atlantic Ocean. He would go right in the opposite direction from that in which India lay. "The way to the East is by the West," said he.

If he should be able to reach India in this way, he would prove that the earth was round and would bring the wealth of the Indies to Europe. The more he thought about this great plan, the more he longed to carry it out. In fact, he thought of it by day and dreamed of it by night. But he was poor and he had few friends. How could he get money and help to make his great dream come true?

At last he laid his plan before King John of Portugal. But the king would not promise to help him. Columbus then took his little son Diego by the hand and started across the mountains to Spain. We may picture father and son hurrying along the rough mountain roads. Columbus could hardly stop to see whether his little boy was tired, so eager was he to find some one to help him.

When he came to a place near the town of Palos, he left Diego with an aunt, and set out alone in search of the king and queen, Ferdinand and Isabella. At that time a war was going on in the south of Spain between the Spaniards and the Moors. So Columbus had a hard time getting them to listen to him.

At last they gave him a hearing. They had asked a number of wise men to be present. Some of them laughed at Columbus for saying that the earth was round like a globe. Others said, "We believe he is right." But the king and queen would not help him. Sick at heart, therefore, he planned to leave Spain and go to France.

Up to this time he had failed. He was poor and had few friends. Men said, "He is a crazy dreamer." When he walked through a village with sad face and threadbare clothing, the boys laughed at him.

But Columbus did not give up hope. He had faith in his plans, and believed that sometime he should succeed. He started bravely, therefore, for the court of France, taking Diego with him.

At that time, we are told, Columbus was a fine-looking man. He was tall and strong, and had a noble face with keen blue eyes. His white hair fell in long wavy locks about his shoulders. Although his clothing was plain and perhaps shabby, there was something in his manner that made people like him.

After father and son had walked about a mile and a half, they stopped at the Convent of St. Mary. Perhaps they wanted some bread and water. Just then the good Prior of the Convent was passing by and the two men began to talk together.

Columbus reasoned well about his plans. The Prior listened closely, and then wrote at once to Queen Isabella, who knew him and believed in him as a wise and good man. This letter proved a help to Columbus, for a little later the queen told him she would furnish him with men and vessels for the voyage.

But even with the queen's help, he still had many trials before him. The ocean was unknown. The sailors were afraid to go out far from land upon the deep, dark waters. In the course of time, however, three small vessels with one hundred and twenty men were ready to start. The vessels were not larger than many of our fishing-boats today. The largest was the Santa Maria and was commanded by Columbus. It was about ninety feet long, and was the only vessel of the fleet which had a complete deck.

A half hour before sunrise on Friday morning, August 8, 1492, the little fleet sailed out of the port of Palos. It was a sorrowful time for the poor sailors and their friends. All believed that the vessels would be lost, and that the sailors would never again see home and family.[4]

1927

Roman Coffman, *The Story of America: The Age of Discovery, Book I*

It is a mistake to suppose that Columbus was the first man, or even one of the first, to believe in the roundness of the earth. The idea of a round earth dates back to ancient Greece. Most of the Greeks, to be sure, thought that the earth was flat, and they used to tell their children that there was "an ocean river" which flowed around the border. There were some Greek thinkers, however, who declared that the earth must be "round like a ball." They were not able to prove the fact beyond doubt, but they had sound reasons for their belief. The famous Aristotle said: "When there is an eclipse of the moon, the shadow is caused by the earth which gets in the way of the sun's light. The shadow is curved, so the earth that makes it must be curved." That reason is still given in school geographies, and it is a good one.

The ancient Greek thinkers had another excellent reason for believing that the earth was not flat. "When we go south to Egypt," they said, "we cannot see some of the stars which are seen at the same time of night in Greece. That must mean that the earth is getting in our way because it is round."

The thoughts of those brilliant men were passed on in their writings. Most persons did not pay attention to them, but a few did. Among those who thought about the question in the fifteenth century, was an Italian named Toscanelli. He felt sure that the earth was round, and drew a map to show how Asia could be reached by sailing west. Another man who believed the same thing was a simple sailor named Christopher Columbus. He seems to have studied the writings of Aristotle; and there is some proof that he was a friend of Toscanelli.

In those days, a book by Marco Polo was widely read. It told of Marco's visits to India, China, and Japan; of the gold, silver, and jewels he had seen. The merchants of Europe were anxious to trade with India, but goods had to be carried a long distance by land when traders went straight east; and there was constant danger of robbery by the Turks. Everyone knew that it would be better to trade with India by ships, which could go all the way by water, and for many years sailors tried to find a route around the south of Africa.

After thinking upon the subject, Columbus asked the king of Portugal for help in finding a western route to Asia, saying: "Your captains have had no fortune in their efforts to reach Asia around Africa. Why not let me find a way by sailing west? I believe the earth is round, and I think I can reach India by a short route if I sail straight west."

The king held a council of the learned men of his kingdom, and they discussed all sides of the question. Some were in favor of the plan, but others declared that even if the earth was round, the westward voyage would be too long for profit. The king decided to refuse the request of Columbus, but he made a plan to test the idea. He did not care to pay Columbus the money he wanted if he found India, and, acting in secret, sent three ships to the west; but they returned with the report that land could not be found.

Columbus left Portugal and went to Spain. There he spent years trying to persuade King Ferdinand and Queen Isabella to let him have ships. The queen was more friendly to Columbus than was her husband; but Spain was busy with a war carried on for the purpose of driving the Moors out of the country. Consequently, Columbus was "put off," until at last he started north to ask aid of the king of France. While he was on his way, a messenger came to him and said: "Come back! The king and queen are now willing to let you try to reach India."

Columbus returned and signed an agreement which said that he was to be called "Admiral of the Ocean," and that he was to receive one-tenth of the gold and silver from the lands he hoped to find.

The old tale of Isabella's selling her jewels to help Columbus, cannot be trusted. It seems to be just one more of the stories of fancy which should never be told as history. Records prove that Columbus obtained two of his ships from the town of Palos, in Spain. The people of that little seaport had acted in a manner which made the Spanish king and queen angry. To punish them, the officials of Palos were ordered to pay the cost of fitting up two vessels for Columbus.

Columbus went to Palos in May. The people there disliked the idea of doing anything for his "wild plan." Sailors did not want to start on a voyage across the "Sea of Darkness," as the Atlantic was often called. They feared that they might fall off the earth when they came to the end, or that sea monsters would sink their ships before the end was reached.

Some sailors were compelled by force to go; others were set free from prison when they promised to sail with Columbus. Martin Pinzon, a Spanish Jew, aided Columbus by giving money to help equip an extra vessel.

Early in August, 1492, Columbus and his three small ships left Palos. Little did the "Admiral of the Ocean" think that he would stumble upon islands near the great continent now known as America.[5]

1948

Irving Robert Melbo, *Our America: A Textbook for Elementary School History and Social Studies*

"Are you very tired, Diego, my son?" asked the man.

"Only a little, father," replied the boy bravely. "Is it much farther?"

"I do not know how far it is to the next town. Perhaps on the other side of that hill is a place where we can spend the night. We must go on yet a little farther."

The man and the boy stopped to rest for a moment. They had walked many miles since morning. The sun with its fierce heat had beaten down upon them all day. There had been many hills to climb. In places the dust had been more than an inch deep. The man looked wearily at the long hill ahead of them. Then he took the boy by the hand. They began to walk on, each footstep raising a little cloud of dust.

And so it was that they came to La Rabida. This was a monastery in Spain not far from the seaport town of Palos. Here they stopped and asked for a bit of food and a place to rest. The monks who lived in the monastery of La Rabida were kind and wise. They lived simply, serving God and helping men whenever they could.

The monks looked carefully at the man and boy and thought, "Surely these two are not common beggars." So they asked them to come in and spend the night.

That evening the man began to talk with one of the monks. "My name is Christopher Columbus," he said. "I was born in Genoa in Italy. My father was a weaver of wool. When I was a boy I liked nothing better than to see the ships come in and to hear the sailors tell their stories. When I was fourteen years old I became a sailor. But I did not want always to be a sailor.

"I learned to sail a ship by the sun and stars. I learned how to read the compass and also how to read and make maps. I studied everything I could find about the oceans and the winds. At last I learned navigation, but even that was not enough.

"It is good to know how to read and write and figure, but it is better to know more. So I began to talk with learned men. They taught me that the earth was round and not flat as so many foolish people believe. I studied their maps and charts and books. I read the accounts of great travelers such as Marco Polo, who spent so many years in China and Asia. I asked questions of the sea captains and sailors. My brother, who is a map-maker, helped me. My wife's father gave me many maps and charts and books.

"The more I studied the surer I became of one thing. The great sea which lies east of Asia is the same ocean that washes our own shores. If this is true, and the world is round, why cannot a ship reach the east by sailing straight west across the ocean? That is what I believe.

"Think how easy it would be for the merchants to trade with the Indies and China if this could only be done. No longer would it be so difficult to get silk and spices and rich jewels from the east. Yes, I am sure a ship can get to the east by sailing west. But there are not many who believe in my idea.

"For many years now, I have talked about my plan. I have been laughed at and made fun of. Many people have called me crazy. If I were rich, I would buy a ship and hire a crew. Then I would prove that I am right.

"I went to see King John of Portugal. I thought perhaps he would help me. I thought he might give me ships with which to make the voyage. But the king's advisers laughed at me. I was disappointed, but I was not discouraged.

"I went to Spain, and got King Ferdinand and Queen Isabella to give me a hearing. They were polite and kind. They seemed to be interested, but a committee of their learned men advised them against the trip. I then tried to get others to help me. Some of them were members of the king's court. A few of them believed that my plan was a good one, but something always happened to keep me from getting help.

"For many years I have been trying to get aid in Spain. Now, I am going to see the king of France. Perhaps he would like to help me find a new route to the Indies by sailing west."

The monk, who was himself a learned man, was very much interested in what Columbus said. He begged Columbus to wait a while before going to France. "I know Queen Isabella," he said. "I once served at her court. I shall ask her to listen to your plan again. Spain must not lose this chance to find a new sea route to the rich cities of China and India."

Before long a message came to La Rabida. Columbus was recalled to the court of King Ferdinand and Queen Isabella. This time he succeeded in making them believe that his plan was worth trying. Queen Isabella especially was interested. She persuaded the king to give Columbus the money he needed.

It seemed almost too good to be true. The many long years of discouragement had been hard on Columbus. Although he was only forty-one years old, his hair had long since turned white. At no time had he quit

trying. Now, at last, he was to get his chance. It was indeed a fitting reward for this man who would not give up and who had such great faith in
himself.

Columbus' troubles, however, were not yet over. He had to get ships
and load them with supplies. Then he must have sailors who were not
afraid to go with him. At that time sailors knew very little about the broad
Atlantic Ocean. Many of them believed that dreadful monsters lived far
out in the ocean. Others were afraid they might never get back if they
went too far from land.[6]

1985

Ernest R. May, *A Proud Nation*

Most sailors thought the best water route to Asia required sailing along
the coast of Africa and past its southern tip. Christopher Columbus did
not agree. He believed that a shorter route could be found by sailing west,
across the Atlantic Ocean.

Christopher Columbus was born in Genoa, Italy, in 1451. Through
sailing on the Mediterranean Sea and along the Atlantic coast, possibly
even to Iceland, he had acquired an outstanding knowledge of the seas
and their currents and winds.

Columbus's idea was simple enough. Since the earth was round, he
could reach the Indies by sailing west. But first Columbus had to find
someone to pay for the ships and sailors and to meet several other demands. This proved difficult. In 1484 Columbus approached King John II
of Portugal. Since the king was more interested in a route around Africa to
Asia, he turned Columbus down.

Next, Columbus went to King Ferdinand and Queen Isabella of Spain,
who would have been happy to beat Portugal to an all-water route to the
Indies. They did not think, however, that Columbus's plan was sound.

The idea of sailing west to reach the East was not the problem. Everyone who knew geography agreed that the earth was round. Distance was
the main problem at that time.

Columbus used Ptolemy's map as well as other inaccurate maps. Also,
he had read Marco Polo's book, which led him to believe that only 3,000

miles or fewer separated Europe from Asia across the Atlantic. Scholars believed the distance was much greater.

For years Columbus talked of little else but sailing westward. A man with a single purpose, he firmly believed in his maps and plans. Never doubting that God intended him to make the trip westward, he knew God would help him reach his goal.

In January, 1492, Columbus pleaded with Ferdinand and Isabella one last time. Again, they refused help. Then the queen abruptly changed her mind. Deciding that she really had much more to gain than to lose, she took a chance and aided him.[7]

DISCUSSION QUESTIONS

1. Provide examples of some of the different reasons textbooks have given over the years for why Columbus went on his famous voyage. If there are differences, explain why different textbooks highlighted diverse reasons for this journey.

2. These textbooks all claim that Columbus was the first man to discover the New World. Research and see if other groups/nations also make this claim. Why do you think this claim is important to the different groups/nations that make it? Explain.

3. According to the textbooks in this section, what reasons were given for why Columbus was turned down by some European leaders to help pay for his voyage?

4. Some of the textbooks in this section discuss the Turks and the Moors. Research who these two groups were and their relationship to Europe in the 1400s and 1500s. Why do you think textbook authors included them in a story about Columbus?

5. While some textbooks asserted that Columbus was the first to claim that the world was round, others wrote that many Europeans had known this for a long time. Conduct your own investigation and find out what these people actually knew about the shape of the world in the 1400s.

6. On a map, trace the path that Columbus took to get to the New World. How far off was he in terms of finding China? Would he ever have been able to find a route from Europe to Asia by sailing west?

Did any other European explorers try to find the same route? If so, explain why they may have done this.

7. The 1948 textbook tells the story of Columbus by quoting his exact words. None of the other textbooks does this, so how does this author seem to know exactly what Columbus said? How would a historian verify whether this was an exact quote or not?

8. Most of the textbooks discuss how Columbus went from nation to nation to find financial backing for his expedition. Research the politics and economics of this period in Europe and explain why some nations' leaders said no while Spain was willing to take a gamble on him.

For years there was a controversy over where exactly Christopher Columbus's remains were buried: some believed it was in Seville, Spain, while others argued it was Santo Domingo, Dominican Republic. In 2003 Spanish scientists conducted DNA tests and concluded that Columbus's final resting spot was in a church in Seville.

3

Pocahontas and Captain John Smith

The story of Pocahontas and the first British colony in the New World has been found in almost every single U.S. history textbook since the late 1700s. That said, most American historians seem to doubt that much of what students have been taught actually happened. It seems the American public is equally mesmerized by this highly embellished story. A cursory search of library holdings on the topic reveals nearly three thousand books that discuss some aspect of Pocahontas. Hollywood has also pitched in with a long string of movies— most portraying the purported relationship between the two star characters, Pocahontas and John Smith. Here, truly, is a case where myth has overtaken history.

1860

Benson J. Lossing, *A Primary History of the United States*

Captain John Smith, a very great soldier, of whom you have heard, I daresay, was one of the Adventurers. He had been in many fights with the Turks in Eastern Europe, and had done wonderful things there. Many of the Adventurers were rather bad characters, and they became jealous of Captain Smith, for they knew he was smarter and better than them.

Smith was accused of wrong intentions during the voyage, and was put in prison on board the ship. When the Adventurers landed, they proceeded, according to King James's orders, to open a sealed box, which he had given them. Then it was found that the king had appointed Captain Smith to be one of the governors of the settlement. Greatly fearing the king's displeasure, they set him at liberty, and for many years Captain Smith was the greatest and best man in the New World.

Newport [Captain Christopher Newport] sailed for England in June, 1607, for more Adventurers and provisions. Soon after he left, the provisions of the settlers became scarce, and the poisonous vapors which arose from the swamps near by, made a great many sick. Before the close of summer, one half of the Adventurers died, and were buried in the round at Jamestown.

Every one now began to think of death and starvation, for the Indians had not received them very kindly, and would not bring them food. The man whom the Adventurers had chosen to be their chief ruler was a very bad one, and it was not long before they asked Captain Smith to take his place.

Smith soon made the Indians respect him, and bring food for his companions. He now resolved to know more of the country he was in. He had already been up the James River to the Falls at Richmond, and had seen a large stream coming in from the north, just above Jamestown. With a few companions he went up that stream, which the Indians called Chichahominy. While away from his boat, in the woods, some of the Indians, who had been watching the white people, sprang forward and made Captain Smith a prisoner.

The great Emperor of the Indians was called Powhatan. Captain Smith was taken from one Indian village to another, so that the women and children might see him. Then he was conducted to the dwelling of the emperor on the York River. He was kindly treated; but when the great men around Powhatan had talked the matter all over, they concluded to kill him.

A huge stone was placed before Powhatan, on which the head of Captain Smith was laid. His hands were tied behind him, and he could not stir. Then two strong Indians raised each a heavy club to kill him, and there appeared no help for him.

Powhatan had a beautiful daughter, ten or twelve years old, named Pocahontas. She sat by the side of her father, who loved her very much. She was a good girl, and pitied poor Captain Smith. Just as the Indians raised their clubs to kill him, she leaped from her seat, clasped the head of the captive in her arms, and begged her father to spare his life. Pocahontas was an angel of deliverance, for Powhatan not only gave Smith his life, but sent a guard of twelve men to conduct him back to his friends at Jamestown.

During his captivity Smith learned much that was useful to him, about the Indians and their country. But he was grieved to find every thing in confusion at Jamestown, and only forty of his companions alive. These were just preparing to leave, but he caused them to remain, and by his own exertions he procured food enough from the Indians, for them all.

Newport arrived with more Adventurers and provisions, the following spring. Then Smith started, in an open boat, to explore the Chesapeake Bay. He visited every bay and river along its coasts; and, on foot, he went up into the wilderness as far as the country of the Five Nations in the southern part of New York.

Altogether this was one of the most wonderful voyages I have ever read about. Smith and his companions were gone three months, and traveled about three thousand miles. That is the distance across the Atlantic Ocean, from New York to London.

A pleasant thing happened not long after Smith's return. Some more adventurers came from England, and with them, two women; the first from Europe ever seen in Virginia. They were very good women, but I am sorry, I can not say the same of the men. Most of those who were in Virginia were very lazy. They would not raise grain for food, but looked for gold, or did nothing, day after day.

Smith coaxed the Indians to give the white people food, or they would have all starved. Finally, when he went to England on account of being badly hurt, the Indians not only refused to let the white people have food, but laid a plan to kill them all. The good and beautiful Pocahontas, like a divine angel, went to Jamestown, told the Adventurers what the Indians thought of doing, and made them prepared to defend themselves.

The Indians did not attack the people at Jamestown. After awhile, an English sailor, named Argall, who was a sort of sea-robber, came there, coaxed Pocahontas on board of his ship, and kept her a prisoner for a long time. Her father was greatly grieved. But the robber would not let her go until her father sent plenty of food to the half-starving Adventurers.

And now another pleasant thing occurred. While Pocahontas was on the ship, a young Englishman, named John Rolfe, fell in love with her. She became a Christian, was baptized, and married Rolfe. This made her father a good friend of the English as long as she lived.[1]

1869

G.P. Quackenbos, *Elementary History of the United States*

Smith was suddenly attacked by Indians. He had ordered his men to stay by the boat while he went out to reconnoiter, but they wandered off, and were killed by the savages. After slaying three of his enemies, Smith, while trying to escape, sunk in a swamp and had to yield. Even then the Indians were afraid to touch him till he had thrown away his arms. He would now have lost his life, if he had not understood the character of the Indians. Taking his compass out of his pocket, he showed them how the needle always points north, and told them about the shape of the Earth and the heavenly bodies.

To increase the wonder of the savages, Smith told them that the next day they would find some articles that he named, in a certain place in the forest. He then wrote to his countrymen at Jamestown to put the articles there. They did so, and when the Indians, who did not understand his writing, saw every thing turn out as he had said, they began to look on him as more than man. They carried him around to their different villages in triumph, and at last brought him to their chief, Powhatan.

Here a solemn council was held, and it was determined that Smith should be put to death. His head was laid on a large stone, to receive the fatal blow. A fierce savage stood beside him, war-club in hand. Just as he was about to strike, Pocahontas, a gentle Indian girl of twelve years, ran forward, threw her arms about the prisoner, and with tears besought the savages to spare his life. She was the daughter of Powhatan, and the favorite of the whole tribe. Smith had amused her during his captivity by making her toys, and telling her about the wonders of nature. She had become fond of the stranger, and now tried to save him.

Moved by the tears of Pocahontas, the Indians spared Captain Smith. They even treated him kindly, and let him go back to Jamestown with promises of friendship. Pocahontas continued to be a firm friend of the English. She often visited them, bringing baskets of corn to relieve their wants. Once, when the Indians had formed a plot to surprise and murder all the whites, she came through the woods by night at the risk of her own life, and warned them to be on their guard.

On his return to Jamestown, Smith found the colonists reduced to forty men, and these were on the point of leaving in despair. He made them remain, and soon after Newport arrived with fresh settlers and supplies. Some of the newcomers were goldsmiths; and, seeing some glittering sand near the town, they fancied it must be gold dust. Newport was foolish enough to load his vessel with this worthless sand, and carry it to England.[2]

1884

Edward Ellis, *The Eclectic Primary History of the United States*

When Captain John Smith left Jamestown, there were five hundred men in the colony. Dreadful times followed. Idleness and famine swept away all but sixty, and they narrowly escaped. That winter is known in history as the "Starving Time."

When spring came, the few survivors believed nothing could save them if they remained. They therefore embarked on their return voyage, doubtful whether they would live to reach their old homes, thousands of miles away.

While drifting down the James, they were amazed to see a ship coming up the river. When they met, the visitor was found to be their new governor, Lord Delaware, who brought with him emigrants and plenty of supplies.

The colonists were glad to return to the homes they had just left. Lord Delaware was a good governor, but his health soon failed, and he went back to England. Other settlers arrived, and Jamestown continued to prosper.

One day a Dutch vessel visited Jamestown. She had twenty Africans on board, who were sold to the colonists. In this manner, negro slavery was introduced into our country.

Pocahontas, of whom I have spoken, was a great favorite with the settlers. When the Indians formed a plot to kill them, she made her way alone through the woods at night to give them warning. While she was visiting a neighboring tribe, Captain Argall bought her, giving a copper kettle in exchange. This outrage made Powhatan so angry that he began preparations to massacre all the whites.

A young English planter, named John Rolfe, had fallen in love with Pocahontas, who was very pretty and bright. He asked her hand in marriage, and she consented. In the quaint little church at Jamestown she was baptized, and, in broken English, repeated the marriage vows as they appear in the service of the Church of England.

This marriage made Powhatan a firm friend of the whites, who were in no further danger from him. Three years later, Rolfe sailed for England, taking his dusky wife with him. Her visit awakened great interest, for she was the first of her race to make such a voyage. In England she was known as Lady Rebecca, for it must not be forgotten that her father was a monarch among his people.

Lady Rebecca was presented to King James, and met her old friend, Captain John Smith, who was then in England. When about to sail for America, she fell ill and died. The husband returned with his infant son, from whom many of the leading families in Virginia are proud to claim their descent.[3]

1885

Thomas Wentworth Higginson, *Young Folks' History of the United States*

Captain Smith, at different times, made expeditions along the coast as far as Maine. He visited the Isles of Shoals in New Hampshire, which were formerly called "Smith's Isles," and on which a monument is now erected to his memory. It was he who first gave the name of "New England" to that part of the country; and the names of "Plymouth" and "Cape Ann" and "Charles River" appear first on a map made by him. He also made expeditions into the interior of the country. On one of these he was made prisoner by the Indians; and his few companions were killed. He, however, amused his captors by showing them his compass, and by explaining to them the movements of the earth and sun; so that they spared him. Then he puzzled them very much by writing a letter to be sent to his friends; for the Indians could not well understand how a message could be put on a piece of paper. Then he was condemned to death by Powhatan, an Indian chief but the chief's daughter Pocahontas, a girl twelve years old, threw herself between the prisoner and the uplifted tomahawk, and Captain Smith was spared. This story has been doubted in later times and may not be true, but it is certain that there was such a person as Pocahontas, and that, when she grew to be a woman, she became a Christian, was married to an Englishman named Rolfe, and went with him to England, where, as an English writer of that day says, "She did not onely [sic] accustom herself to civilite [sic], but carried herself as the daughter of a king."

She died soon after. Capt. John Smith also went to England in 1609, to be cured of a severe wound; and he never returned to the colony. After his departure, things grew worse and worse among the emigrants; and in six months they left Jamestown in despair, meaning to return to England forever.[4]

1909

William H. Mace, *A Primary History: Stories of Heroism*

The king had made Smith an officer of the new colony, but the other officers would not permit him to take part in governing Virginia. John Smith was not a man to sulk and idle his time away, but resolved to do some thing useful, by visiting the Indians, and gathering food for the colony.

While on an expedition up the Chickahominy, Smith's party was attacked by two hundred Indians. Smith seized his Indian guide, tied him in front for a shield, and with his gun was able to hold the Indians at bay until he fell into a swamp and had to surrender.

He immediately showed the red men his ivory pocket compass. They saw the little needle tremble on its pivot, but could not touch it. He wrote a letter to Jamestown. An Indian returned with the articles asked for in the letter. This was still more mysterious than the compass.

The Indians marched him from one village to another to show off their prisoner. This gave Smith a chance to learn a great deal about the Indians. Some of them lived in houses made of the bark and branches of trees; others had rude huts to shelter them. Now and then a wigwam was seen large enough to hold several families.

The Indian warriors painted their bodies to make themselves look fierce. They carried bows and arrows and clubs as weapons, for they had no guns at that time. The men did the hunting and fighting, but in other things they were lazy. The Indian women not only cared for the children, did the cooking, and made the clothes, but also gathered wood, tilled the soil, and built the wigwams. The Indian wife was the warrior's drudge.

Smith saw a more wonderful sight still, when he was led to the village where lived Powhatan. The old chief had prepared a real surprise for this Englishman. Powhatan, tall, gaunt, and grim, was wrapped in a robe of raccoon skins. He sat upon a bench before the wigwam fire. His wives sat at his side. Along the walls stood a row of women with faces and shoulders painted bright red, and with chains of white shells about their necks. In front of the women stood Powhatan's fierce warriors. This council of Indians was to decide the fate of Smith.

Two big stones were rolled in front of Powhatan, and a number of powerful warriors sprang upon Smith, dragged him to the stones, and forced his head upon one of them. As the warriors stood, clubs in hand, ready to slay Smith, Pocahontas, the beautiful twelve-year-old daughter of Powhatan, rushed forward, threw her arms around the prisoner, and begged for his life.

Pocahontas had her way. Powhatan adopted Smith as a son and set him to making toys for the little maid. This was strange work for the man who had fought the Spaniards and slain the Turks, and who was to save a colony. This story is doubted by some people, but is believed by many good historians.

After a time Smith returned to Jamestown only to find the settlers facing starvation, and the officers planning to escape to England in the colony's only vessels. He promptly arrested the leaders and restored order. In a few days, the hungry settlers saw a band of Indians, led by Pocahontas, enter the fort.

They were loaded down with baskets of corn. The fear of starvation was now gone, because every few days the little maiden came with food for the settlers. Ever afterwards they called her "the dear blessed Pocahontas." She was the good angel of the colony.

When winter came on, Smith resolved to secure another supply of corn. But Powhatan had noticed the increase of settlers and the building of more houses. He feared that his people might be driven from their hunting grounds. Smith knew that Powhatan's women had raised plenty of corn, and immediately sailed up the river to the old chief's village.

Powhatan bluntly told Smith he could have no corn unless he would give a good English sword for each basketful. Smith promptly refused, and compelled the Indians to carry the corn on board his boat. That very night, at the risk of her life, Pocahontas stole through the woods to tell Smith of her father's plot to kill his men. They kept close watch all night, and next morning sailed safely away.

But Smith needed still more corn, and stopped at another Indian town. Suddenly he found himself and men surrounded by several hundred Indian warriors. A moment's delay and all would have been over. Smith rushed into the chief's wigwam, seized him by the scalp, dragged him out before his astonished warriors, pointed a pistol at his breast, and demanded corn. He got it; and the English sailed back to Jamestown with three hundred bushels of corn on board.

When spring came Smith resolved that the settlers must go to work. He called them together and made a speech declaring that "he that will not work shall not eat. You shall not only gather for yourself, but for those that are sick. They shall not starve." The people in the colony not only planted more grain, but repaired the fort and built more and better houses. Thus they grew happier and more contented with their home in the Virginia woods.

Unfortunately for the colony, Smith was wounded so badly by an explosion of gunpowder that he had to return to England for medical treatment. The settlers again fell into idleness after he left, and many of them died. Still the colony had gained such a foothold that it was strong enough to live.

Some years later, Smith sailed to America again, explored the coast from Penobscot Bay to Cape Cod, drew a map of it, and named the region New England. This was his last visit to America.

After John Smith left, Pocahontas did not visit the English any more. One time she was seized by an Englishman, put on board a vessel, and carried weeping to Jamestown.

Before long an English settler, John Rolfe, fell in love with her and she with him. What should they do? Did not this beautiful maiden of eighteen years have a strange religion? But she was anxious to learn about the white man's religion, so the minister at Jamestown baptized her and gave her the Christian name of Rebecca.

The wedding took place in the little wooden church. No doubt it was made bright with the wild flowers of Virginia and that all the settlers crowded to see the strange event. Powhatan gave his consent, but would not come to the wedding himself. But we may be sure that the sisters and brothers and the Indian friends of Pocahontas were there.

It was a happy day for Jamestown, for all the people, white and red, loved Pocahontas. The marriage of Pocahontas and John Rolfe was taken to mean the uniting of the Indians and settlers by ties of peace and friendship. For several years white men and red men lived as good neighbors. Rolfe took Pocahontas to England, where she was received "as the daughter of a king." The fine people, lords and ladies, called on her; and the king and queen received her at court as if she were a princess of the royal blood.

How different the rich clothes, the carriages, and the high feasting from her simple life in the woods of Virginia! Here, too, she met her old friend, John Smith. He called her "Lady Rebecca," as did everybody. But the memory of other days and other scenes came before her mind. She covered her face with her hands for a moment, and then said he must call her "child," and that she would call him "father." Smith must have thought of the days when she brought corn to Jamestown to feed his starving people.

When about to sail for her native land, Pocahontas died (1617). Her son, Thomas Rolfe, returned to the land of his mother and became the ancestor of many noted Virginians; among these the best known was the famous orator and statesman, John Randolph of Roanoke.

So ended the life of one who had indeed been a good and true friend of the people of Virginia. Her name, Pocahontas, meant "Bright Stream Between Two Hills."[5]

1923

Henry Eldridge Bourne and Elbert Jay Benton, *Story of America and Great Americans*

[John] Smith's most interesting adventure was at Powhatan's town. Some persons do not believe it ever happened because he did not tell it until many years later. On one of his trips for corn he left his large boat and went on with two companions, guided by two Indians. Suddenly he was attacked by other Indians and his companions were killed. He tried to defend himself, but stumbled into a quagmire and was seized. He was now taken before an Indian chief who was about to have him killed when Smith took out a compass, something which an Indian had never seen. The Indian was so interested that he changed his mind. He sent Smith to the great chieftain Powhatan.

For several days there was feasting in Powhatan's town, as if Captain Smith were an honored guest. At the end when all were gathered in Powhatan's house, Smith was seized, thrown on the ground, and his head was placed upon a great stone. Near by stood stalwart Indians, their war clubs raised, ready to beat out his brains at a signal from the king. Suddenly Powhatan's favorite daughter, Pocahontas, a girl of twelve or thirteen, rushed forward and clasped Smith's head in her arms so that the Indians could not strike. Powhatan consented to spare Smith's life. He sent Smith back to Jamestown, making him promise to give the messengers guns and grindstones. This is the story. What we know is that Pocahontas remained the friend of the settlers. But Powhatan did not get either guns or grindstones.[6]

1946

George Earl Freeland and James Truslow Adams, *America's Progress in Civilization*

The Virginia colony in time became very successful. The marriage of John Rolfe to Pocahontas, daughter of the great "werowance" Powhatan, brought peace with the Indians and made it safe to settle outside of Jamestown. From the first the colonists had had ministers of the English church. One of them baptized Pocahontas and solemnized her wedding. By 1620 the colony was made up of eleven distinct settlements and had a population of over 4000. The most important product was tobacco, which Europe had come to use extensively. Any Virginian who raised a good crop was on his way to wealth.[7]

1977

JoAnne Buggey, *America! America!*

Captain John Smith had taken the role of a leader in the colony, although he had no authority to do this. And Smith had decided to lay down the law to his followers. He told them that those who refused to work would not eat. Many of the older men found this young man's self-confidence maddening. Still, after much grumbling, the men responded by planting new crops, cutting down trees, and repairing their dwellings. By the end of the second year, 50 houses had been built, and the little town had been surrounded by a 15-foot wall.

Supply ships, carrying provisions and additional settlers, began to arrive from England. Two women were aboard the second supply ship, and five men from Poland had been brought to start the processing of pitch, tar, and turpentine in the Virginia colony.[8]

1986

Lewis Paul Todd and Merle Curti, *Triumph of the American Nation*

Slowly, after 1610, the conditions [at Jamestown] began to improve. Much to everyone's surprise, tobacco saved the colony.

Europeans first learned about smoking tobacco from the Indians. By the early 1600's, the habit of smoking was spreading throughout England and the rest of Europe.

Until Jamestown was settled, the Caribbean islands supplied all the tobacco smoked by the English and other Europeans. Then around 1612 John Rolfe (who later married the Indian princess Pocahontas) learned how to grow and cure tobacco in Virginia. Within a few years, the colonists were shipping large quantities of this valuable product to England. By 1619 there were more than 1,000 colonists in Virginia, and most were raising tobacco.[9]

DISCUSSION QUESTIONS

1. As the textbooks in this section mention, some historians do not believe the stories that John Smith told about himself, Jamestown, and/or Pocahontas. Do your own research on this story and try to uncover what actually happened there. How much of what John Smith and these history textbooks said do you think is accurate?

2. The 1869 textbook claimed that the Native Americans saw John Smith as being "more than a man." In the next paragraph this textbook claims that a council of Native Americans ordered his death. Did this actually happen? If so, why did the Native Americans seem to change their mind about him? If they didn't, why would an author put this story in a textbook?

3. Some of the textbooks in this section discuss the "Starving Time" in Jamestown Colony. What happened during this time and what did the survivors have to do to live through this?

4. The textbooks in this section seem to disagree about events in Pocahontas's life. Research and explain whether Pocahontas was a hostage, bought by one of the English settlers, a close friend of Jamestown, all of the above, or none of the above.

5. After researching Jamestown Colony explain whether or not you think James Smith had a positive or negative impact on this colony. What impact did Pocahontas have on this colony?

6. What was life like for Pocahontas when she went to England? Was she treated like royalty, as some of these textbooks claim?

7. After researching the story of John Smith, Jamestown, and Pocahon-

tas, tell the story from the perspective of the Powhatan Indians, as if they had been writing the history textbooks for the past two hundred years. How might the story change?

8. Some of these textbooks emphasize the fact that once she was married Pocahontas became a Christian. Looking at the years in which these particular textbooks were published, explain why you think that part of the story was highlighted.

John Smith left Jamestown in 1609 and returned to England, where he began to write books about his adventures in the New World.

4

Anne Hutchinson

Born in England to a Puritan minister, Anne Hutchinson migrated to the new British colonies in 1634 with her husband and fourteen children. Having been educated and raised in a minister's home, Anne decided to hold Sunday meetings where she discussed the minister's sermon and Bible readings. These meetings quickly attracted attention, not all of it positive. After finding herself caught up in a political fight, Anne was excommunicated and banished from the colony.

Although frequently overlooked in history textbooks, the story of Anne Hutchinson has been cited by some as the founding moment of religious freedom in the New World, or by others as an instance of early feminism. It is most often held up as a classic example of the American spirit of independence.

1860

Benson J. Lossing, *A Primary History of the United States*

A smart woman, named Anne Hutchinson, offended the ministers greatly, and the rulers first put her and her family into prison, and then drove them into the wilderness among the Indians. They wandered through the woods, almost to Manhattan Island, and lived in a hut. There all but one of them were murdered by the Indians, who hated the white people.[1]

1885

Thomas Wentworth Higginson, *Young Folks' History of the United States*

Many such persons came to him [Roger Williams], and settled in different parts of the colony he founded. Among these were Anne Hutchinson, a famous woman-preacher of those days, whom the Massachusetts magistrates had exiled; and Samuel Gorton, another independent religious teacher. Another was William Coddington, who bought the island of Rhode Island, then called Aquidneck, from the Indians. Indeed, so many people of various opinions went there, that it used to be said that any man who had lost his religion would be sure to find it again at some village in Rhode Island.[2]

1930

William Backus Guitteau, *Our United States: A History for Upper Grammar Grades and Junior High School*

Williams had spent much time among the Indians, teaching them the Word of God. He said that the soil of the New World belonged to them, and that the settlers could obtain a valid title to it only by purchase, instead of by a grant from the king. A serious dispute at once arose. The Puritan leaders feared that the king, who was already inclined to take away their charter, might hear of this bold denial of his authority. Williams was ordered to return to England in 1636; but instead of obeying, he fled to the woods and took refuge with his Indian friends. Another dissenter, Mrs. Anne Hutchinson, was likewise teaching new religious doctrines and boldly criticizing the magistrates. She, too, was banished.[3]

1946

George Earl Freeland and James Truslow Adams, *America's Progress in Civilization*

In 1638 Williams' colony became a refuge for Anne Hutchinson and a group of followers. Mrs. Hutchinson preached doctrines contrary to Puritanism and was convicted of heresy and banished from Massachusetts.[4]

1977

JoAnne Buggey, *America! America!*

Anne Hutchinson was another person who spoke out against official Puritan beliefs in Massachusetts. Hutchinson held small meetings in her home, at which she analyzed and commented on sermons of the local ministers. Hutchinson was able to attract a large number of followers, including many well-known men.

The Puritan officials could not accept Hutchinson's religious views. In addition, some of the men in the colony objected that no woman should "meddle" with religious affairs. As a result, the General Court banished Hutchinson from the colony for being "a woman not fit for our society."

Hutchinson, her husband, and her family, along with a band of followers, traveled southeast and founded a settlement which they named Portsmouth in an area which became part of Rhode Island.[5]

1986

James West Davidson and John E. Batchelor, *The American Nation*

Among those who fled to Rhode Island was Anne Hutchinson. Hutchinson and her husband, William, arrived in Boston in 1634. She worked as a midwife, helping to deliver babies. She was herself the mother of 14 children.

Hutchinson was an intelligent and devout churchgoer. Often, she met with friends at her home after church to discuss the minister's sermon. These meetings worried Puritan officials. They believed that only clergymen were qualified to explain God's law. When Hutchinson claimed that many ministers were teaching incorrect beliefs, she was put on trial.

At her trial, Hutchinson answered the questions put to her by Governor Winthrop and other Puritan officials. Winthrop found that she had "a nimble wit and active spirit." Time after time, she showed up the weakness in his arguments. And he could not prove that she had broken any Puritan laws or religious teachings. Finally, after two days of questioning, Hutchinson made a mistake. She said that God had spoken directly to her. To

Puritans, this was a terrible error. They believed that God spoke only through the Bible, not to individuals.

In 1638, the General Court sent Hutchinson away from the colony. With her family and supporters, she went to Rhode Island. Later, she moved to the Dutch colony of New Netherland, where she and most of her family were killed by Indians.[6]

DISCUSSION QUESTIONS

1. There are a number of different stories of what actually happened to Anne Hutchinson and her followers after she was banished from the Massachusetts colony. Conduct your own research on the Hutchinson story and try to find out what you think happened to her after she was banished from the Massachusetts Colony.
2. According to the textbooks in this section, is questioning an established religion a good or bad thing?
3. Do you think Anne Hutchinson is considered a hero or villain in these textbooks? Explain.
4. Research and explain what happened at her trial. Why exactly was she put on trial? How did her beliefs contradict those of the other Puritans? Were the Puritan leaders tolerant of others' ideas? What of other people such as the Native Americans?
5. Some argue that feminist movements influenced how this story is told to students. Find out when these feminist movements happened and explain whether or not they did have an effect on the story of Anne Hutchinson found in history textbooks.

Today, one can find a statue of Anne Hutchinson outside the Massachusetts State House on the base of which she is referred to as a "courageous exponent of civil liberty and religious toleration."

5

The Pequot War

Most historians today agree that the Pequot War of 1636–1638 was a pivotal moment in the history of the colonies. It is a reminder of the violence that often lay at the heart of the New World experience. For students, it is perhaps the first time they are asked to grapple with the causes of interethnic strife—and to think about the much longer history of genocide and oppression in the Americas.

1832

Noah Webster, *History of the United States: To Which is Prefixed a Brief Historical Account of our [English] Ancestors, from the dispersal at Babel, to their Migration to America, and of the Conquest of South America by the Spaniards*

Principal Indian Tribes in New England

The settlers at Plymouth and Massachusetts had no trouble with the Indians in their neighborhood for many years. But westward of the Narraganset bay, lived many powerful tribes, which had not been reduced by the malignant fever. These were the Narragansets who possessed the country between the river of that name and the Paucatuc, which territory is now a part of Rhode Island—the Pequots, a warlike nation, inhabiting the territory between Paucatuc and the Connecticut, now a part of

Connecticut, by the names of Stonington and Groton—the Mohegans who resided on the west of the river Mohegan, and owned the land, now a part of New London and Norwich. Of these the Pequots were the most warlike, ferocious, and formidable to the other tribes, with whom they were often at war.

Occasion of the Pequot War

In the year 1634, the Pequots killed Capt. Stone and all his companions, being seven in number who were bound up the Connecticut, merely for compelling two of the nation to be their guides. In 1636, Capt. Oldham was killed at Block Island, where he went to trade. Some others were killed the same year; and in April 1631 a party of Indians went up the Connecticut in canoes, and surprising a number of persons in Wethersfield as they were going into the field, killed nine and took two young women prisoners. These murders called upon the inhabitants to take measures for their safety, and it was determined to make war on the Pequots.

Beginning and Progress of the War

The murder of Capt. Oldham induced Massachusetts to send ninety men under Gen. Endicott to reduce the Indians on Block Island, and then to demand of the Pequots, the murderers of Capt. Stone, and a thousand fathom of wampum, by way of satisfaction, with some of their children as hostages. In October 1636, they landed on the isle and the Indians fled, but their wigwams were all destroyed. The party then sailed to the Pequot country, where they could not effect their purposes, and after burning a number of huts, they returned. This expedition from Massachusetts gave offense to the settlers at Plymouth and Connecticut; who complained to the governor that it would exasperate the savages, without being of any use towards subduing them. But the continued murders of the Pequots induced all the colonies, the next year, to unite in an expedition against them.

Destruction of the Pequots

In April 1637, the Connecticut people sent letters to the government of Massachusetts, expressing their dissatisfaction at the expedition of the former year; but urging a continuance of the war to a more decisive conclusion. Preparations accordingly were made in all the colonies. But Connecticut was beforehand in executing the design; for early in May, Capt. Mason with ninety men from Hartford, Wethersfield and Windsor, went down the river, being joined by Capt. Underhill at Saybrook and by Uncas, sachem of the Mohegans, the enemy of the Pequots. Sailing round to the Narraganset shore, they landed, and being joined by five hundred Indians of that tribe, who wished to see the Pequots exterminated, they marched by moonlight to the Pequot fort, and attacked it by surprise. Capt. Mason entered, set fire to the huts, and slew or took most of the Indians, amounting to six or seven hundred, with the loss of only two of his own men. Those who escaped fled and took refuge in a swamp now in Fairfield. A body of men, being joined by the troops from Massachusetts, under Capt. Stoughton, pursued them, killed some, took others and dispersed the rest, so that the tribe became extinct.[1]

1860

Benson J. Lossing, *A Primary History of the United States*

The Pequods, from time to time, murdered several white people. The Adventurers in the Connecticut valley, seeing no chance for peace with them, resolved to kill them all. The settlers in Massachusetts agreed to help them, and they got the Indians who lived on Narraganset Bay, in Rhode Island, to join them.

In May, 1637, full five hundred warriors, white people and Indians, were marching toward the country of the Pequods, whose great sachem and chief, Sassacus, felt no fear. He had a strong fort a few miles from the present New London, and could call around him almost two thousand warriors. But Sassacus felt stronger than he really was.

Captain Mason, a famous Indian fighter, commanded the army that marched against Sassacus. One morning before daylight, he surrounded the Indian fort, set it on fire, and, when the sun arose, more than six hundred men, women, and children had perished in the flames, or by the sword and spear. Only seven escaped.

Sassacus was amazed; and when he heard that other soldiers were coming from Massachusetts, he fled westward with his remaining warriors, to a great swamp near Fairfield. There a severe battle was fought, and the Indians were nearly all slain. Sassacus again fled, and took refuge with the Mohawks, one of the Six Nations, where he was murdered. The whole territory of the Pequods was desolated, and the tribe was destroyed.

The white people who followed the Pequods in their flight, discovered the beautiful country along Long Island Sound. Adventurers soon came from Massachusetts to examine it. In the autumn they built a log hut on a little stream near a bay, and spent the winter there.

The next spring the Adventurers were joined by John Davenport and others. Davenport was a Gospel minister, and preached his first sermon to the people under a large oak tree. They purchased the land of the Indians, made a covenant by which they agreed to be governed, and called their settlement New Haven.[2]

1869

G.P. Quackenbos, *Elementary History of the United States*

Connecticut was inhabited by many powerful tribes of Indians. Among these were the Pequods, who lived in what is now the south-eastern part of the state, near the mouth of the Thames River. When the Pequods saw the white men spreading over their pleasant hunting-grounds, they were filled with jealousy and alarm; and the whites, seeing how the Indians felt, distrusted them in turn. Up to this time, there had been peace between the whites and Indians; but this suspicion soon produced war.

One day, a trader, sailing off the coast, saw a boat which he knew belonged to one of the settlers named Oldham. It was full of Indians, and he suspected there was something wrong. So, although he had only two boys with him, he made for the boat. The Indians were frightened when they saw him, and as he approached they jumped over into the water. The trader went on board, and under a fishing-net he found Oldham's body, all mangled and bleeding.

The people of New England determined to punish the murderers. A body of men started for the Pequod villages. The Indians had fled, but there were their wigwams and cornfields. Setting fire to these, the settlers laid waste the country far and wide. This roused the Pequods to a bloody revenge. Dividing into small parties, they surrounded solitary houses, cut off travelers, shot down the men as they worked in the fields, and scalped women and children at their own firesides. They spared none.

Resolving to cut off all the English settlers, the Pequods tried to induce another tribe, the Narragansetts, to join them. When the people of Boston heard of this, they were greatly frightened. Knowing that Roger Williams, whom they had driven out shortly before, was much beloved by the Narragansetts, they sent to him, begging that he would dissuade his friends from joining the Pequods. This good man, on receiving their message, set out alone in his canoe, in a violent storm, for the Narragansett village. He found the Pequod chiefs already there; but he pleaded so earnestly, that after wavering several days, the Narragansetts refused to join the Pequods, and declared themselves friends of the English.

The settlers now sent a body of men against the Pequods. Reaching one of their forts just before sunrise, they surprised its inmates, and set fire to their wigwams. They then formed a ring around the wigwams, and as the flames drove the Indians out, shot them down without mercy. Six hundred Pequods perished in an hour. The next morning, the rest of the tribe, who had been at another fort, came in sight and renewed the battle. They fought bravely, but were defeated by the English. The few that survived were pursued from place to place, and the whole tribe was destroyed.[3]

1885

Thomas Wentworth Higginson, *Young Folks' History of the United States*

The first Connecticut settlers found fiercer tribes to deal with than the Pilgrims; and they had very early a war with the Pequots, in which all the New England colonists were involved. It would have been much more serious than it was, but that Roger Williams used his influence over the Narragansett tribe to keep them from joining the war. A council of the Indians was being held and Roger Williams, in order to save the very men who had banished him from Massachusetts, went many miles in a canoe in a severe storm. The Pequots were enraged with Williams for interfering, but after four days of delay, the Narragansetts refused their aid. The Pequots kept up constant attacks upon the Connecticut settlers; and at last an expedition was sent against them (in 1637), consisting of ninety white men and several hundred Indian allies, under command of Capt. John Mason. Their object of attack was the chief fort of the Pequots, which lay near in what is now Stonington, Conn.

The fort covered more than an acre, which was enclosed by trunks of trees, about twelve feet high, set firmly in the ground, close together. Within these were some seventy wigwams, covered with matting and thatch, and arranged in two lanes. There were two entrances; and Captain Mason stationed himself at one of these, and the next in command, Captain Underhill, at the other, each having a portion of the colonists with him, while the Indian allies were arranged outside. As they were taking their positions, a dog barked, and they heard the cry from within, "Owanux, Owanux" ("Englishmen, Englishmen!").

Then the attack began. The roofs of the Indian cabins were set on fire, and the greater part of the Indians were killed; while only two white men were slain, many, however, being wounded. It was the first great blow inflicted by the whites on the Indians; and for forty years after it there was much more peace between the two races in New England.[4]

1888

John J. Anderson, *New Grammar School History of the United States*

They [English settlers] had come to a country pleasant to look upon, and of fertile soil, but troubles were before them. The Dutch called them intruders, and threatened to drive them away. Governor Stuyvesant was not yet in New Netherland. The Indians were still to be feared. These were the Pequods, or Pequots, the most powerful tribe in New England. They could muster a thousand warriors. The first settlers found the Pequods friendly, but, in the strife for furs, small bands of Indians committed hostile acts. A force sent against them burned their wigwams, and destroyed their corn and canoes.

Smarting under the belief that their punishment was not deserved, the

Pequods resolved upon revenge. They tried to get the Narragansetts to join them, but the good Roger Williams, who had fled to Rhode Island from Puritan persecution, at great risk to his life prevented the alliance. The infant towns on the Connecticut united for protection, but not before thirty of their inhabitants had fallen under the tomahawk. About a hundred colonists, with some friendly Indians, went against the Pequods, surprised them in the early morning, and set fire to their fort. Muskets, swords, and fire never before made destruction more complete. The bodies of six hundred men, women, and children were in the smoking ruins (1637).

The surviving Pequods hid in swamps. Being pursued and captured, the men were put to death or sent to the West Indies to be sold into slavery. The women and children not sent away were given to friendly Indians, or disposed of as slaves to the colonists. Sassacus, the chief of the tribe, escaped, and put himself under the protection of the Mohawks, in New York; but, influenced by the Narragansetts, the Mohawks basely killed him, and sent his scalp to Boston. The Pequod tribe was no more.

> "No more for them the wild deer bounds,
> The plough is on their hunting grounds;
> The pale man's axe rings through their woods,
>   The pale man's sail skims o'er their floods."[5]

1905

Thomas B. Lawler, *A Primary History of the United States*

In eastern Connecticut lived a powerful tribe of Indians named Pequots. From time to time they went on the warpath and put the settlers to death with terrible tortures. The colonists at last resolved to put an end to this warfare.

With a band of friendly Indians the Connecticut and Massachusetts soldiers marched (1637) against the Pequot stronghold. This was a fort surrounded by a wooden fence. Here were gathered seven hundred members of the tribe. On a bright moonlit night the colonists silently drew near. The sleeping Pequots did not dream of danger until burning torches were thrown over the high fence, or palisade, that surrounded the fort.

The huts became at once a mass of flames, and as the warriors rushed out they were killed by the bullets of the English or tomahawked by the Indians. Of all within the fort only five escaped. The Pequot nation was utterly destroyed, and New England had no further Indian wars for thirty-eight years.[6]

1913

Wilbur F. Gordy, *Stories of Early American History*

While the French were exploring Canada and the West and were living mostly as traders among the Indians, the English were planting settlements along the Atlantic Coast from New England to Georgia.

Most of them paid the Indians for their land; but the red men did not know at first that the English would cut down the forests, and so take away their hunting-grounds.

When they came to understand this, they seized the first excuse for trying to drive them off again. So there was much fighting between the English and the red men. A large part of this took place in New England.

Soon after Thomas Hooker and his company came to the Connecticut Valley, they had a war with the Pequot Indians, a fierce and powerful tribe then living in the southern part of what is now Connecticut.

These Indians killed two traders from Massachusetts, and stole their goods. When the people in Massachusetts tried to punish them, the Indians began to torture and murder all the men, women, and children they could lay their hands on. They killed over thirty, and the settlers in the valley of the Connecticut saw that they must either conquer the Pequots or leave the country.

So they prepared at once to send a body of men against the Pequot fort. They sailed down the Connecticut River and along the coast eastward, landing near the mouth of the Thames River. There they pitched their tents for the night.

Before daybreak the next morning, they advanced slowly and silently upon the Indians, who were still asleep in their stronghold. This was a village of wigwams, surrounded by a palisade, ten or twelve feet high, having only two doors, each just wide enough for one man to pass through.

The first alarm was the barking of a dog, next came the cry of a waking Indian. Quickly the white soldiers hurried to the openings to keep the Indians from escaping. Some rushed into the fort and others threw firebrands among the wigwams from the outside and set them on fire.

The red men fought bravely, but in vain. Many were burned alive, and others were killed as they rushed to the gates or jumped over the palisade. Only fourteen survived, of whom seven were captured. The others escaped.[7]

1955

Clyde B. Moore, Fred B. Painter, Helen M. Carpenter, and Gertrude M. Lewis, *Building Our America*

The Pequot Indians in Connecticut were not friendly. They raided the settlements, burning houses and killing more settlers. An army of settlers was raised, and, with the help of friendly Indians, attacked the main village of the Pequots. The village was set on fire just before dawn. Almost six hundred Indian men, women, and children were burned or shot before their warriors could get ready to defend themselves. Indian trouble in Connecticut was ended for a long time.[8]

1977

Lewis Paul Todd and Merle Curti, *Rise of the American Nation*

By 1635, the most powerful Indians in southern New England, the Pequots, realized that the rapid expansion of white settlements threatened their way of life and even their very existence. Mounting tension between the two races led to the Pequot War of 1635–37. After attacking two villages, the Pequots were surrounded in their own main fort. The fort was burned and nearly 400 Pequots were shot as they tried to escape. Others were hunted down, killed, or sold into slavery. Only a few Pequots survived the war. Smoldering hatred among the remaining Indian tribes toward the white settlers of New England was fanned by the contempt shown by most whites toward Indians. Their bitterness was increased by efforts among the white settlers to force Indians to live by Puritan standards.[9]

1986

James West Davidson and John E. Batchelor, *The American Nation*

When settlers ignored Indian land claims, fighting broke out. In the 1630s, the English accused the Pequots of killing two traders in the Connecticut Valley. Colonists decided to punish the Pequots. They attacked a Pequot town when most of the men were away and killed hundreds of unarmed men, women, and children.

In the war that followed, most of the Pequots were killed, and the English took over the rich lands of the Connecticut Valley.[10]

DISCUSSION QUESTIONS

1. In the 1832 textbook students learned that the Pequots were a "ferocious" and "warlike" people. Research the culture of the Pequot people and see if this statement is true or false. Defend your answer.

2. Do the textbooks from the 1800s make the extinction of the Pequot people sound as if it was a horrible event in history? How do you think students reading these textbooks in the 1800s would have reacted to hearing these stories?

3. *Genocide* means the deliberate killing off of an entire religious, ethnic, or national group. As these textbooks claim, one goal of the Pequot War was to kill off all the Pequots in New England. Was this the only time this happened in U.S. history? Explain.

4. The textbooks in this section all seem to disagree over what actually caused this war. Conduct research and see if you can find out what may have caused it. Who do you think was to blame for starting the fighting? In the 1946 textbook the authors claims that there was cruelty on both sides during this war. Is that true? Explain.

5. Explain why you think this story seems to get less and less attention over time in our history textbooks.

6. On a map of New England find and label all the places mentioned in

these textbook selections. What role do you think geography played in the events that transpired?

The 1910 census recorded that there were only sixty-six living Pequot people remaining. Today their number is estimated at between one thousand and two thousand.

6

The Salem Witch Trials

There are as many different explanations of why the Salem witchcraft trials oc-
curred as there are books written on the subject. What seems to be consistent
about this story in most history textbooks is that the authors usually tried to por-
tray the young girls, or the citizens of Salem, as being "silly," "delusional," or
even "hysterical." That they were a sane, rational people does not seem to be an
argument that many textbooks make.

Soon after the final trial of a suspected witch, in 1695, many family members
of the accused (and later their descendents) began to try to clear their family
names. It is interesting to note that even by 1695 there were those in the British
colonies who questioned how justifiable these trials were. Today the historical de-
bate continues over what exactly took place in and around Salem during this
time as well as the true cause of the bizarre behaviors that seemed to develop.

1875

John J. Anderson, *A Grammar School History of the United States*

During the war, King William, refusing to restore to Massachusetts the
charter which James II had taken away, granted a new one, which united
Plymouth, Massachusetts, Maine, and Nova Scotia in a royal government. Upon Phipps was conferred the office of governor.

One of the first acts of the new governor was the formation, in 1692, of a court to try certain persons who, because of their real or supposed strange conduct, were accused of practicing witchcraft. Most of the inhabitants of Salem and vicinity, where the accused parties lived, believed the accusations to be true; and, before the delusion was dispelled, twenty persons were put to death, more than fifty were tortured or frightened into confessing themselves guilty, and many suffered imprisonment.[1]

1884

Edward Ellis, *The Eclectic Primary History of the United States*

One of the strangest facts in the history of the colony was the Salem witchcraft. The folks in Salem suddenly seemed to have lost their senses with respect to this matter; but they were not much worse than people living in England at that time.

Some poor old woman was generally fixed upon as the witch, and it was thought that she had the power to change herself into the form of a cat or some other animal. Many of the ignorant people believed, too, that she rode through the air on a broomstick to a place where she met a party of demons, and helped them form plans of mischief.

The delusion began in the house of a minister, where a company of girls had met to study the black art, as it was called. They were suddenly affected with a nervous twitching of the face and muscles, and accused an old Indian servant of bewitching them.

She was whipped until she confessed the crime. A fast day was ordered, and the excitement spread everywhere. Magistrates were kept busy punishing those who were arrested, and it was unsafe even to express a doubt of their guilt.

Fifty-five persons were tortured, and twenty put to death, before the people awoke to their sin and folly. Then the persecutions ended, and those who had taken part in them bitterly repented the great wrong they had done.[2]

1930

William Backus Guitteau, *Our United States: A History for Upper Grammar Grades and Junior High School*

The Witchcraft Delusion

The colonists of the seventeenth century brought with them from Europe the belief in witchcraft. Superstitions die hard; and from earliest times, men believed in the existence of evil spirits that sometimes entered the bodies of people, usually friendless old women, and caused them to work harm to their neighbors. In England, Parliament actually passed a law which punished with death any one guilty of "Witchcrafte and dealing with evill and wicked Spirits." Cotton Mather, one of the leading ministers of Boston, wrote a long treatise on witchcraft; and his book helped to promote the strange delusion that seized upon the people of Salem in 1692.

The trouble began when the children of one Samuel Parris indulged in strange antics, saying that certain persons whom they or their father disliked had bewitched them. Soon there were accusations on all sides, and scores of people were arrested and brought before a special court for trial. Many confessed their guilt; they had actually talked to the devil, who took the form of a tall black man with a high-crowned hat. To others, a black dog had appeared and said, "Serve me." One woman related that she was riding on a broom-stick with another witch, when suddenly the stick broke; but by holding fast to the witch in front of her, she reached her destination safely. So overwrought were the minds of the people that they actually believed these silly tales. When the craze came to an end, twenty persons had been convicted and put to death, fifty-five had been pardoned after confessing their guilt, and one hundred and fifty more were in jail awaiting trial.[3]

1977

JoAnne Buggey, *America! America!*

The people who came to America from Europe brought with them many fears and superstitions. During the seventeenth century there had been a series of witchcraft epidemics in Europe. Hundreds of people had been put to death because they were believed to have supernatural powers or to be possessed by supernatural powers.

Some of the Puritans in New England were especially fearful of witchcraft and had passed laws against witches. Massachusetts and Connecticut were the scenes of two waves of persecution against people believed to be witches.

In Salem and other communities on the north shore of Massachusetts, hundreds of people were thrown into jail. People worried about their neighbors, not knowing who might be the first to point an accusing finger. Death was usually the penalty for being found guilty. This was thought to be in keeping with the teachings of the Bible. The book of Exodus states, "Thou shalt not suffer a witch to live."

By the time the witch hunts ended in 1693, 14 women and 5 men had been put to death because of testimony of 5 teen-age girls. Another 8 persons had been found guilty of witchcraft and were "awaiting hanging." Under pressure, 50 had confessed, 150 were in prison, and 200 more had been accused but had not as yet been arrested. Many innocent people confessed rather than risk a trial.[4]

1999

Beverly J. Armento, Jacqueline M. Cordova, J. Jorge Klor de Alva, Gary B. Nash, Franklin Ng, Christopher L. Salter, Louis E. Wilson, and Karen K. Wixson, *America Will Be*

The tension in the Massachusetts Bay Colony reached a high point in 1692. Two young Puritan girls, Elizabeth and Abigail, began acting strangely. They both would scream and fall to the floor as if they were unable to control themselves. They said they saw rats and other creatures swarming around them. A colonial doctor decided that Elizabeth and Abigail were victims of witchcraft.

Many people in Salem got caught up in the witch craze. First children and then older people were calling their unpopular neighbors "witches." When a person was accused, a trial would be held in the town.

Within a year, 19 people, mostly old women, were found guilty of witchcraft and hanged. Historians are not sure why the people of Salem became so hysterical about witchcraft. Some historians believe that poor farmers accused rich merchants of being witches out of jealousy. Other historians think that Puritan officials used the popular belief about witches to get rid of outspoken older women who challenged their authority. There is even a possibility that moldy grain was the cause. Such grain might have brought on an illness in people that made them seem to be possessed by devils.

After about a year, the witchcraft craze in the New England colonies died down. During that time, however, many people suffered and died because of the Puritans' fear of the devil and their beliefs about witchcraft.[5]

DISCUSSION QUESTIONS

1. Research this historical event and explain why you think the people of Salem were so convinced that there were witches when few if any historians since have seemed to agree with them.

2. If the study of history is about learning lessons from the past, what do you think these textbooks wanted students to learn about the Salem witch trials?

3. The 1977 textbook claims that Connecticut also had a witchcraft craze at about the same time as Salem. Research witchcraft trials in colonial America and see if this was a common or uncommon event during that period. What about in Europe?

4. After researching the Salem witch trials, explain who or what you think was to blame for causing this hysteria.

5. Since the late 1600s this event has been analyzed by looking at the fields of psychology, sociology, economics, political science, and geography. Explain how these different fields would interpret this event.

Do you think any of these textbooks would agree with how these different fields have interpreted this historical event?

On October 31, 2001, the acting governor of Massachusetts officially exonerated the remaining five young women accused of being witches during the Salem witch trials. Other former accused witches had been exonerated in the early 1700s and in 1957.

PART II

The American Revolution

7

The Boston Massacre

The events of March 5, 1770, are essential reading for any American student who takes a U.S. history class. Nearly every textbook explains how common American colonists stood up to the British soldiers on that cold night in Boston. What makes this topic so interesting, then, are the differences that appear in the various tellings of the story, putting into question the whole concept of students learning historical "facts" from their history textbooks.

1832

Noah Webster, *History of the United States: To Which is Prefixed a Brief Historical Account of our [English] Ancestors, from the dispersal at Babel, to their Migration to America, and of the Conquest of South America by the Spaniards*

To a free and high spirited people, the presence of an insolent military could not but be extremely irksome and provoking, and it was not possible that harmony could long subsist between the inhabitants of Boston, and the British troops. A slight affray took place between them on the second of March 1770; but on the night of the fifth, the enmity of the parties burst forth in violence and blood. A body of troops being ordered to disperse a number of the citizens of Boston, who were collected in Cornhill, the populace pelted them with stones, upon which the troops fired among

them, killed three and wounded five, two of whom died. With great difficulty the soldiers were saved from the fury of the enraged populace. But
this outrage inflamed the animosity of the Americans against Great Britain, and hastened a most important crisis. To commemorate this melan-
choly tragedy, an anniversary oration was instituted in Boston, and was
annually pronounced by some distinguished citizen on the fifth of March,
till the close of the revolution.[1]

1860

Benson J. Lossing, *A Primary History of the United States*

General Gage, who, you remember, was made governor at Montreal,
was then in Halifax with an army. He went to Boston, with many soldiers,
to compel the people to pay the duties or tax. It was a quiet Sabbath morning in September, 1763, when he marched into the town, with flags flying
and drums beating, as if it had been a conquered city. But the people,
strong in the right, felt no dismay.

The colonial governors became more proud, insolent, and overbearing,
when they saw the determination of the English government to force the
Americans into obedience. They treated them as rebels, and in every way
the Americans were irritated beyond endurance. Yet they acted manly and
respectful, while they were firm and unyielding.

Even the children partook of the boldness of their fathers and mothers.
On one occasion, in Boston, the soldiers had beaten down some snow-
hills which the boys had raised. This had been done before, and the lads
determined not to endure it longer. The larger boys held a meeting, and
several of them were appointed to see General Gage about it.

When the boys entered Gage's room, he asked why so many children
had called upon him. "We come, sir," said the tallest boy, "to demand satisfaction." "What!" said the general, "have your fathers been teaching you
rebellion, and sent you to exhibit it here?" "Nobody sent us, sir," replied
the boy, while his eyes flashed, and his cheeks reddened, at being accused
of rebellion.

The lad then told Gage how the soldiers had broken down their snow-
hills, and how, when they complained, they were called young rebels. "Yes-

terday," he continued, "our works were destroyed the third time, and we will bear it no longer." The general's heart was touched by the noble courage of the boy. "The very children here," he said to an officer at his side, "draw in a love of liberty with the air they breathe." He then assured the boys that their snow-hills should not be touched again.

The soldiers in New York and Boston became very insolent, and they and the citizens frequently quarreled. In the latter city, on the 5th of March, 1770, a quarrel took place, and that evening there was a riot. Three citizens were killed, and four were dangerously wounded, by the soldiers.

The excitement was very great. All the bells of the city were rung, and no doubt there would have been a great deal of bloodshed, if the governor had not promised justice to the people. They demanded the instant removal of the troops from Boston. This was done, and quiet was restored. The "Boston Massacre," as it was called, was long remembered.[2]

1873

John J. Anderson, *A Grammar School History of the United States*

When the day came on which the Stamp Act was to go into effect, there were no officials courageous enough to carry it into execution, and, besides, all the stamps had been concealed or destroyed. Business continued to be conducted without stamps, and the colonial merchants agreed to import no more goods while the obnoxious measure remained a law. A change in the British ministry occurring, the act was repealed in 1766.

Parliament, still claiming the right to tax the colonies, passed a bill, in 1767, for levying duties on glass, paper, painters' colors, and tea. The news of this and other obnoxious measures of the British government, produced a revival of the feelings which had been caused by the passage of the Stamp Act; and non-importation associations were formed.

The opposition of the people of Boston being particularly bold, two regiments were ordered by Gen. Gage from Halifax to overawe them. The presence of the troops exasperated the people and affrays ensued, in one of which, called the "Boston Massacre," occurring on the 5th of March,

1770, the soldiers fired upon the populace, killing three men and wounding others.

The opposition to the revenue measures induced Parliament to revoke all the duties laid in 1767, except that of three pence per pound on tea; but as the people were contending against the principle of "taxation without representation," and not against the amount of taxes imposed, the concession was not satisfactory.[3]

1885

Thomas Wentworth Higginson, *Young Folks' History of the United States*

In Boston the troops made themselves still more unpopular. There was quite a quarrel between them and the boys; for the soldiers used to destroy the snow-slides that the boys had prepared for their sleds. After appealing in vain to the captain, the boys finally went to the British general, and complained.

"What!" he said, "have your fathers been teaching you rebellion, and sent you here to exhibit it?"

"Nobody sent us, sir," said one of the boys. "We have never injured nor insulted your troops; but they have been spoiling our snow-slides, so that we cannot use them any more. We complained; and they called us 'young rebels,' and told us to help ourselves if we could. We told the captains of this, and they laughed at us. Yesterday our slides were destroyed once more; and we will bear it no longer."

The general ordered the damage to be repaired, and told Governor Gage, who said that it was impossible to beat the notion of liberty out of the people, as it was rooted in them from their childhood.

But the British troops in Boston had already got into more serious trouble. The young men of the town used often to insult the red-coated soldiers, calling them "lobsters," "bloody-backs," and such names, and threatening to drive them from the town. On the other hand, the soldiers used to be allowed, by their officers, to stray about the town in the evening, carrying their guns, and without any proper authority to control them. One moonlight evening (March 5, 1770), some soldiers were going about in this way, and got into a quarrel, as they often did. As they were taunting the people, and calling, "Where are they? Where are the cowards?" some boys began to snowball them, crying, "Down with them! Drive them to their barracks!" The noise increased, until the guard was called out, commanded by Captain Preston.

He came roughly through the crowd, with six or eight men, whom he drew up in line. Many of the people fell back, but about a dozen men, some of whom had sticks, advanced to meet the soldiers, and spoke angrily to them; and some, it was said, struck at the muskets with sticks. The noise increased every moment, till at last Captain Preston gave the word, "Fire!"

When the smoke had cleared away, there were eleven men stretched upon the ground, of whom eight were wounded, and three killed. Among these last was Crispus Attucks, a mulatto, and the leader of the mob. This affair made an intense excitement; and Captain Preston was tried for murder. But some of the leading lawyers of Boston, who were also eminent patriots, defended him on the ground that he had done his duty as an officer and he was acquitted. The public indignation was, however, so great over the whole affair that the two regiments of troops were soon removed to the barracks at Castle William, and were not allowed to stray about the streets. But this bloodshed never was forgotten, and the "Boston Massacre" was another step towards the Revolutionary War.[4]

1909

William H. Mace, *A Primary History: Stories of Heroism*

The king now sent two regiments of soldiers to Boston to force the people to pay the Tea Tax. There were frequent quarrels between the soldiers and the people. One evening in a street quarrel the soldiers killed three men and wounded eight others (1770). Immediately the fire bells rang and great crowds of angry people filled the streets. The next day they filled to overflowing Faneuil Hall, the "Cradle of Liberty." A still larger meeting in the Old South Church cried out that both regiments of soldiers must leave town.

Adams and other leaders were sent to the king's officers to tell them what the people had said. Before the governor and the general, backed by the king's authority and by two regiments, stood plain Samuel Adams, with only the voice of the people to help him.

The governor, unwilling to obey the demand of the people, said he would send one regiment away. But Samuel Adams stood firm and said: "Both regiments or none!" The governor finally gave up, and Samuel Adams, the man of the people, was a greater leader than ever before.

The king now tried to trick the Americans into paying the tax by making tea cheaper in America than in England, but leaving on the tax. But the people everywhere declared that they did not object to the price, but to the tax.[5]

1955

Glenn W. Moon and John H. MacGowan, *Story of Our Land and People*

The Boston Massacre created bitter feelings. Just before the repeal of the Townshend duties, a serious clash occurred between British troops and a group of colonists. It happened in Boston where feelings between Red Coats and townspeople were growing.

One cold March day in 1770 some carefree boys had a snowball fight in Boston. On their way home they saw a soldier walking back and forth on guard duty. They promptly began to throw snowballs at him. To them it was just fun, but the soldier became frightened. He called for help. Soldiers rushed to aid him.

The noise brought men and boys running from all directions. Both sides hurled insults back and forth. Suddenly an excited young officer yelled a command. The soldiers thought he said "Fire!" They fired their muskets. When the smoke lifted, eleven of the crowd lay dead or wounded in the snow.

This was the Boston Massacre. It was the first time blood was shed in the quarrel between Great Britain and the colonists. Some people call the Boston Massacre of 1770 the opening fight of the War of Independence.

Boston was in an uproar after the Massacre. Angry citizens, led by Samuel Adams, told the governor to get the troops out of Boston. The governor did not want any more trouble, so he sent the soldiers to an island in Boston Harbor.

News of the Boston Massacre spread quickly. People in the other colonies asked themselves, "Will we be next?" The feeling against Great Britain became more bitter. Repeal of most of the Townshend duties—soon after the Boston Massacre—helped restore good relations. But the Massacre was not forgotten.[6]

1966

Harold H. Eibling, Fred M. King, and James Harlow, *History of Our United States*

Purpose of the Troops

The third measure of England's new colonial policy was the plan to station 10,000 soldiers in the colonies. England told the colonists that the troops were to protect them against Indians and enemy countries. The Americans were expected to provide living quarters for this army and to pay part of the expense of maintaining it.

Since there was no longer any grave danger from the Indians, the French, or the Spanish, the colonists felt that the real purpose of the troops was to prevent the growing opposition to English laws. It had been a fairly simple matter to say "No!" to a single tax agent armed with nothing more than a quill pen and a stern look. It would not be so easy to ignore a squad of soldiers.

Bloodshed in Boston

Inasmuch as the colonists did not want a British army in their midst, it was only natural that trouble should develop between the colonists and the soldiers. Clashes occurred in Charleston, New York, Boston, and other towns where English troops were quartered.

The regiments of British soldiers stationed in Boston probably behaved themselves well enough. But their coats were red, their ways British, and the people could not forget that they were there to watch the colonists. Little things were easily magnified. In time little things piled up on both sides until there was no longer friendliness between the soldiers and the people.

On the evening of March 5, 1770, a false fire alarm brought many people into the streets, especially boys. You can picture these boys, disappointed at finding no fire, scooping up snow and making snowballs. What better target than a redcoated sentry standing motionless on his post of duty! They pelted the sentry before the customhouse door and called him names. Frightened, he called for help.

Captain Preston and seven men responded. A crowd gathered. Captain Preston warned the colonists to break up and go home. Insults were called. A group, led by Crispus Attucks, pushed against the alarmed soldiers. A soldier was knocked down. Another was hit by a club. Amid the shouting and confusion the soldiers fired! With a cry of terror, the crowd melted away and sought the safety of carts and doorways.

The soldiers, back to back, made ready to meet another attack. At their feet lay three dead colonists and eight wounded. Two of the wounded died.

The news of this bloodshed swept through the colonies. It came to be called the "Boston Massacre," by American patriots. People began to look with new distrust on the British soldiers. A great town meeting held in Boston demanded removal of the troops. The royal governor, anxious to avoid further trouble, took the soldiers out of the city and stationed them on an island in the harbor.[7]

2001

Wayne E. King and John L. Napp, *United States History*

One evening early in March of 1770, a crowd gathered near a group of British soldiers. The crowd began throwing stones and snowballs at the soldiers. The soldiers then fired a round of shots into the crowd. The first to fall was a free African, Crispus Attucks. A few colonists were killed, and several were wounded.

News of the Boston Massacre, as it was called, spread throughout the colonies. The people of Boston demanded that the British soldiers be removed from the city. The governor of Massachusetts agreed to remove the soldiers to prevent more trouble. The same day, all of the Townshend taxes were repealed except for the tax on tea. Great Britain had lost a good deal of money due to the boycotts. It was believed that the tax on tea was kept mainly as a symbol of the British right to rule.[8]

DISCUSSION QUESTIONS

1. Use library and Internet resources to research this topic and then create a timeline showing what events led up to the shooting in Boston that night.

2. After researching this story, explain exactly how many people were killed and wounded that night. Discuss in class what the word *massacre* means. Does this event meet your standards of what a massacre is? Explain.

3. What punishment did the British soldiers receive for shooting into the crowd? Do you agree with this verdict? Explain.

4. Write and present a biography of Crispus Attucks. Describe why you think U.S. history textbooks didn't mention him until the late 1880s, and then in mostly negative terms. Would you consider him the "leader of the mob," as some of these textbooks do?

5. The 1966 textbook mentions other clashes between British soldiers and colonists in the cities of Charleston and New York. Research these other events. Why do you think these historical events didn't make it into the history textbooks and the Boston Massacre does?

6. Find paintings of the Boston Massacre. When were these paintings done and by whom? Do the images in these paintings all tell the same story? Explain.

7. Some of the textbooks in this selection discuss the role of the children of Boston and how they too wanted their independence from England. Look at your current history textbook and see if these same children are mentioned. Explain why certain textbooks over time have included this story while others have not. What impact do you think the story of the children standing up to British authority may have had on some of the students reading these textbooks?

Paul Revere was the artist who created the famous engraving of the Boston Massacre that helped enrage many American colonists against the British troops. Interestingly enough, Revere was not there the night of the violence and very likely used the work of another engraver, Henry Pelham, as the basis of his own.

8

Lexington and Concord

A story that no U.S. history textbook can do without: what transpired on Lexington Green, Massachusetts, in April 1775. This is one event that every schoolchild has learned about since the creation of the first U.S. history textbook. It is a story that has helped generations of Americans learn what it is to be an American. Fraught with patriotic significance, it is nevertheless no more than a piece of history, as open to interpretation as any other.

1832

Noah Webster, *History of the United States: To Which is Prefixed a Brief Historical Account of our* [English] *Ancestors, from the dispersal at Babel, to their Migration to America, and of the Conquest of South America by the Spaniards*

Attack on the Militia at Lexington

An attempt of a party of British troops to take some cannon which were lodged at Salem, threatened to open the awful scene of hostilities, but the persuasion of its worthy clergyman induced the provincial troops to withdraw their opposition, at the drawbridge in the town; the British troops marched over, and not finding the cannon which had been previously removed, they marched back unmolested. But in April, a body of troops was ordered to march to Concord to destroy the military stores, which the Americans had collected at that place. The march, though in the night, was discovered, and early in the morning of the 19th of the month, about seventy of the Lexington militia assembled on the green. Major Pitcairn, who commanded the British troops, rode up to the militia, and addressing them by the name of rebels, ordered them to disperse. Not being obeyed, he discharged his pistol, and ordered the troops to fire. Eight men were killed and some others wounded. Thus began the sanguinary contest which dismembered the British empire, and ended in the establishment of the independence of the colonies.

Return of the Troops to Boston

Having dispersed the militia at Lexington, the British troops proceeded to Concord, destroyed some flour and other stores, and returned to Boston. But the exasperated patriots in the vicinity collected, and with such arms as they had, annoyed the troops on their march, by firing from behind fences and walls; and it is doubtful whether the detachment would not have been all killed or taken had not a reinforcement arrived and joined that body at Lexington on its retreat. On the part of the Americans, fifty men were killed, and a number wounded. Of the British forces sixty five were killed, and one hundred and eighty six wounded.[1]

I 860

Benson J. Lossing, *A Primary History of the United States*

When the trees budded, in the spring of 1775, there were three thousand British troops in Boston, sent there to frighten the Americans. Yet they were not frightened. They saw that they must fight for freedom, or be slaves, and they resolved to defy the fleets and armies of Great Britain.

With all these soldiers, Gage felt strong. Hearing that the patriots were collecting powder and balls, muskets and provisions, at the village of Concord, he sent a party of soldiers, on the night of the 18th of April, to seize them and carry them to Boston.

These troops reached Lexington at daylight. A good many Minutemen were watching for them there. A sharp fight took place, and eight of the patriots were killed, and the rest driven away. This was the beginning of the old War for Independence.

The British now marched on to Concord to seize the stores, and there they had another fight with the patriots. They soon found that the Minute-men were coming from all quarters, so they turned and fled to Boston as fast as their feet could go. When they got there, they found that two hundred and seventy-three of their number had been killed or wounded.

When the news of this bloodshed became generally known, there was great excitement among the patriots all over New England and elsewhere. Hundreds of people, armed and unarmed, started for Boston; and, before the 1st of May, full twenty thousand men were there, building fortifications to keep the British army from coming out of the city.[2]

1869

G.P. Quackenbos, *Elementary History of the United States*

In 1775, the war, long foreseen, broke out. It is known as the Revolutionary War. Early in that year, the British Parliament declared that Massachusetts was in rebellion, and sent out more troops. General Gage had already fortified Boston Neck, which connects the city with the mainland. The patriots had some trouble in getting their ammunition out of Boston. They hid their cannon in loads of manure, and their powder and cartridges in market-baskets and candle-boxes. Thus they passed the sentinels unsuspected.

The patriots collected most of their stores at Concord, a few miles from Boston. Hearing of this, General Gage one night sent a force of eight hundred men to destroy them. It was done very secretly; yet the patriots found out what was going on. The British, as they advanced towards Concord, heard bells ringing and guns firing in the surrounding country. These were signals for the minute-men to assemble.

A little more than half way between Boston and Concord was the village of Lexington. Here the British arrived shortly after daylight. They found a body of minute-men on the green. "Disperse, ye rebels!" said the British leader, riding up to them and discharging his pistol. His men then fired. Several of the Americans fell. The rest gave way. This was the first blood shed in the Revolution.

The British went on to Concord. Here some of them held the bridge, while the rest went to destroy the stores. Meanwhile some American militia-men came up, and a skirmish took place at the bridge. Several fell on both sides; and, as soon as their companions came back, the British were glad to commence their homeward march. They had destroyed two cannon, had thrown a great number of cannon-balls into the river and wells, and had broken to pieces about sixty barrels of flour. Most of the stores had been carried off to a place of safety before they arrived.

A large quantity of flour was saved by a miller named Wheeler. It was stored in his barn, along with some of his own. When the soldiers came to search the place, Wheeler told them that he was a miller, and made his living by grinding grain. Then putting his hand on a barrel which belonged to himself, he said: "This is my flour; surely you will not destroy private property." The soldiers thought from what he said that it was all his, and went away without doing any injury.

The British suffered sorely on their return. The alarm had spread, and the brave men of the surrounding country came up from all sides. Posting themselves behind barns and houses, trees and fences, they poured in a deadly fire on the retreating British. In vain the latter tried to return it. All the way to Boston, they were thus harassed. Their ranks kept thinning, and they were ready to sink with fatigue. They would never have reached the city, had not fresh troops been sent to their aid.

The news of the battle of Lexington was the signal for a general rising. The farmer left his plough and the mechanic his workshop. Even old men and boys hastened to arm themselves. The wife girded the sword about her husband. The mother blessed her son, and bade him go strike a blow for his country.[3]

1884

Edward Ellis, *The Eclectic Primary History of the United States*

General Gage was royal governor of Massachusetts, and commander-in-chief of the British troops. He had three thousand soldiers in Boston. Learning that the Americans had stored some military supplies in Concord, a few miles distant, he sent Colonel Smith and Major Pitcairn with a body of soldiers to destroy them.

As soon as the patriots learned his purpose, they sent messengers to warn the minute-men along the route. The British reached Lexington early in the morning, and found the minute-men hastily gathering on the village green.

Major Pitcairn rode forward on his horse, and ordered them to disperse. They did not obey; whereupon he discharged his pistol at them, and commanded his men to fire. They did so, and seven of the patriots were killed.

A scattering and ineffective fire was returned, and the Americans dispersed. The British continued their march to Concord, destroyed the stores, and started back to Boston.

But the massacre on the village green had aroused the patriots, and, catching up their guns, they rushed to the attack. From behind fences, trees, and stone walls, they poured in their bullets upon the invaders as they hurried toward Boston.

So deadly was the fire that all the British would have been killed had not re-enforcements been sent them. When the first battle of the Revolution was ended, the Americans had lost forty-nine killed and thirty-four wounded; and the British, nearly three hundred killed, wounded, and missing.

The tidings of the battle roused the colonies to arms. Men left their plows and workshops, seized their flintlocks, bade their families good-bye, and hurried to Cambridge. Israel Putnam, a staunch patriot of Connecticut, was building a wall on his farm when the news reached him. He immediately set off toward Boston without waiting to change the checkered shirt in which he had been working. In a short time, thousands of men were throwing up entrenchments to keep the British in the city. Large re-enforcements also arrived for the enemy. Every one saw that a battle must soon be fought.[4]

1912

Henry William Elson, *A Guide to United States History for Young Readers*

In April, 1775, the British commander sent an army to destroy military stores at Concord, sixteen miles from Boston. But the people were roused by Paul Revere, who galloped out at midnight and shouted, "The British are coming, the British are coming!"

Next day, April 19th, occurred the first battle of the Revolution—the battle of Lexington. The British destroyed the stores at Concord, but they came near being destroyed themselves. The farmers fired on them from behind the fences, trees, bushes, and boulders, as they ran back to Boston, and the road was strewn with redcoats along the way.

This battle roused the New England farmers, when the news reached them, as nothing had ever done before. Israel Putnam left his plow in the field, hurried to his house to say good-by to his family, and started for Boston. Matthew Buell, a Connecticut farmer, did the same thing. John Stark, of New Hampshire, was sawing logs at his mill in his shirt sleeves, and he started for the scene of conflict without a coat and without going to the house. On the way he gathered an army of twelve hundred men. Nathanael Greene came from Rhode Island with a thousand followers ready to give their lives for their country.

But this was not all. The women did their share.

Mrs. Draper, the wife of a farmer near Dedham, Massachusetts, urged her husband and their sixteen-year-old boy to go, and when they had gone said to her daughter: "Kate, we have work to do, too. There will be hundreds of men passing here within a few days. They will be hungry. We must feed them."

The great outdoor oven was soon in operation. All that day, all night, and the next day the two women and a servant worked. They soon had a large stock of provisions ready. They made a long rough table of boards, and loaded it with bread and cheese and cider. Hundreds of would-be soldiers came along and partook of Mrs. Draper's bountiful store. Some of them, though half starved with their long walk, were so anxious to fight the British that they could scarcely be persuaded to stop long enough to satisfy their hunger.

The people took the leaden weights of their clocks and window shades, spoons and leaden dishes, and sent them to the army to be melted into bullets; many women sent their blankets and even their own flannel clothing to be made into men's shirts.

A lady in Philadelphia wrote: "My only brother I have sent to the camp with my prayers and blessings, and had I twenty sons and brothers, they should all go. I have retrenched all extra expenses, have drunk no tea since Christmas, and spend my time making clothing for the soldiers."

So it was all over the colonies. The people were so roused against the British oppression that they were willing to make any sacrifice for liberty. Patrick Henry, of Virginia, had said in a great speech, "I know not what course others may take, but as for me, give me liberty or give me death."[5]

1930

William Backus Guitteau, *Our United States: A History for Upper Grammar Grades and Junior High School*

Lexington and Concord, April 19, 1775

Meantime, affairs in Massachusetts were moving swiftly toward a crisis. General Gage with a force of five thousand men held Boston in sullen submission; but he dared not provoke a conflict by arresting Hancock and Adams, or by attempting to disarm the inhabitants. While the British were throwing up fortifications around Boston, the colonists were not idle. In the near-by towns, companies of minutemen were drilling on each village green; stores of muskets and powder and ball were collected and hidden away for the conflict that seemed at hand; and by the spring of 1775, eastern Massachusetts had become an armed camp.

Now or never, Gage must strike. He determined on a secret expedition which should arrest the patriot leaders, Hancock and Adams, at Lexington, then destroy the military stores hidden at Concord. Toward midnight on April 18, 1775, eight hundred British soldiers crossed the Charles River in boats, and started on the road to Lexington. But the patriots were on the watch. Signal lanterns hung in the belfry of the Old North Church flashed out the warning to swift-riding messengers. Far ahead of the British troops rode Paul Revere, and his warning shouts awakened the farmers along the Lexington highway. Signal fires were lighted on the hilltops; soon the whole countryside knew that the British soldiers were coming. Warned by Revere, Adams and Hancock made their escape from Lexington and started for Philadelphia, where the Second Continental Congress was soon to meet. At daybreak of April 19, the British reached Lexington, where they were confronted by about sixty minutemen. Their commander, Captain Parker, told his men: "Don't fire unless you are fired on; but if they want a war, let it begin here." A shot was fired, by which side is not certain; then came a volley from the British soldiers which killed eight men and wounded many others. Unable to oppose a force that outnumbered them ten to one, the minutemen fell back in confusion.

The British Retreat to Boston

From Lexington the British forces marched on to Concord, only six miles away, where they destroyed a few cannon and other military supplies. Toward noon they began their retreat to Lexington. The countryside was aroused by this time. From the shelter of trees, rocks, and fences, a deadly fire was poured on the British regulars, until the retreat became a rout. At Lexington they must have surrendered had not strong reinforcements under Lord Percy come to their rescue. With nearly two thousand men under his command, Percy had to fight every foot of his way back to Boston along a highway swarming with deadly marksmen. The fighting did not end until nightfall, when the wearied British soldiers found shelter in Charlestown under the guns of the king's ships.

As a result of this memorable nineteenth of April, all America realized that war had actually begun. From every hill and valley of New England, men left their farms to aid the patriots of Massachusetts. Within three days after Lexington, General Gage was no longer a besieger; he was himself surrounded in Boston by an untrained army of 16,000 men.[6]

1946

George Earl Freeland and James Truslow Adams, *America's Progress in Civilization*

It was inevitable that the armed forces of Massachusetts would clash with the British troops. The British heard that the colonists had a supply of arms and powder at Concord, a small town about twenty miles from Boston. They decided to send a force of soldiers to destroy those supplies. The troops also had orders to capture John Hancock and Samuel

Adams, who were staying with a friend at Lexington, near Concord. Both Hancock and Adams were guilty of treason for being colonial leaders.

In order to surprise the colonists, the British troops left Boston during the night. The Minute Men were aroused, and Hancock and Adams were warned in time to make their escape. "Paul Revere's Ride," written by Henry Wadsworth Longfellow, describes one of the ways by which it is said the countryside was alarmed. The first clash came at Lexington, where Minute Men were assembling. The British commander ordered them to disperse and when they refused, he commanded his troops to fire. Eight Americans were killed, and after returning the fire, the Americans left the field.

At Concord bridge the real fight began. Minute Men, most of whom were expert riflemen, arrived from every direction. As the British retreated toward Boston, they were fired upon by the Americans who were in ambush behind trees and stones along the way. Finally the British retreat became flight. They were saved by the arrival of fresh troops, and retired into Boston. During the next few days from North, South, and West, new arrivals swelled the ranks of the Americans until 20,000 men, hardened by the rough outdoor colonial life, surrounded the British in Boston.[7]

1970

Kenneth Bailey, Elizabeth Brooke, and John J. Farrell, *The American Adventure*

General Gage knew that Samuel Adams and John Hancock, a wealthy Boston banker, had formed a new patriotic organization called the Minutemen. The members of this organization were to be ready at a minute's notice to take action against British forces.

The Minutemen had been collecting rifles and gunpowder in Concord. When Gage learned of this large supply of weapons and ammunition, he ordered that it be seized and that Adams and Hancock be arrested.

In April, 1775, Gage sent Colonel Francis Smith and seven hundred men to Concord. The Massachusetts governor did not know it, but his men were being carefully watched. The patriots had signals to use whenever the British troops made a move.

One of the Minutemen was Paul Revere, a silversmith who had partici-
pated in the Boston Tea Party. On the night of April 18, a messenger told
Revere that two light signals had been seen from the tower of the Old
North Church. Two signals meant that the British army was moving by
ship from Boston harbor. Revere was to arouse the neighboring patriots
and get to the town of Lexington to warn Hancock and Adams.

Paul Revere started his famous ride from Boston to Lexington with
two other patriots, William Dawes and Dr. Samuel Prescott. After they
warned Hancock and Adams of the approaching troops, the three patriots were stopped by British troops halfway between Lexington and
Concord. In Revere's own words: "Just as I reached it (a barrier set up by
the British) out started six [British] officers, seized my bridle, put their
pistols to my breast, ordered me to dismount, which I did." Dawes and
Prescott managed to escape and carry the news of the British advance.
Contrary to legend, Paul Revere was forced to walk and never finished the
ride.

Colonel Smith and his men reached Lexington at dawn on April 19.
An advance unit was led by Major John Pitcairn. The major found seventy
armed Minutemen waiting on the village green. Pitcairn told his men to
hold their fire. Captain John Parker, leader of the Minutemen, also told
his men to hold their fire.

When a shot rang out from the American side, the British soldiers
started firing. By the time order was restored, eight Americans were dead
and eight more were wounded. Only one British soldier was hurt. Smith
and his men continued on toward Concord.

At Concord's North Bridge, the redcoats faced a group of angry patriots. The Americans attacked and fourteen British fell. Smith decided to
turn back to Boston. On the way back, the British were attacked on all
sides by the colonial militiamen. Smith and his troops got reinforcements
in Lexington and hurried back to Boston.

The colonists had killed the king's soldiers—a serious offense. The battles at Lexington and Concord were more than local skirmishes. Pam-
phlets and protests had given way to rifle fire. Ninety-three Americans
were dead, wounded, or missing. The British counted 273 casualties. By
midday on April 20, thousands of patriots had gathered in Boston to try to
force the British to leave. As the word that Massachusetts was at war with
Britain spread, Americans banded together to help.[8]

1991

Carlton L. Jackson and Vito Perrone, *Two Centuries of Progress*

During the winter and spring of 1774–1775, Britain sent more soldiers to Boston. No one knew what the next move would be. But the Massachusetts radicals were getting ready for anything. They began training soldiers and gathering military supplies.

The British commander in Boston, General Thomas Gage, decided to act. On April 19, 1775, he sent British soldiers to capture powder and guns at nearby Concord. Next the soldiers were to arrest the radical leaders, Samuel Adams and John Hancock, at Lexington. Warned by Paul Revere and William Dawes, groups of farmers challenged the British soldiers at both Lexington and Concord. These colonists, ready to fight at short notice, were called minutemen. The clash, and the British retreat to Boston ended with 273 British soldiers dead wounded, or missing. The Americans lost 93.

The news went out through the colonies that Massachusetts farmers had been massacred by British soldiers. These wild stories convinced most colonists that Britain wanted war.[9]

DISCUSSION QUESTIONS

1. In the 1832 textbook the author discusses events that happened in Salem, Massachusetts. Research what happened in Salem in April 1775. Explain why you think most history textbooks do not mention this event.

2. Investigate and explain why the story of Paul Revere does not appear in history textbooks until after the 1860s.

3. The story of Lexington Green and the battle that followed is essential reading in every U.S. history textbook. Why do you think textbook authors treat this as such an important story?

4. Many of the textbooks in this section discuss how the American colonists shot at the British Army from behind trees, fences, and rocks. Explain why the American militia did not stand in an open field and fight the British troops face-to-face.

5. Some historians claim that the battle of Lexington and Concord was

a unifying moment for the American colonists. Looking at these text-books, give examples explaining whether or not you think these text-book authors feel this was or was not a unifying moment in history.

The events of April 19, 1775, are probably best remembered by many Americans through poetry. In 1836 Ralph Waldo Emerson wrote "Concord Hymn" and in 1860 Henry Wadsworth Longfellow wrote "The Midnight Ride of Paul Revere."

9

The Battle of Trenton

One of the more famous battles of the Revolutionary War, the Battle of Trenton pitted a demoralized American army against the Hessians, allies of the British. Often considered a key turning point in the early stages of the war, this victory was a huge public relations win for George Washington.

1832

Noah Webster, *History of the United States: To Which is Prefixed a Brief Historical Account of our [English] Ancestors, from the dispersal at Babel, to their Migration to America, and of the Conquest of South America by the Spaniards*

Retreat of General Washington, and His Victory at Trenton

The American army being greatly reduced by the loss of men taken prisoners, and by the departure of men whose enlistments had expired, General Washington, was obliged to retreat towards Philadelphia; General Howe, exulting in his successes, pursued him, notwithstanding the weather was severely cold. To add to the disasters of the Americans, General Lee was surprised and taken prisoner. Due to the surprised state of affairs many persons joined the British cause and took protections. But a small band of heroes checked the tide of British success. A division of

Hessians had advanced to Trenton, where they reposed in security. General Washington was on the opposite side of the Delaware, with about three thousand men, many of whom were without shoes or convenient clothing; and the river was covered with floating ice. But the General knew the importance of striking some successful blow to animate the expiring hopes of the country; and on the night of December 25th, crossed the river, fell on the enemy by surprise, and took the whole body, consisting of about nine hundred men. A few were killed, among whom was Colonel Rahl, the commander.[1]

1884

Edward Ellis, *The Eclectic Primary History of the United States*

The British threatened Philadelphia, and Washington hastened into New Jersey to check them; but his force was reduced to three thousand men, and he could do almost nothing. He retreated slowly before Cornwallis, the British commander, and crossed the Delaware at Trenton, taking all the boats, so that the enemy could not follow.

But while so many patriots lost heart, the great and good Washington never despaired. He knew his cause was just, and he prayed to heaven to give it success. He did his utmost to encourage his soldiers, and he infused hope in many hearts. After crossing the Delaware into Pennsylvania, he was joined by fifteen hundred volunteers from Philadelphia.

Washington felt that the time had come to strike a telling blow against the enemy. He, therefore, prepared to recross the Delaware with three divisions, and attack the British in Trenton. The river was so full of floating ice, that only his own division was able to force its way across the river. The patriots landed on the New Jersey shore a few miles above Trenton.

At daybreak, Washington surprised Colonel Rall and his Hessians in the town of Trenton. The Hessian leader was mortally wounded. Sixteen others were killed, and seventy-eight wounded, while none of the Americans were slain. Nearly a thousand of the Hessians were taken prisoners.[2]

1909

William H. Mace, *A Primary History: Stories of Heroism*

Those were, indeed, dark days for the Americans. Hundreds of Washington's soldiers had gone home discouraged, and many other faint-hearted Americans thought the cause lost, and were again promising obedience to George III. But the people did not yet know Washington.

On Christmas night, with two thousand five hundred picked men, Washington took to his boats, and crossed the Delaware in spite of the floating ice. Nine miles away, in Trenton, lay the Hessians, those soldiers from Hesse-Cassel, in Europe, whom George III had hired to fight his American subjects, because Englishmen refused to fight Americans. On went the little army in spite of the biting cold and blinding snow. Two men froze to death and others were numb with cold.

"Our guns are wet," said an officer. "Then use the bayonet!" replied Washington. There was a sudden rush of tramping feet and the roar of cannon in the streets. The Hessian general was killed, and one thousand of his men surrendered.

These were a strange lot of prisoners. Not one could speak a word of English nor cared a thing for George III. No doubt they wished themselves at home on that morning. But the Hessians were not more surprised than the British generals in New York.

Cornwallis, the British commander, hurried forward with troops to capture Washington, but rested his army at Trenton. That night Washington's army stole away, and Cornwallis awoke in the morning to hear the booming of Washington's cannon at Princeton, where Washington was defeating another part of the British army. Cornwallis hastened to Princeton. It was too late. Washington was safe among the heights of Morristown, where Cornwallis did not dare attack him.

These two victories turned the tide and aroused the Americans. Reinforcements and supplies made Washington's army stronger and more comfortable.[3]

1923

Henry Eldridge Bourne and Elbert Jay Benton, *Story of America and Great Americans*

Washington showed how skillful he could be when he captured a garrison which the British had stationed at Trenton, now the capital of New

Jersey, on the eastern bank of the Delaware River. It was made up of German troops which the British hired to fight the colonists. The battle took place at Christmas, the year Independence was declared. Washington thought the Germans would be celebrating Christmas joyfully and would not be on the watch for an attack. His little army was on the western bank of the river, and it was hard to cross on account of the floating ice.

Once across, the Americans marched eight or nine miles in the rain and sleet. They reached Trenton before the Germans heard of their approach and captured nearly all. Not an American was killed. Washington took his prisoners to Philadelphia, and then re-crossed the river and put to flight three regiments of British at Princeton, not far from Trenton. The result was that the British withdrew from New Jersey and remained for months in New York.[4]

1955

Glenn W. Moon and John H. MacGowan, *Story of Our Land and People*

Americans won surprising victories at Trenton and Princeton. The British believed they had crushed the rebellion. But Washington fooled them. He suddenly turned, in New Jersey, and made two attacks.

In those days, armies did not usually fight in the winter. When snow began to fall, they settled down in a town or a fort. They made this their "winter quarters."

Howe and his men settled comfortably in New York City. Only a few regiments remained in Trenton and Princeton to hold the New Jersey colony. Scouts reported to Washington that two of the hated Hessian regiments were stationed in Trenton on the Delaware River.

On Christmas night, 1776, the Hessian soldiers were drinking and making merry. Snow was falling; the river was full of ice. This was the night Washington chose to strike.

With a few companies of picked men, he crossed the river by boat. He attacked in the morning. The Hessians, in drunken sleep, were taken completely by surprise. They had to surrender. The Americans captured nearly a thousand prisoners.[5]

1961

Edna McGuire and Thomas B. Portwood, *Our Free Nation*

With the army in retreat many soldiers thought their cause lost and went home. There was little money with which to buy supplies for those who remained. Winter found the army hungry, cold, and without shelter.

Howe followed the retreating Americans across New Jersey. He stationed some of his Hessian soldiers at Trenton. But the general, who loved good living, returned to New York to celebrate the Christmas holidays. This gave Washington his opportunity. Let us see how he used it.

The commander's own force has been made stronger by the arrival of fresh troops. A bold plan takes shape in his mind. He will cross the Delaware River in the night and attack Trenton in the early morning. Knowing how well Germans like to eat and drink at the holiday season, he decides to make his attack on the morning after Christmas Day. Then, he hopes, the Hessians may be sleeping soundly after their feasting. Christmas Night brings a terrible storm. Sleet falls, covering the roads with a sheet of ice. The Delaware is filled with cakes of floating ice.

A less-determined man might turn back, but not George Washington. He has set out to cross the Delaware, and cross he does. Among the troops are a number of fishermen from New England. With these men at the oars the boats move safely among the floating ice cakes. But ten precious hours are required to get all the company across. With this done, the men form two columns and set out on a nine-mile march to Trenton. A blinding storm of snow and sleet whips at their faces. The wind rages about them. Yet the men march on, never pausing. For Trenton must be reached before the Hessians are out of bed if Washington's plan is to succeed.

As the Americans approach the town, they capture the guards. Quickly American guns are planted so that they command the main streets. As the alarm is sounded, surprised Hessians tumble out of bed. They seize their weapons and make such defense as they can. Shots ring out. Men drop, killed or wounded by the bullets of the Americans. But in less than an hour the battle is ended and nearly a thousand Hessians have surrendered.

This has been a good night's work for the Americans. At the cost of four men, two frozen to death and two killed in battle.[6]

1991

Clarence L. Ver Steeg and Carol Ann Skinner, *Exploring America's Heritage*

After the recent victories, many of the British soldiers thought the war was almost won. On Christmas night 1776, they certainly did not expect trouble. But Washington had a daring plan. With about 2,500 troops, he dashed back across the Delaware to attack the British in Trenton.

The night was bitterly cold. The wind whipped up the river, and great chunks of ice bumped against the small boats that carried the soldiers. The bad weather slowed the crossing by several hours. Yet Washington's army surprised the soldiers in Trenton. The Continentals captured the city in a 45-minute battle.[7]

DISCUSSION QUESTIONS

1. Most U.S. history textbooks have described the Hessians as a group of brutal mercenaries hired by the British to help them fight the war against the colonists. Investigate who the Hessians were, and what happened to them after the war was over. Are U.S. history textbooks correct in calling them savage mercenaries? If possible, try to find out what German historians say about this same group of people.

2. Most of the textbooks in this section mention how this victory was a turning point in the American Revolution. Create a timeline of events before and after the Battle of Trenton and explain why you think historians believe this was such an important event.

3. Why do you think the 1923 textbook uses the word *German* to describe the soldiers that Washington was fighting, rather than the word *Hessian*, which was more commonly used in textbooks up through the 1800s?

4. Geography seems to play an important role in this story. Some textbooks discuss how troops would go into "winter quarters" during the Revolutionary War. Research what this means, and explain why they did it and how the Battle of Trenton plays into that.

5. Some textbooks claim that one reason why Washington won this battle so easily was that the Hessian troops had partied and drunk too much the night before. According to your research, is this correct?

6. Explain why you think the Battle of Trenton receives so little attention in the 1991 textbook as compared to earlier ones.
7. After reading these textbooks and doing your own research, explain exactly how many Americans were killed during this battle.

Starting in the later 1800s, the now famous painting Washington Crossing the Delaware *became an almost mandatory picture in U.S. history textbooks. Originally completed in 1851 by Emanuel Leutze, it has also been picked apart by historians for a number of inaccuracies found in it. Historians point out that Washington would not have been standing, that it was actually raining that night, and—probably the greatest sin of all—that the American flag as we know it had not been created yet. Even with that, schoolchildren for decades have been given this image as a historical depiction of that great moment in American history.*

10

George Rogers Clark

A number of individuals made a name for themselves on the American frontier, such as Davy Crockett, Daniel Boone, Meriwether Lewis, and William Clark. Their exploits have a prominent place in our national memory. Yet others have been forgotten, among them William Clark's older brother, George Rogers Clark. Why does historical memory favor some people and not others? Over the past two hundred years, history textbooks have sometimes portrayed the story of George Rogers Clark and his men, but their exploits have been all but forgotten today. Still, it's a story with uncommon bravery, sacrifice, daring, and significance for the new nation—one that is still worth considering.

1888

John J. Anderson, *New Grammar School History of the United States*

The vast region north of the Ohio was, during the first years of the war, in the undisputed possession of the English. Its governor, General Hamilton, from his headquarters at Detroit, offered rewards for scalps, but not for prisoners. Thus incited, the savages scoured the country in every direction to murder its unprotected settlers. No person was spared, for the scalp of a woman or child brought as big a reward as that of a man. Having made bargains with various tribes of Indians, Hamilton planned an expedition against what was then the western part of Virginia and known as the County of Kentucky. Before, however, he could put his plan into execution, Colonel Clark, a backwoodsman of the county, was leading a party of volunteers to frustrate him. On rafts and flatboats the Kentuckians floated down the Ohio, and, when within a few miles of its mouth, landed, and, marching northward, captured Kaskaskia, the oldest town in Illinois. Other posts were also captured (1778).

On hearing of these events, Hamilton left Detroit and began a march toward Kaskaskia. It took him more than a month to get to Vincennes, the oldest town in Indiana, and, as has been supposed, "the seat of empire of the mysterious race known as Mound Builders." Though the middle of winter had come, and there were many miles between the two commanders, Clark resolved to seek his enemy. After a toiling march of sixteen days, five of them in crossing the "drowned lands of the Wabash," his men often wading up to their breasts in water and holding their rifles and powder-horns above their heads, he appeared before Vincennes. "The hair-buyer," as Hamilton was called, made a stubborn defense, but in vain. He and his troops became prisoners of war (February, 1779). It has been said that, "except for George Rogers Clark and his victories, the Northwest would today be a British Canadian province."[1]

1905

Thomas B. Lawler, *A Primary History of the United States*

George Rogers Clark's Expedition

Here and there throughout the vast territory that now forms the states of Ohio, Indiana, and Michigan, the British held many fortified posts. From these forts they urged the Indians to go on the warpath against the American settlers.

George Rogers Clark planned an expedition to capture these forts, destroy the Indian alliance, and add the territory to his native colony of Virginia.

With a force of one hundred and fifty men Clark sailed down the Ohio to a point forty miles from its mouth, where he landed. One hundred miles away was Fort Kaskaskia. The way there led through forests and swamps.

Clark with his little band pushed on through the pathless woods and silently drew near the fort. Soon they heard the sounds of music. A ball was in progress and all the soldiers were there. Clark's force silently surrounded the fort while he quietly walked in at the open gate and stood in the door watching the dancers. He had been there but a moment when an Indian, seeing him, gave the war whoop. In an instant all was confusion. The women screamed and the soldiers ran to get their guns. It was too late. "Go on with your dance," said Clark calmly; "but remember you now dance under the flag of Virginia."

Capture of Vincennes

Father Peter Gibault, a loyal friend of the Americans, now went to Vincennes and persuaded the French as well as the Catholic Indians to join Clark's colors. Without firing a shot Clark took the fort through Father Gibault's influence.

When the British heard of Clark's victories they marched from Detroit and recaptured Vincennes. They held it but a short time. With only one hundred and thirty men Clark waded through the swamps and overflowed lands of the Wabash and suddenly appeared before the fort once more. For twenty four hours his men kept up a steady fire upon the British works. The British saw that their position was now hopeless, and surrendered, hauling down their flag (February 23, 1779) amid great rejoicing by the sturdy frontiersmen who made up Clark's little army.

One of the greatest results of Clark's victory was that at the close of the Revolution the Great Lakes instead of the Ohio River became our boundary on the north, and the Mississippi river marked the extent of our territory on the west.[2]

I 9 2 3

Henry Eldridge Bourne and Elbert Jay Benton, *Story of America and Great Americans*

While Washington was fighting the British in New Jersey and New York, the settlers on the frontiers of Pennsylvania and Virginia were struggling with the Indians who believed this to be the time to drive the white man from their hunting grounds. The Indians received help from the British who held forts at Detroit and other places captured in the earlier war with the French.

Patrick Henry was governor of Virginia. He sent George Rogers Clark, a hunter and Indian fighter in Kentucky, to attack the British forts. With 150 men Clark boarded several flatboats and floated down the Ohio River. When he reached the region which is now Illinois he marched northward. The Fourth of July, 1778, he celebrated by capturing Kaskaskia on the Mississippi River. His greatest exploit was the capture of Vincennes early the next spring when the rivers were high and the lowlands were flooded. His men often waded in icy water, sometimes up to their chins. The Indians called him the "Big Knife Chief." His successes were the reason for his being named also the "Conqueror of the Northwest." [3]

1951

Clyde B. Moore, Fred B. Painter, Helen M. Carpenter, and Gertrude M. Lewis, *Building Our America*

George Rogers Clark was sent to Williamsburg, Virginia, by the settlers along the Ohio River to ask for help against Indian raiders. He returned with gunpowder and decided to attack the English forts. These were the old French forts that were turned over to England after the French and Indian War.

Clark, with two hundred woodsmen, started down the Ohio River in the spring of 1778. He surprised the British at Fort Kaskaskia on the Mississippi while the officers were giving a dancing party. Clark posted his men around the fort and boldly walked into the dance hall. The women and officers became excited. Clark ordered them to go on with the dance. "Hereafter," he added, "you must dance under the American Flag."

Later, Clark took Fort Vincennes on the Wabash River.

This gave the American colonies control of the land north of the Ohio River and east of the Mississippi (the Northwest Territory). [4]

1970

Kenneth Bailey, Elizabeth Brooke, and John J. Farrell, *The American Adventure*

The British felt that it was very important to hold the wild country in the Ohio Valley, especially if the Americans should win their independence. Every effort was made by the British to drive the settlers out of the valley, and to keep the country under military rule.

A brave and daring backwoodsman from Virginia, George Rogers Clark, set out with a band of only two hundred men to capture the British posts. In October, 1778, Clark and his men reached the forts along the Ohio and Mississippi Rivers.

Clark's courage and persistence were amazing. With his small army, he managed to defeat the British forces in all the important forts. His victories at Kaskaskia, Cahokia, and Vincennes were all hard won. The capture of Vincennes was especially interesting. Clark knew he was outnumbered by the enemy. To trick the British commander into thinking there were many more Americans, he told his men to tie twenty American flags to poles; each pole was to be carried by a single man. The men were to spread out so that when the British looked out over the horizon and saw twenty flags approaching, they would think a large army was coming.

The plan worked and the British surrendered. The spring of 1779 found the Ohio Valley in American hands, where it was destined to remain.[5]

1991

Clarence L. Ver Steeg and Carol Ann Skinner, *Exploring America's Heritage*

While fighting went on in the North, settlers had moved west of the Appalachians. Patrick Henry, governor of Virginia, ordered Colonel George Rogers Clark to protect them.

Clark and an army of fewer than 1200 men captured a British outpost at Kaskaskia, in the southern part of Illinois. Then they captured a British fort at Vincennes on the Wabash River. With these victories, Clark had won the land west of the Appalachians for the Patriots.[6]

DISCUSSION QUESTIONS

1. On a map of Indiana and Illinois, mark the areas mentioned in this selection and show the route that George Rogers Clark took to

Vincennes. Also, on a map of North America, show what the United States would have looked like physically had Clark not won the Battle of Vincennes and the United States wasn't able to claim this territory.

2. Most of these textbooks tell the story of George Rogers Clark and his expedition to Vincennes, but few mention the actual fighting there. Study this battle and explain why you think it is rarely discussed in history textbooks.

3. Research what relations were like between white settlers and Native Americans in the Northwest Territory prior to and during the American Revolutionary War. Investigate what George Rogers Clark's attitude was toward Native Americans before and during this battle.

4. Almost every textbook in this selection mentions the importance of Clark's expedition in allowing the new United States to expand and grow. If this battle had such an important impact on U.S. history, why is it not mentioned along with other great Revolutionary War battles?

Tucked away in the city of Vincennes, Indiana, is the National Park Service's memorial to George Rogers Clark and the Battle of Vincennes. Even though the U.S. victory in this battle had long-term and significant implications for the new country, this historic site is basically a secret to most Americans.

I I

Women in the American Revolution

Women have usually been ignored by U.S. history textbooks. The rare exception is the coverage of women's roles during the American Revolutionary War. The most prominent cases are addressed in these selections.

1869

G.P. Quackenbos, *Elementary History of the United States*

Washington's men suffered intensely at Valley Forge. A great part of them could not move out of their huts for want of clothes. Many had no shoes. Some were without blankets, and had to rest at night in their rags on the bare frozen ground. Sickness set in. Food could hardly be obtained. Most of the people in the neighborhood were Tories, who sold their produce to the British at high prices. Washington had no gold or silver, and the paper money issued by Congress was worth but little. This was indeed a trying hour.

There were some kind hearts, however, that felt for the poor American soldiers. One devoted woman, Mary Knight, used to cook provisions for them, and carry them herself to the camp in the depth of winter, disguised as a market-woman, that she might pass the British outposts. Her brother was a general in the American army. The British set a price upon his head;

but this brave woman saved him by heading him up in an empty cider hogshead in the cellar, and feeding him through the bunghole. He stayed there three days, and the British searched the house four times for him without success.[1]

On the day of the battle [of Monmouth, 1778] the heat was intense. Many of the British soldiers died from its effects. When Monmouth is mentioned, the name of Molly Pitcher must not be forgotten. Her husband served at one of the American cannon. While she was bringing him water from a spring, a ball struck him, and he fell. There was no one to manage his gun. Springing forward, she took his place, and performed her duty in the most heroic manner. Washington appointed her a sergeant in the army, and she was afterwards well known as "Captain Molly."[2]

1906

Oscar Gerson, *History Primer*

American Women During the War

When we study about the War for Independence it seems as though everything was done by the men. We must not forget that while the men were fighting in the army, their wives and families were left at home.

The women had to work very hard to take care of the children without the help of their husbands. Many men who went to the war were killed in battle. Their poor wives and children never saw them again.

Lydia Darrah

The women as well as the men were anxious to win the fight against England. There was one woman in Philadelphia who helped the Americans at a time when they greatly needed help. Her name was Lydia Darrah.

Lydia was the wife of a Quaker school teacher. She used to nurse the sick. Many people in Philadelphia knew and loved her, because she was so kind and tender hearted.

Meetings Held in Lydia Darrah's House

When the British army was spending the winter in Philadelphia some of the officers held meetings in a back room in Lydia Darrah's house. They chose this room because they could meet there quietly and make secret plans without fear of being disturbed.

Lydia Overhears the British Plans

One afternoon they told Lydia Darrah to have the room ready by seven o'clock that evening. One of the officers said to her:

"Be sure to have your family go to bed early. When we are ready to go, I shall let you know so that you can put out the candles."

Lydia thought this was a strange order but said she would do as she was told. She was afraid the British officers were getting ready to make a secret attack on the American army at Valley Forge.

The Darrah family went to bed early as Lydia had promised. She was so worried that she did not undress. She threw herself on the bed but did not go to sleep.

When all was still, Lydia slipped off her shoes and went quietly to the door of the meeting room. She could hear the British officers talking over their plans. She heard them say that they were going to slip out quietly at night to surprise and capture Washington's army. Lydia had heard enough. She crept softly back to bed.

In a little while one of the officers knocked on her door. She pretended to be asleep. After he had knocked again, she got up, put on her shoes, and came to the door yawning, as if only half awake.

When the British officers left the house Lydia put out the lights. She went back to bed but could not sleep. She made up her mind that she would keep the secret even from her family and friends. She meant to let Washington know as soon as possible.

Washington Warned of His Danger

Early in the morning Lydia Darrah told her husband that she must go to the mill to buy some flour. The flour mill was five miles away. At last she reached it and left her sack to be filled. She then hurried off.

Luckily she soon met a scout from Washington's army. She told him her secret and hurried back to the mill for her flour. The scout rode off as fast as he could to warn Washington of the danger.

The British Plan Fails

The British carried out their plans as far as they could. They marched off quietly in the darkness. At last they reached the place where they expected to surprise Washington and his men. But they did not catch them napping. They found the army ready for a fight. Their plans had failed, and they marched back disgusted. They wondered how their plans had been found out. Of course Lydia Darrah knew but she said nothing.[3]

1922

John W. Wayland, *History Stories for Primary Grades*

Nancy Hart's Dinner

Nancy Hart lived in Georgia, long ago. Her house was a little cabin, away out in the wild woods. She and her children lived in that cabin in the woods, but they were not afraid.

Nancy was tall and strong. She was over six feet in height, and she was stronger than some men. She was also very brave, and she could ride a horse and shoot a gun. She would shoot deer, catch fish, and trap rabbits and other animals. In these ways she got food for herself and her children. I suppose she also had a garden in which she grew corn, potatoes, and maybe some watermelons. You know Georgia is a great place for watermelons.

One day five soldiers came to Nancy Hart's cabin. It was war time, and soldiers were all over the country.

Those five soldiers who came to Nancy Hart's cabin had on red coats. That meant that they were British soldiers. Nancy did not like British soldiers, but she did not tell them so.

She smiled and said, "Come in." She had a sweet voice.

The soldiers came in.

"We want dinner," they said.

"All right," replied Nancy, "sit down and rest. I'll get dinner for you in a jiffy."

She flew around and soon had dinner on the table. The redcoats were much pleased. "She is our friend," they thought. They stood their guns up against the wall and sat down to dinner.

Nancy waited on them in fine style. She was here, there, and everywhere, just as polite as she could be. The soldiers thought:

"What a good dinner! What a nice time we are having!"

But the next thing they knew Nancy had hidden their guns! Then she stood in the door and said, "Finish your dinner, gentlemen, you are my prisoners."

When two of them tried to get away she shot them. Then the other three sat still.

One thing that helped Nancy was the fact that she was cross-eyed. This is what people say; and so they say that the British soldiers couldn't tell which way she was looking; they couldn't tell which way she might shoot next time.

Nancy sent word to her neighbors and they came to help her. Not one of the five soldiers got away.

The people of Georgia love Nancy Hart because she was brave and because she did what she could to help her country.[4]

Betsy Ross's Needle

I am going to tell you about Betsy Ross and what she did with her needle.

Betsy Ross was a pretty young woman. Her husband was dead. He had been a soldier and had died in the army.

Mrs. Ross lived in a little house in a big town. The town was Philadelphia. Betsy Ross could sew well. She made nice things with her scissors and her needle.

One day three gentlemen called at Betsy Ross's house. One of those gentlemen was General George Washington. Those gentlemen wanted Mrs. Ross to make a flag—a nice, new flag, with stars and stripes on it.

General Washington told Mrs. Ross what he thought would make a nice flag. He showed her what kind of stars he would make.

The stars he made had six points. Mrs. Ross said:

"General, stars do not have six points—they have only five points."

With her sharp scissors Mrs. Ross clipped out a star with five points.

When General Washington saw it he said:

"You are right, madam; make the stars with five points."

After the gentlemen left Mrs. Ross worked fast on the new flag. She put on it long stripes of white and red. In one corner she sewed on a big square of blue, and on the square of blue she sewed thirteen white stars. Each of the white stars had five points.

When General Washington and the other gentlemen saw the new flag they were very much pleased with it. They said that it was a fine flag and that Mrs. Ross was a good hand at making flags.

Betsy Ross had no sewing machine (nobody had sewing machines in those days), but she made her fingers fly. Her needle seemed to dance merrily on the red and the white and the blue.

Mrs. Ross made many other flags, just like the first one. Our flags today are very much like those she made.[5]

The Tea Party at Edenton

You remember about the Boston Tea Party, do you not? That was in December, 1773. A few months later a famous tea party was held at Edenton, in the Old North State—North Carolina. Edenton is at the head of Albemarle Sound; ships may easily reach the place; and in the days of long ago it was an important tea market.

In those days nearly everybody drank tea. Frequently ladies and gentlemen would meet together and spend an evening talking and drinking tea. Such a party was called a tea party.

But the Boston Tea Party and the Edenton Tea Party were different. At Boston it was a men's party—the ladies did not participate; at Edenton it was a ladies' party, but they did not use any tea!

The ladies of Edenton, like the men of Boston, were more or less angry. They did not believe that the king's government had a right to tax their tea. In fact, they went so far as to say that the king ought not to tax anything they used unless he let them take part in making the laws.

So the ladies of Edenton had a meeting—a party. Fifty-one of them met at the house of Mrs. Elizabeth King. They elected a chairman and had one speech after another.

One speaker said that she did not think the ladies of Edenton ought to use tea at all while the king was taxing it.

"I, for one," she exclaimed, "will never use it again unless the tax is removed."

Another said that her tea cups should be empty of tea unless the tax were soon taken off. A third declared that she would rather drink tea made of raspberry leaves than of tea that had the British tax on it.

All who spoke seemed to agree that if they should drink tea and pay the hated tax they would be giving up their liberties.

"Therefore," they declared, "we will not drink tea—we will not buy anything from England until the tax is taken off."

Somebody wrote those brave words down, and all the ladies put their fair hands to them. That is to say, each lady signed her name to the paper.

It must have been hard on the people of Edenton to do without tea, but they, like the people of Boston and many other places, did do without it. They drank no more tea, they had no more tea parties, till the Revolutionary War was over and they could buy tea again without paying tax to the king.[6]

1934

Rolla M. Tryon, *The American Nation: Yesterday and Today*

Women must always look after new tasks and duties, keeping the affairs of life as nearly normal as they can when their men go off to war. In the Revolution many women ran the farms and shops at home, besides doing as much as they could of their regular work. Those near the battlefields made bandages for the wounded and took them into their homes for care when they could. There were no hospitals in those days.

Prices went higher and higher, and made it more and more difficult for the mother of a family to get proper food and clothing for herself and the children. In any city such as Boston, New York, Philadelphia, Charleston, and Savannah a bombardment or attack always brought suffering for the women and children. If they did not hurry out of the town, taking whatever valuables they could, they had to undergo the danger of cannon shot and burning buildings. When Boston was being held by the British, for example, there was danger every minute of the day and night. Mrs. John Adams wrote to her husband how disease spread, how children and old people fell sick, and how many of her neighbors died because of the epidemics. Sometimes alarms were given in the night (as was done just before Lexington and Concord), and the men leaped out of bed, seized their muskets, and went hurriedly away. Their families might or might not ever see them alive again.[7]

1946

George Earl Freeland and James Truslow Adams, *America's Progress in Civilization*

In the years of the quarrel with England the colonial women entered into the spirit of resistance heart and soul. After the Stamp Act was passed, the women organized societies and made goods at home that otherwise would have been taxed by the English. When the tea dispute arose, they formed leagues against using tea as long as it was taxed. Several of the leading newspapers were owned by women, who were as brave as men in promoting the cause of the colonists.

A famous and oft-quoted letter from a lady in Philadelphia to a friend in the English army stated: "I have retrenched every superfluous expense in my table and family; tea I have not drunk since last Christmas nor bought a new cap or gown since your defeat at Lexington; and what I never did before, have learned to knit and am now making stockings of American wool for my servants; and in this way do I throw my might to the public good. I know this—that free I can die but once; but as a slave I shall not be worthy of life. I have the pleasure to assure you that these are the sentiments of all my sister Americans."

While the men were fighting, women tilled the fields, spun, wove, made uniforms and hospital supplies, and made munitions, often using their pewterware for bullets. They served in hospitals, and some even went on the field of battle to care for the wounded. A few fought in the ranks with the men.

In Philadelphia, Esther De Berdt Reed and Sarah Franklin Bache formed America's first woman's relief organization in 1780, and supplied destitute soldiers with clothing. The women did their part without thought of promotion or pay.[8]

1977

Lewis Paul Todd and Merle Curti, *Rise of the American Nation*

This faith and devotion was shared by many women Patriots. Even before 1776, women played an important part in boycotting British goods. In the struggle for independence, women found many ways to support the Revolution. Mercy Otis Warren published plays that satirized the British and Loyalists, and started writing her history of the American Revolution. Many women collected lead and helped manufacture bullets. Others made uniforms for the soldiers, or collected and distributed medical and hospital supplies. Still others accompanied the troops, helping as cooks, doing laundry, and serving as nurses. A few performed dangerous missions as spies and messengers.

There are many legends about women who fought in the ranks, but it seems well established that Margaret Corbin and Molly Pitcher took the places of their wounded husbands. Deborah Sampson, a young Massachusetts girl, disguised herself in soldier's clothing and took part in several battles.[9]

1999

Beverly J. Armento, Jacqueline M. Cordova, J. Jorge Klor de Alva, Gary B. Nash, Franklin Ng, Christopher L. Salter, Louis E. Wilson, and Karen K. Wixson, *America Will Be*

Many colonial women managed their households alone while their husbands were away fighting in the war. These women still did their traditional work, such as spinning cloth, making clothes, tending the garden and the dairy, and caring for the children and the house.

But they also took over many jobs normally done by men. Some women rose at dawn and rode out on horseback to tell farm workers what to do. Others ran businesses, such as flour mills or tailor shops. At first, many men wrote letters home telling their wives what crops to plant and what bills to pay. But as time went on, husbands came to depend more and more on their wives' judgment.

For their part, women got used to making decisions for their families. Like Abigail Adams, they had no wish to return to the time when husbands and fathers had complete authority over their wives and children.

Among the decisions women had to make was how to manage the family's money. This grew more difficult as the war went on. The army bought tons of meat and flour to feed the soldiers. They also purchased large quantities of shoes and clothing. The army's large purchases created shortages of many essential items at home. Women and other civilians had a hard time finding such things as coffee, tea, and grain to buy. The little that was available was very expensive, and prices rose higher every year.[10]

DISCUSSION QUESTIONS

1. Research the stories of Molly Pitcher, Lydia Darrah, Nancy Hart, and Betsy Ross. Explain whether the stories these textbooks give are historical fact or fiction.

2. Look at the history textbooks used in your school. Does your current textbook mention any stories about women during the American Revolutionary War? What about American women in other wars? Explain.

3. The Tea Party at Edenton is a story rarely mentioned in history textbooks. After investigating this story, explain why you think the Boston Tea Party is the more famous of the two.

4. The 1946 textbook briefly mentions that some women "fought in the ranks." If women weren't able to serve in the military, how could they have "fought in the ranks"? Research Deborah Sampson and see if her biography helps explain this question.

5. Research the role of women in the United States after the American Revolution. All the textbooks in this section discussed the important

WOMEN IN THE AMERICAN REVOLUTION

contributions women made to the war; did these contributions help women improve their status in society after the war?

All of these textbook selections discuss white women who served the cause of the patriot leaders. Missing from this narrative are the stories of loyalist women, African American women, and Native American women.

PART III

Founding a Nation

12

Shays' Rebellion

At the conclusion of the Revolutionary War, things were not as perfect in the new nation as many had hoped. Many of the new citizens were not pleased with the United States' lack of financial stability or the new government's inability to raise needed money. There was also discontent brewing in the countryside. Many citizens felt the blame was to be firmly placed on their new constitution, the Articles of Confederation, which were considered weak by most at the time. These weaknesses were put to the test by a major armed rebellion, led by the farmer Daniel Shays.

1869

G.P. Quackenbos, *Elementary History of the United States*

The war had ceased. The United States were free. But they were still surrounded with great difficulties. They owed an immense debt to foreign governments, as well as to their own soldiers and officers. How was this to be paid? Congress had no money, and no power to raise any from the different states, which considered themselves independent, and looked with jealousy on each other and on the general government. England, too, complained that her merchants could not collect what was owed to them in America. It seemed at one time as if the war would be renewed.

The people continued to suffer. All kinds of business were dull. The taxes laid in some of the states, though light in themselves, were looked upon as a burden, because money was so scarce. In Massachusetts, a number of people rose in arms and resisted the government. Shays, who had been a captain in the Revolution, took command of them, and the movement was called Shays' Rebellion. For a time they gave some trouble; but the militia were called out, and Shays and his men found it best to submit. The ringleaders came near being hanged, but were finally let off.

It was clear that some stronger government was needed. Accordingly, a meeting of delegates from each state was called, for the purpose of drawing up a constitution. In May, 1787, the convention met at the same old state-house in Philadelphia in which the Declaration of Independence had been signed. It contained the wisest men in the country. Washington was elected its president.[1]

1888

John J. Anderson, *New Grammar School History of the United States*

The States of the Union were held together by the compact known as the Articles of Confederation, but experience had proved it to be of little worth. It did not meet the needs of government. Congress had borrowed money, but did not have power to procure funds to pay the debt. If the States were called upon for money, and did not respond, there was no power to compel them. They had war debts of their own, in addition to their every-day expenses, and could not easily raise money for general purposes. Congress could not regulate commerce with foreign countries, nor even between the States. Such were some of the defects in the existing form of government.

The men who with word, pen, or sword had fought the battles of the Revolution saw with deep concern that the Ship of State, as then rigged, was not suited to the voyage before her. A serious outbreak, known as Shays's Rebellion, occurred in Massachusetts. People there were dissatisfied with their State government. They said that the taxes were burdensome, that the governor's salary was too high, and that the legislature was aristocratic. Two thousand men in arms, with Daniel Shays as their leader, defied the rightful authority (1787). This outbreak was put down with little bloodshed, but might not another, a more serious one, occur, and who could tell what the consequences would be?

It was agreed that the Articles might be so altered as to give Congress greater power. With that object delegates from the States met in Philadelphia. Washington was drawn from his retirement, and, by the unanimous vote of the delegates, was chosen to preside over the convention. Before him sat statesmen and soldiers, of whose service in the cause of freedom the people were justly proud. Among them were James Madison, afterward President of the United States; Alexander Hamilton, soon to be the first Secretary of the Treasury, and the venerable Dr. Franklin, now more than eighty years of age.[2]

1934

Rolla M. Tryon, *The American Nation: Yesterday and Today*

People were discontented all over the United States, particularly in Massachusetts. Many people were deeply in debt, and they found it hard to pay their bills because money was scarce. The debtors were frequently put into prison. Finally, under the leadership of Daniel Shays, the people of central Massachusetts seized arms, broke open the jails, and let the debtors out. Only with difficulty was this rebellion stopped.[3]

1977

Lewis Paul Todd and Merle Curti, *Rise of the American Nation*

Led by Daniel Shays, the Massachusetts farmers demanded that the state legislature end the foreclosing of farms and give farmers a larger representation in the legislature. A group under Shays also tried unsuccessfully to seize the arsenal at Springfield in an effort to secure guns.

Frightened by this defiance of the law, citizens of Boston raised funds to equip a militia to put down Shays' Rebellion. The troops hunted Shays and his men through the snowy woods, killing many and driving some across the state boundary into what is now Vermont. The rebellion was crushed. Nevertheless, many Americans were thoroughly alarmed. Armed revolt threatened law and order and might even destroy the new nation.[4]

1999

Beverly J. Armento, Jacqueline M. Cordova, J. Jorge Klor de Alva, Gary B. Nash, Franklin Ng, Christopher L. Salter, Louis E. Wilson, and Karen K. Wixson, *America Will Be*

Farmers in the western part of Massachusetts had an especially hard time paying their bills. Massachusetts farmers owed about one-third of their income for state taxes, and the Massachusetts legislature refused to issue paper money as other states had done. Those farmers who could not pay their taxes had their farms taken away by state courts. Court officials then auctioned off the farms and used the money from the sale to pay the taxes. Farmers who could not pay their personal debts were often put into prison.

The farmers asked the Massachusetts legislature to lower taxes and let them pay taxes and other debts with farm produce. They begged the legislature to stop jailing people who could not pay their debts. Instead the legislature listened to merchants and bankers to whom the farmers owed money. It refused to pass laws to help the farmers.

Because they could not get help through legal means, a group of farmers decided they had no choice but to rebel. Their leader was Daniel Shays, former Revolutionary War captain. In the fall of 1786, Shays led armed farmers in marches outside county courthouses in Springfield, Northampton, and other towns in western Massachusetts. The purpose was to keep the courts from meeting. If the courts did not meet, bankers and others to whom farmers owed money could not take away their farms.

In January 1787, Shays's men attacked a Springfield building where the government stored guns. The governor of Massachusetts sent soldiers paid for by wealthy Boston merchants to fight the rebels. The soldiers shot and killed four, and soon the rest of Shays's followers fled. Several rebel leaders were caught. These men were brought to trial, found guilty, and sentenced to death. Later the court set them all free, including Shays.

Shays's Rebellion failed. But it made many Americans think a stronger central government was needed to prevent such rebellions in the future.[5]

DISCUSSION QUESTIONS

1. The Articles of Confederation are mentioned in many of the textbooks in this section, and each time this document is accused of being too weak. Find a copy of the Articles of Confederation and try to find out why history textbooks consider it so weak. Are these history textbooks correct? Explain.

2. Some textbooks from the 1800s claim that Shays' Rebellion was actually a minor affair, while textbooks in the 1900s begin to claim that it was a difficult rebellion to put down. Research what was going on in Massachusetts with Shays and his men and explain whether this was a minor or major historical event.

3. If you had been a citizen in Massachusetts during Shays' Rebellion, which side of the argument do you think you would have been on? Explain why you would or would not have supported Daniel Shays.

4. Do these history textbooks portray Daniel Shays and his men as heroes? Explain.

Charged with treason and condemned to die, Daniel Shays fled to Vermont, from which he later petitioned the government for amnesty in 1788. The amnesty was granted by John Hancock.

13

The Barbary Pirates

America's first great foreign policy challenge came when pirates off the coast of North Africa, with and without approval from national leaders, forced foreign ships to pay tribute in order to sail in the Mediterranean Sea. In 1801 President Jefferson decided to not pay this tribute and soon after found the United States involved in a war against these pirates.

1860

Benson J. Lossing, *A Primary History of the United States*

The sea-robbers in the Mediterranean . . . were yet giving the merchants and traders a great deal of trouble, and the United States Government resolved not to pay any more money every year to them. Then Tripoli, one of the robber governments, declared war against the United States. Jefferson at once sent strong ships there to protect our merchant vessels, and soon there was fighting.

One day the United States frigate *Philadelphia*, commanded by Captain Bainbridge, a brave war-sailor, struck on a rock in the harbor of Tripoli. Bainbridge and his officers were made prisoners, while his men were all made slaves, and suffered dreadfully.

Early in 1804, Lieutenant Decatur, who was afterward one of the best men in the navy, sailed into the harbor of Tripoli with a small vessel, on a dark night, drove the Tripolitans from *Philadelphia,* set the vessel on fire, and escaped without losing a man. This bold act alarmed the Bashaw, or governor of Tripoli.

The Bashaw was a bad man. His place belonged to his brother Hamet, whom he had compelled to flee to Egypt. Hamet readily joined the Americans against his wicked brother, and at the head of a number of Mohammedan soldiers, he accompanied some seamen, under Captain Eaton, across the deserts from Alexandria in Egypt. They captured a Tripolitan town on the Mediterranean, and were marching directly for Tripoli, when the terrified Bashaw made peace with the American agent there. So the war was ended.[1]

1869

G.P. Quackenbos, *Elementary History of the United States*

In the north of Africa, on the Mediterranean Sea, lie what are called the Barbary States. For a long time they were the home of pirates, who used to scour the sea, capture merchant vessels, and sell their crews into slavery. For a while the United States paid a yearly tribute to secure its vessels from these outrages. But at last the pirates became so insolent that a fleet was sent out under Commodore Preble to punish them.

While reconnoitering the harbor of Tripoli, the *Philadelphia*, one of the American vessels, struck on a rock. She was immediately taken by the Tripolitans. But Lieutenant Decatur, one of the bravest officers in the service, resolved they should not long enjoy their triumph. One evening, in a little vessel disguised as a coaster, he boldly sailed up to the *Philadelphia*, and asked permission to moor his boat beside her. Before the Tripolitans found out what was going on, he and his men were on board. After driving off the pirates, they set the ship on fire and made good their retreat.

Soon after this, the Americans attacked the Tripolitan fleet and bombarded the city. The gallant Decatur again fought like a lion. In boarding one of the enemy's boats, he was met by the captain, and a desperate struggle ensued. While they were thus engaged, another Tripolitan rushed up with drawn sword and was about to dispatch Decatur, when a gallant sailor saved his life by interposing his person and receiving the blow himself. After being pretty severely handled, the bashaw of Tripoli thought it best to come to terms. For some years after this, the American flag was treated with respect.[2]

1884

Edward Ellis, *The Eclectic Primary History of the United States*

If you will examine the map of Africa, you will see a number of divisions in the northern part called the Barbary States. At the beginning of the present century, they were in the habit of sending out pirates, who captured the ships of Christian nations, and held the crews as slaves until large sums were paid for their ransom or release.

After a time, the pasha, or ruler, of Tripoli seemed to think all nations were afraid of him and his pirates. When we complained of his action, he declared war against us, but he was soon taught his mistake.

Our government sent a fleet to the Mediterranean, which bombarded the city of Tripoli. The pasha was very glad to make peace on our own terms.[3]

1930

William Backus Guitteau, *Our United States: A History for Upper Grammar Grades and Junior High School*

Today it seems almost beyond belief that the small Mohammedan states of northern Africa were able for many years to plunder the commerce of Christian nations. Not only did these pirates attack vessels, but they often seized the crews and passengers and held them for ransom. Instead of declaring war on the Barbary States, the maritime powers of Europe purchased peace by paying them an annual tribute. This situation resulted from the mutual jealousy of the European powers. Each nation chose to buy peace for itself, rather than go to war; for after peace was purchased, the pirates were left free to prey upon the commerce of other nations. The United States at first followed this shameful example, and for sixteen years paid annual tribute to the rulers of Tripoli, Morocco, Algiers, and Tunis. Early in Jefferson's administration, still larger payments were demanded, and even the peace loving President concluded that war was less expensive than "tribute and ransom." Commodore Preble's little squadron soon compelled Tripoli to agree to peace without tribute. This taught the other Barbary States a lesson, and they no longer molested our commerce.[4]

1961

Edna McGuire and Thomas B. Portwood, *Our Free Nation*

Tunis, Algiers, Tripoli, and Morocco, four small countries on the northern coast of Africa, were called the Barbary states. For years they had made a practice of sending warships into the Mediterranean Sea to rob trading vessels. European nations paid tribute to these pirates to keep their vessels free from attack. The United States followed this course for a time, but President Jefferson sent American warships to the Mediterranean. After meeting the American ships on several occasions, the Barbary pirates were ready to make peace.

However, a few years later the ruler of Algiers made trouble again. In 1815 Stephen Decatur sailed into the Mediterranean with a fleet of ten American ships. He compelled the Barbary states to release prisoners and give up claims to tribute. From that time on, American shipping was safe in the Mediterranean Sea. A successful blow had been struck for "the freedom of the seas," a principle which America was to defend more than once.[5]

1970

Kenneth Bailey, Elizabeth Brooke, and John J. Farrell, *The American Adventure*

Many United States goods went to the Mediterranean Sea to be sold in southern European ports. But many of these ships were beset with pirate problems.

The kingdoms of Algiers, Morocco, Tripoli, and Tunis forced all ships entering the area to pay money to pass.

Washington and Adams both had paid the pirates. But in 1801 Thomas Jefferson decided to stop this expensive practice. The pirates of Tripoli then declared war on the United States.

The American navy blockaded the pirate ships and attacked Tripoli. Stephen Decatur, a young American commander, led many of the attacks on pirate ships.

In 1805 a peace treaty was signed with the Pasha (leader) of Tripoli. This greatly increased the prestige of the United States Navy. Although the amount of tribute paid by the United States to the pirates was greatly reduced as a result of this war, the tribute payments did not stop completely until 1816.[6]

1986

James West Davidson and John E. Batchelor, *The American Nation*

American trading ships ran great risks, especially in the Mediterranean Sea. For many years, the rulers of the Barbary States on the coast of North Africa attacked American and European ships. The United States and many European countries were forced to pay a yearly tribute, or bribe, to protect their ships from attack.

The ruler of Tripoli, one of the Barbary States, wanted the United States to pay an even bigger bribe. When President Jefferson refused, Tripoli declared war on the United States. In response, Jefferson ordered American ships to blockade the port of Tripoli.

One of the American ships, the *Philadelphia*, ran aground near Tripoli. Tripoli pirates swarmed on board and imprisoned the crew. The pirates planned to use the *Philadelphia* to attack other ships. But a brave American officer, Lieutenant Stephen Decatur, had other plans. Late one night, Decatur and his crew sailed quietly into Tripoli harbor. They boarded the captured ship and set it on fire so that the pirates could not use it.

Meanwhile, a force of American marines marched 500 miles across North Africa to make a surprise attack on Tripoli. The war with Tripoli lasted until 1805. In the end, the ruler of Tripoli signed a treaty promising to let American ships alone.[7]

DISCUSSION QUESTIONS

1. In some of the early textbooks the authors refer to people of the Muslim faith as Mohammedans. How were Muslims (which included the Barbary pirates) portrayed in these textbooks? Compare this to how Muslims are portrayed in your current history textbook. Have the images of these people improved over time or not? In your opinion, what impact do recent news stories have on how Muslims are currently portrayed?

2. In the 1869 textbook, the author points out at the end of the story that "for some years after this, the American flag was treated with respect." Research what was going on with the United States during the 1860s and 1870s in terms of international relations and explain why having the American flag treated with respect around the world was important for this author.

3. On a map of Africa draw in where the Barbary states were located. Looking at the map, explain why this was such a great area for "pirates." Explain why it was such an important area for the U.S. and Europe during this time as well.

4. Do any of these textbooks portray religion as being important to this story? Cite examples.

5. In the 1961 textbook the author makes a reference to the need for the United States to protect the "freedom of the seas," and then goes on to state that this was a principle that Americans have had to defend "more than once." Investigate and find examples of other times when the United States has had to defend the open seas. Was everyone involved in agreement that the United States should have done this?

6. The 1970 textbook is the only book that claims that the United States continued to pay the tribute even after Stephen Decatur's heroics in North Africa. Research this story and see if this is accurate.

In 1786 Thomas Jefferson (U.S. ambassador to France), John Adams (U.S. ambassador to Britain), and Sidi Haji Abdul Rahman Adja (Tripolitan ambas-

sador to Britain) met in London to negotiate a peace treaty and protect the United States from the threat of Barbary piracy. During that meeting Jefferson was presented with a Koran as a gift from the Tripolitan ambassador. In January 2007, Minnesota representative Keith Ellison, the first Muslim-American elected to the U.S. Congress, used that same Koran to be sworn into the U.S. House of Representatives.

14

Sacagawea

Most historians today agree that any concrete historical information about Sacagawea—the Shoshone woman who helped guide the Lewis and Clark expedition—is scarce at best. Historians usually have had to rely upon the journals that Meriwether Lewis and William Clark left, which give testimony to her pivotal role in the Lewis and Clark Corps of Discovery.

1869

G.P. Quackenbos, *Elementary History of the United States*

West of the Rocky Mountains, on the Pacific, lay a province of Mexico called California. North of this was an extensive tract, now forming the state of Oregon and the territory of Washington. Little or nothing was known of this region; and, during Jefferson's term, a party of soldiers and hunters was sent out to explore it. They were gone two years, and met with many adventures. They traveled six thousand miles, and thoroughly explored the valley of the great Columbia River.[1]

1909

William H. Mace, *A Primary History: Stories of Heroism*

The company spent the winter on an island sixteen hundred miles from St. Louis. The men built rude homes and fortified them. The Indians were friendly and the explorers spent many evenings around the wigwam fires listening to stories of the country the Indians had to tell them.

In the spring they bade the Indians good-by, passed the mouth of the Yellowstone, and traveled on till the Rocky Mountains with their long rows of snow-covered peaks came into view.

On the thirteenth day of June they beheld wonderful pictures of the "halls of the Missouri." The water tore through a vast gorge a dozen miles or more in length.

On they went until their boats could go no farther. They had reached rough and rugged hills and mountains. They climbed the heights as best they could. From now on the suffering was very great indeed.

One day Captain Lewis went ahead with three men to find Indian guides for the party. They climbed higher and higher until finally they came to a place where the Missouri River takes its rise. They went on and at last came to the western slope of the mountains, down which flowed a stream toward the Pacific.

Finally Captain Lewis came upon a company of Indian women who could not get away. They all bowed their heads as if expecting to be killed. They led the white men to a band of Indians who received them with all the signs of kindness they could show.

Now they all turned back to find Clark and his party. When they reached Clark the Indians smoked the "pipe of peace" and Lewis and Clark told the Indians why the United States had sent them out.

They were the first white men these Indians had ever seen. They looked the men over carefully and took a deep interest in their clothing, their food, and in their guns.

The mountains were now rough and barren and the streams ran through deep gorges. The explorers took an old Indian guide and crossed the Bitter Root Mountains into a valley of the same name. They followed an Indian trail over the mountains again and into the Clearwater. They suffered for want of food and on account of the cold. When they reached a tribe of the Nez Perce (Pierced Nose) Indians they ate so much they were all ill.

In five log boats, which they had dug out of trees, they glided down the Clearwater to where it meets the Snake River. They camped near the spot where now is the present town of Lewiston, Idaho. Then they embarked on the Snake River and floated down to where it joins the mighty Columbia.

They were among the Indians again, who had plenty of dried fish. Here is the home of the salmon, a fish found in astonishing numbers. The men had never seen so many fish before.

The number of Indians increased as they went toward the Pacific. Finally the party of explorers passed through the Cascade Mountains and were once more on the smooth current of the Columbia. They soon beheld the blue waters of the Pacific.

During their five months' stay on the Pacific, Captain Clark made a map of the region they had gone through. They repaired their guns and made clothes of the skins of elk and of other game.[2]

1930

William Backus Guitteau, *Our United States: A History for Upper Grammar Grades and Junior High School*

Even before Louisiana came into our possession, President Jefferson was planning an exploring expedition into the vast unknown country beyond the Mississippi. To penetrate the great West, with its mighty rivers and majestic mountains, its plains covered with herds of buffalo, its valleys peopled with warlike Indians,—this was indeed an exploration to thrill the hearts of its leaders. So thought Meriwether Lewis and William Clark, the two young Virginians chosen to command the expedition. These pathfinders were to follow the Missouri River to its source, then cross the Rocky Mountains, and descend the nearest stream flowing to the Pacific.

Lewis and Clark started up the Missouri from a point near St. Louis in May, 1804. There were forty-five men in all, in three boats. After a difficult journey of sixteen hundred miles, the party reached the villages of the Mandan Indians, in North Dakota, where they spent the winter. In the following spring the explorers reached Great Falls, where the Missouri passes over a series of cataracts, forming thirteen miles of cascades and rapids. Hauling the boats and luggage around the falls was no easy task; but at last the expedition reached the highest source of the Missouri. Here the boats were hidden, and the leaders prepared for the difficult journey across the mountains. Fortunately, a friendly band of Shoshone Indians was at hand, from whom Captain Lewis secured horses. Then followed weeks of hardship and hunger, while his men worked their way through the forest-clad passes of the Rockies. They finally came to one of the branches of the Snake River, where canoes were built in which the entire party soon reached and floated down the swift-flowing Columbia. On November 7, 1805, the roar of breakers was heard in the distance. The explorers had reached their goal at last. On the shore of the Pacific they built a camp, where they passed a second dreary winter.[3]

1951

Clyde B. Moore, Fred B. Painter, Helen M. Carpenter, and Gertrude M. Lewis, *Building Our America*

The Lewis and Clark party reached a large village of the Mandan Indians in October. Captain Lewis decided to spend the winter there. The Mandan Indians lived in houses that looked like huge mud tepees. Unlike their Sioux neighbors, they grew crops on the rich bottom land of the Missouri. The explorers found the Mandans getting ready for winter. Pumpkins, cut in strips, were drying in the sun. Great holes in the ground were being filled with corn, beans, and squash for use during the cold weather. Dried plums, wild chokecherries, sunflower seeds, and dried tobacco leaves were stored in the wigwams.

Mandan warriors rode their swift little ponies on buffalo hunts. The hunters would ride up along the side of a running buffalo and shoot arrow after arrow into the huge beast. When an arrow reached the heart or lungs, the buffalo went down.

The Indian squaws skinned the buffaloes, dried the meat, and tanned the hides. In zero weather the buffalo robes kept the Indians warm. But when the temperature dropped to thirty or forty degrees below zero, the Mandans stayed in their lodges.

There was a Frenchman living in the Mandan village. His name was Charbonneau. His young wife was only fifteen or sixteen years old. Charbonneau had bought her from another tribe of Indians who had taken her as a prisoner. She was a Shoshone and came from the headwaters of the Missouri River. She could speak the Shoshone languages and knew the country over the Rocky Mountains. Her name was Sacajawea. This means "Bird Woman" in the Shoshone language.

Captain Lewis hired Charbonneau to guide them over the mountains. When the men had finished building their log fort, Charbonneau and his Indian wife moved into one of the cabins. A baby boy was born to Sacajawea in February.

Wild ducks and geese were seen flying north in March. The men in the little Mandan fort made ready to travel. In early April one boat was sent back to St. Louis with a report to President Jefferson. Lewis and Clark, with the rest of the party, pushed on up the Missouri. Now was to come the hardest part of their trip. Would they be able to cross the Rocky Mountains? Would they finally succeed in reaching the Pacific Ocean?

The nights were frosty, and the river was high with water from the melting snow. Sacajawea, with her baby tied on her back, shared the hardships with the men. Charbonneau called the baby "Baptiste," but Sacajawea and the other men called him "Pomp." In the Shoshone language, Pomp means "the firstborn son."

When they reached the three forks of the Missouri (above the present Helena, Montana), Sacajawea knew which one led to the top of the Continental Divide. (The divide is the high part of the mountains which separates the waters running east from the waters running west.) When they met some Shoshone Indians, she told them that the white captains were their friends. They met her brother who was a chief of one of the Shoshone tribes. The Shoshones furnished horses to pack the supplies over the great divide to the headwaters of the Snake River.

For days the party followed the high, rocky trails over the mountains. These were between the headwaters of the Missouri and Columbia rivers. It snowed on the last day of August. The nights were cold. Game was scarce, and there was little grass for the horses. Some of them were killed to feed the men. At last the trail started down, and the party came to a plateau where there was grass for the horses.

They came to an Indian village about September 20. The friendly Snake Indians gave them food. Perhaps the starving men ate too much, for the food made them sick. When they reached the headwaters of the Snake River, they built canoes. The horses were left with Chief Twisted Hair to keep for the trip back over the mountains. Secretly, the men buried powder and shot and pack saddles.

In a few days they floated down the Snake River to the Columbia River. They were wet with a cold rain most of the time. They lived on wild ducks and geese, and salmon and roots which they got from the Indians.

These were a tribe of Indians who followed a queer custom. They bound the heads of their babies between boards, which made them flat, coming to a peak at the top. These Indians were friendly, but dirty and unhealthy. Many of them were blind, and they all had very bad teeth. Unlike the Sioux, Mandans, and Shoshones, these Indians helped their women with some of their work, especially in drying salmon.

The swift rivers took the explorers' canoes toward the Pacific. The men had to carry the canoes around rapids and waterfalls. This was the hardest work of the journey. At last they reached the tidewater from the Pacific on November 3, 1805.

Sacajawea, her husband, and little Pomp stayed at the Mandan village where Lewis and Clark had found them. Little Pomp was now able to run and dance to the music of the violin. Clark wanted to adopt him as a son, but his mother and father would not part with him.[4]

1966

Harold H. Eibling, Fred M. King, and James Harlow, *History of Our United States*

That first summer they traveled about 1,600 miles up the Missouri. They were near a village of Mandan Indians (in what is now North Dakota) when ice began to form in the river. The Indians were friendly, so the party built a stockade and spent the winter near them.

During their stay with the Mandans, Lewis and Clark met the French fur trapper, Charbonneau. His Shoshone Indian wife, Sacajawea or "Bird Woman," had come to the Mandans as a prisoner and wanted to see her family in the Idaho country again. Lewis and Clark thought it would be of great help to the expedition to have a person guide them into the mountains who knew something about the language of the tribes they would meet.

The other men of the expedition were displeased to learn that Lewis and Clark had invited Charbonneau and Sacajawea to travel with them into the mountains. They complained that the trip was going to be rough enough without a squaw with a papoose on her back to slow them up.

The men were wrong, as they soon found out. Sacajawea not only kept up with the party, but she turned out to be their guide. Without her help, it is doubtful that the expedition would have accomplished its entire mission.

When the snow began to melt on the plains and the ice broke up in the river, some of the men started off for St. Louis. They carried with them the reports, maps, and specimens the party had already gathered for President Jefferson.

The other explorers, with their new guides, proceeded up the river. When they met Indians, Clark would tell his servant, York, what he wanted to say. Since York spoke French, he translated the message to Charbonneau. Charbonneau then put the idea into the speech of his Indian wife, who in turn talked to the Indians. You can see there were no lively conversations between Lewis and Clark and the people they met.

When they came to the Rocky Mountains, it was no longer possible to proceed by boat. By one of those strange coincidences that read like a fiction adventure story, Sacajawea discovered that the chief of the local Indians was her long-lost brother. She persuaded him to help the American explorers with horses and supplies.

Nights grew cold. There was little game. The men were hungry and very weary when they reached the headwaters of the Snake River. Here they built boats, left their horses with some Indians, and began the long boat trip down the Snake and Columbia rivers into the Oregon country. The Louisiana Purchase lay behind. In November of 1805 the little party reached the Pacific. Years later this early boat ride was to give the United States one of its strongest claims to the disputed territory.[5]

1985

Ernest R. May, *A Proud Nation*

Talleyrand's offer had taken the Americans by complete surprise. Months before, though, Congress had secretly considered sending an expedition to explore the land west of the Mississippi River. It wasn't until May, 1804, after the Louisiana Purchase had been approved, that the expedition actually began. Under the command of two army officers, Meriwether Lewis and William Clark, the group left from St. Louis.

The more than forty members of the group were young yet seasoned. George Shannon was only seventeen. All were healthy, single and willing to take serious risks for their pay—five dollars a month. Clark's slave, York, and a French-Indian interpreter, Drewyer, also proved invaluable to the group.

For two years and four months, the Lewis and Clark expedition crossed the continent to the Pacific and then recrossed it to reach St. Louis. Despite dangers and sickness, only one man on the expedition died, probably of a ruptured appendix. Along the way the explorers collected valuable information about the natural life and geography of western North America. Clark tried to describe an unfamiliar animal in his journal. "Joseph Fields killed and brought in an Anamale . . . [which] burrows in the ground and feeds on [prairie dogs] bugs and vigatables. His shape and size is like that of a Beaver, his head and mouth is like a dogs with short ears, his tail and hair like that of a ground hog." This animal is called a badger today.

Amazingly, the Lewis and Clark expedition had few problems with Indians. In fact, the Indians were a great help. Sixteen-year-old Sacajawea, a Shoshone, served as guide and interpreter. She was able to get needed food and horses from Indians for the expedition to return home. Congress voted double pay for each member of the party, and York received his freedom. Jefferson was elated with the expedition's results. Sacajawea was honored with a medal by the government.[6]

DISCUSSION QUESTIONS

1. Explain why you think that most of the textbooks in the 1800s failed to mention Sacagawea and her role in this expedition.
2. Find copies of the Lewis and Clark journals and do your own historical research. What do they say about Sacagawea and her role in this expedition?
3. On a map trace the route that Lewis and Clark took. Locate on a map where Lewis and Clark would have found Sacagawea. Research the geography from where Sacagawea joined them to the Pacific Ocean. Explain why Lewis and Clark would have needed a guide through this area.
4. The 1951 textbook gives a great deal of detail when discussing the

Mandan Indians. Investigate the history of this tribe and check to see
if this textbook was accurate in its details.

5. Explain what reasons these textbooks give for why Sacagawea decided to go along with Lewis and Clark. According to your research,
are these reasons accurate?

*Even before she was a teenager Sacagawea had lived an eventful life. She was
originally a member of the Shoshone nation, but when she was approximately
twelve a band of Hidatsa Indians kidnapped her and brought her back to their
villages, located just north of modern-day Bismarck, North Dakota. Later, she
was sold as a slave to a French Canadian fur trader by the name of Toussaint
Charbonneau, who made Sacagawea and another woman his wives.*

1 5

Tecumseh

The great Shawnee leader Tecumseh has often been given special treatment in textbooks that otherwise seem to go out of their way to portray Native Americans as savages. For most textbook authors, as well as people such as Governor William Henry Harrison, his genius seemed to come from the fact that he was a powerful leader who was able to get a great many Native Americans to follow him and his ideas.

1860

Benson J. Lossing, *A Primary History of the United States*

I have told you how the British, in the West, a long time before, had caused the Indians to attack the Americans. Now they did the same thing again, and in the spring of 1811, Tecumseh, a great Indian warrior, united several of the western tribes in a league, in which they agreed to drive the white people from the country between the Ohio River and the Lakes.

General Harrison, who was afterward President of the United States, was then Governor of the Indiana Territory. He saw the gathering danger, and caused the people to arm themselves, and prepare for war. In the summer he marched these armed men into the Indian country, and for several months he watched the savages closely. Finally, on a dark night early in November, while he was on the banks of the Tippecanoe River, the Indians fell upon him and his men. They had a very hard fight until morning, when the Indians were driven away. The battle of Tippecanoe was one of the severest ever fought with the Indians.[1]

1869

G.P. Quackenbos, Elementary History of the United States

The territory of Indiana was at this time governed by William Henry Harrison, afterward, President of the United States. The crafty Tecumseh thought he would commence the war by striking a blow at Governor Harrison. So, going to the capital of the territory with several hundred warriors, he asked for an interview. On a given signal, his men were to fall upon the whites who were present, and let none escape. Governor Harrison met him as desired, but, suspecting treachery, took such precautions that Tecumseh, bold as he was, durst not give the signal.

Tecumseh had all the pride of his race. At the meeting between him and Harrison, a chair was placed for him by the interpreter, who said, as he offered it, "Your father [meaning Harrison] requests you to take a chair." "The sun is my father," replied Tecumseh, proudly, "and the earth is my mother; on her bosom will I repose." And, wrapping his blanket around him, he sat down on the ground.

Wishing to unite the Red Men in one common cause, Tecumseh visited the Creeks, who lived in Alabama and Georgia. Many of them listened to him and promised their aid. But before the Creeks could take the field, and while Tecumseh was still absent, an army under General Harrison approached the Tippecanoe River. They intended destroying the prophet's town, unless a satisfactory treaty was signed.

Here Harrison was met by several Indian ambassadors, who said that their nation desired peace, and would sign a treaty on the next day. That very night the war-whoop was suddenly heard, and the army was attacked by savages on every side. Harrison, however, was prepared. He had directed his men to encamp in order of battle, and now he hurried from one point to another, urging them to stand their ground till daylight.

The Indians, hidden in the long prairie-grass, poured in a deadly fire with the rifle. They had chewed their bullets, so that they would tear the flesh, and every volley they fired caused the wounded to scream with pain. Very few of Harrison's men had been in battle before; still, throughout that terrible night, they kept their line unbroken. When day dawned, they charged the savages. The latter fought desperately. Their prophet had assured them that they would gain the battle, and they believed him. But prophets sometimes make mistakes, and so they found in this case.

A vigorous charge drove the Indians from their cover. They fled in all direction. The prophet's town was destroyed, and the army returned in triumph. General Harrison was as merciful as he was brave. Shortly before the battle, a negro deserter, who had been hired by the Indians to murder the general, was seized while lying hidden near his tent. He was condemned to death, and secured, till the sentence could be carried out, by fastening his feet, like a wedge, between the sides of a log that had been partially split.

As he thus lay, he kept his eyes sadly fixed on the general. Harrison's feelings were moved. He could not bear to have the negro executed, and asked his officers to pardon him. They were unwilling to do so. They felt that the wicked man deserved to die. Yet when their general, who had the greatest cause to condemn him, pleaded in his favor, they could not refuse, and the wretched negro was spared.[2]

1888

John J. Anderson, *New Grammar School History of the United States*

After cutting off Ohio from the Northwest Territory, the rest was called the Indiana Territory. General William Henry Harrison was its governor. The wild tribes of the forest were again dissatisfied. They were not getting good prices for their furs, the white settlements were crowding them off their lands, game was scarce. Tecumseh, a great warrior, and his brother, commonly known as the Prophet, were trying to form a union of the tribes. Both were opposed to selling any more land to the whites. They wanted to see their race restored to its ancient power. Tecumseh was an orator as well as a warrior. He was crafty, and he never stopped at the means for carrying out his plans. His brother also was an orator. As a "medicine man," regarded as a medium between the Great Spirit and the Indians, the Prophet's influence among his people was almost unbounded. "They believed that he could make a pumpkin as big as a wigwam spring out of the ground at a single word."

Wanting blankets and other things, some of the tribes met Harrison, and sold to the government a large tract of land along the Wabash River. Tecumseh and his brother would not consent to the transfer. They said that all the Indian lands belonged to all the Indians, and for that reason, none could be sold without the consent of all. Being told that the Prophet was making preparations for war, Harrison, with a body of troops, marched against his town on the Tippecanoe River, in the western part of Indiana. Messengers from the Prophet met him. "What is the meaning of this?" they asked. "We do not want war. Halt where you are, and tomorrow we will have a talk with you." The troops halted and formed a camp, but, suspecting treachery, slept on their arms. It was a fortunate precaution, for just before daybreak, the Indians, with fearful yells, rushed upon the camp. The contest was brief. The assailants were repulsed, and the town was destroyed (November 7, 1811).[3]

1916

Charles Morris, *Primary History of the United States: The Story of Our Country for Young Folks*

Wayne and Harrison

General Wayne, a brave soldier of the Revolution, was then sent against them [Native Americans]. He defeated them so badly that they were glad enough to make peace and give up some of their land. One of the officers in Wayne's army was named William Henry Harrison. On the side of the Indians was a brave warrior named Tecumseh. At that time these were both young men, but they were to be enemies and to fight battles with each other in later years.

The Plan of Tecumseh

Tecumseh got to be a great leader among the Indians. He told them that it was wrong to sell their land to the whites, and he tried to get all the tribes to join together and drive the strangers from the country. He went far to the north and the west and the south, and talked wisely to the leaders of the tribes, and got many of them to agree with him in his plan.

How the Houses Fell

In one village of the South the chiefs would not agree to join him. This made him angry and he told them that when he got back to Detroit he would stamp his foot on the ground and the houses in their village would fall. Soon afterwards there was an earthquake and some of their houses fell down. The Indians were greatly scared, and said, "Tecumseh has stamped his foot. He is a great magician, and we must join him against the palefaces."

A False Prophet

Tecumseh had a brother who was an Indian prophet, or one who said he could tell what would happen in the future. He said to the red men, "Stop drinking fire-water and you will be strong enough to kill all the palefaces; when you have killed them I will bless the earth. I will make your pumpkins grow to be as big as wigwams, and will make the ears of corn so large that one of them will make a dinner for a dozen hungry men."

Harrison's March

William Henry Harrison was governor of the western country at that time. He saw that the Indians were getting ready to go to war and tried to stop them. When he found that he could not do it, and that they were dancing the war-dance in their villages, he started to meet them with a body of soldiers. He kept on until he was near an Indian village called Tippecanoe, and here the soldiers went to sleep in their camp in the woods.

The Sacred Beans

Tecumseh was away in the South, but the Prophet was in the village, where he had gathered the Indians to fight. He showed them some beans, and said, "These are sacred beans. Touch them, and no white man's bullet can hit you." The Indians crowded up to touch the magic beans.

The Prophet's Plan

"Now," he said, "take your tomahawks and your guns, and creep through the tall grass till you get to the edge of the woods. You will find the soldiers fast asleep, and you can jump among them and scatter them like so many rabbits."

A Night Alarm

It was near morning, and General Harrison was putting on his boots in his tent and getting ready to go out and waken up the army, when he heard a shot followed by an Indian war-whoop. One of the sentries had seen the tall grass wave as the Indians crept through it. He fired into the grass, and the warriors sprang up with their wild cries.

The Indians Defeated

The soldiers jumped up and ran for their guns, and they put out their camp-fires so that the Indians could not see them. There was a hard battle in the darkness, but in the end the white men won, and the Indians were driven back. Their village was set on fire and burned to the ground. After that the Indians would not believe in the Prophet and his wonderful stories about beans and pumpkins and corn.

What Tecumseh Did

Tecumseh had given the Indians of the South bundles of sticks painted red. They were to throw away one stick every day, and when the last stick was gone they were to attack the white men. But when he got back and found that his brother had spoiled his plans by fighting too soon he was very angry. He seized the Prophet by his long hair and shook him till the teeth rattled in his head. It was too late now to do anything, for the whites were armed and ready.[4]

1930

William Backus Guitteau, *Our United States: A History for Upper Grammar Grades and Junior High School*

The ill-feeling against Great Britain was increased in 1811 as a result of the Indian attacks on our western frontier. The Shawnee chief, Tecumseh, and his brother, the "Prophet," formed a plan to unite all the Indian tribes of the country against the steady advance of the white settlers. This project came to a sudden end when William Henry Harrison, governor of Indiana Territory, routed Tecumseh's braves at Tippecanoe. Harrison reported that the Indians had been armed and equipped from the British post at Malden. The frontiersmen firmly believed that the British government was behind this work, and there was strong feeling for a counter attack on Canada.[5]

1966

Harold H. Eibling, Fred M. King, and James Harlow, *History of Our United States*

After Jefferson became President, he wanted more land opened to settlement. His Indian agents were told to convert the western tribes to farming or to move them to land beyond the Mississippi. The governor of Indiana Territory, William Henry Harrison, carried out Jefferson's wishes so well that by 1809 nearly 110 million acres of hunting land had come into the white man's hands through sharp dealings with the Indians. Harrison took large sections of land from one small tribe or another, and pushed the displaced Indians farther west.

Very few of the Indians wanted to be farmers, and many of them did not want to be moved west to poor land. A great Shawnee Chief, Tecumseh, saw that his people suffered because small tribes could not stand up to Harrison alone. With his brother, the Prophet, Tecumseh began uniting the Indians to stop the white man's advance. They traveled about explaining their plan to the various tribes. If all the Indians would unite in a confederation, he said, and if each member tribe promised to make no cession of land without the consent of all they could resist the American demands. As tribe after tribe joined the confederacy, the Prophet and some Indian braves set up fortified headquarters where the Tippecanoe and Wabash rivers meet. Frontier settlers were disturbed by this Indian activity. The people of Vincennes persuaded Harrison to take action. Harrison watched the Indians, and when Tecumseh was away in the South, the governor marched his men toward the Indian village. He reasoned that without Tecumseh at hand to hold them back, the young warriors at Prophetstown would be defeated before Tecumseh could complete his plan.

Harrison's men camped outside Prophetstown. That night they slept on their rifles. As he had forecast, a band of Indian warriors attacked before dawn. The Americans beat off the attack, formed lines, and poured a deadly fire into the Indians. The Indians fell back when Harrison's cavalry attacked. After the skirmish, the white men burned Prophetstown.

The Battle of Tippecanoe, as the skirmish was called, scattered the angry Indians from Prophetstown and so launched a serious Indian war in the Northwest. The Americans blamed the British; said the British had armed the Indians and stirred them up against the Americans. That claim was one of the causes of the War of 1812 which the Americans were soon to fight with Great Britain. During the War of 1812 Tecumseh was killed while fighting for the British. The Indian power between the Ohio and Wabash rivers was broken.[6]

1986

James West Davidson and John E. Batchelor, *The American Nation*

Many Native Americans were furious over this treaty. They claimed that the men who signed it did not have the right to sell the land. Among those angered by the sale were two Shawnee leaders: Tecumseh and his brother, called the Prophet. The two men wanted to keep settlers from taking more Indian land.

Tecumseh had fought at the Battle of Fallen Timbers. In the early 1800s, he organized many Native American nations into a confederation. The Prophet provided spiritual leadership for the confederation.

Tecumseh and the Prophet urged Native Americans to preserve their traditional ways. Many white customs, they said, were corrupting the Indian way of life. They took a strong stand against whiskey. White traders used gifts of whiskey to trick Indians into selling land and furs cheaply.

Tecumseh earned the respect of Native Americans. He convinced them to unite against white settlers. "Until lately," he said, "there was no white man on this continent. . . . It all belonged to red men." The whites have "driven us from the great salt water, forced us over the mountains. . . . The way—and the only way—to check and to stop this evil is for all the red men to unite in claiming a common equal right in the land."

Even white leaders saw how much influence Tecumseh had among Native Americans. Harrison grudgingly admitted, "He is one of those uncommon geniuses which spring up occasionally to produce revolutions and overturn the established order of things."[7]

DISCUSSION QUESTIONS

1. How do history textbooks usually portray Tecumseh? Compare what these textbooks say about Tecumseh to what history textbooks said about Native Americans in the first section of this book. Are there any differences? Explain.

2. How do the history textbooks in this selection portray Tecumseh's brother Tenskwatawa (often called "the Prophet")? Do Tenskwatawa and Tecumseh receive the same recognition? Explain.

3. Research the Battle of Tippecanoe. Do the textbooks in this section get this story right? Explain. Who is to blame for starting the fighting between these two sides?

4. Research how General Harrison used the Battle of Tippecanoe later on in his life. Explain its significance to the 1840 presidential campaign.

5. Some textbooks in this section claim that the British may have been behind all of these events and were actually encouraging the Native Americans to fight the American settlers. Is this true? Explain.

One of Tecumseh's main arguments against Governor William Henry Harrison was that Harrison negotiated treaties to take land with individual tribes and/or minor chiefs. Tecumseh argued that such transactions could be valid only if all Native Americans agreed with the treaty.

PART IV

Westward Expansion

16

The Monroe Doctrine

The key architect of this pivotal doctrine, proclaimed on December 2, 1823, was actually John Quincy Adams, not President James Monroe, whose name it bears. Originally invoked to stop Europeans from colonizing any more of the Western Hemisphere, the Monroe Doctrine has since become a cornerstone of American foreign policy.

1873

John J. Anderson, *A Grammar School History of the United States*

An important event of Monroe's administration was the recognition of the independence of the South American republics. In his annual message of 1823, Monroe declared that the American continents "are henceforth not to be considered as subjects for future colonization by any European power." This is known as the "Monroe Doctrine." [1]

1885

Thomas Wentworth Higginson, *Young Folks' History of the United States*

Monroe's administration had expressed great sympathy for the new republics formed in South America, and had announced the opinion that the United States should thence forward never allow any European government to plant a colony on the soil of North or South America, or to interfere in American affairs, but that the people of the different parts of the continent should govern themselves. This has always been called "the Monroe doctrine," and is considered one of the most important results of this president's administration.[2]

1905

Thomas B. Lawler, *A Primary History of the United States*

Two questions of great importance came before President Monroe. The first question dealt with Russia. That nation claimed a large part of the Pacific coast southward from Alaska and had already begun to send settlers into the territory as far south as California. Mexico at this time owned California, and we were, therefore, in danger of being shut off entirely from the Pacific ocean. The American nation for this reason viewed with great alarm the activity of Russia on the Pacific coast.

The second great question was with Spain. Many of the Spanish colonies in the New World had rebelled against the mother country and had become independent republics.

It was now believed that the monarchs of Europe, alarmed at the growth of these republics, had joined hands to help Spain regain her lost colonies.

President Monroe in a message to Congress (December 2, 1823) declared that European nations must try no longer to colonize America. He also declared that they must not attempt to overthrow American republics in the interests of European monarchs.

This was the famous Monroe Doctrine. It had two great results: First, Russia gave up all attempts at colonizing the Pacific coast south of Alaska. Second, the struggling republics of the New World were allowed to work out their own destiny, free from the interference of European nations.[3]

1930

William Backus Guitteau, *Our United States: A History for Upper Grammar Grades and Junior High School*

Clearly, the time had come for the United States to take a decided stand on the question of European interference in American affairs. Great Britain had held aloof from the Holy Alliance. She was not in sympathy with absolute government, and her commerce would benefit by a free South America. Her minister of foreign affairs, George Canning, now proposed that Great Britain and the United States should unite in a declaration that we would not permit an attack upon the new republics. But John Quincy Adams, our Secretary of State, advised President Monroe that the United States should act alone on what was clearly an American question. The President decided to adopt this course, and in his famous message to Congress on December 2, 1823, announced to the world the famous Monroe Doctrine:

(1) As heretofore, the United States "will not interfere in the internal concerns" of any European power.

(2) European governments must not meddle in American affairs or attempt the conquest of the young republics.

(3) European nations must not attempt to set up any new colonies on either American continent.

Thus the "Monroe Doctrine" is really a declaration of home rule—America for the Americans. Russia heeded the warning, and by a treaty signed in 1824, gave up her claim to the territory south of the parallel 54° 40'. Nor did the Holy Alliance venture to attack the countries of South America at the risk of war with the United States. From Monroe's day to the present, the doctrine which bears his name has been a shield for the liberties of the western world.[4]

1946

George Earl Freeland and James Truslow Adams, *America's Progress in Civilization*

In 1823 President Monroe started the "Monroe Doctrine," which has been important in shaping American policies throughout our history. The

Spanish colonies in Latin America had revolted and declared their independence. Prussia, Austria, Russia, and France were considering joining forces to restore these possessions to Spain. England refused to join in this conspiracy and suggested that the United States stand with Great Britain to prevent such action.

Confident that Great Britain would "support" him, President Monroe and his Secretary of State, John Quincy Adams, decided to take a stand alone. In December, 1823, the President made a statement of the Monroe Doctrine. He said that the American continents were not to be regarded as a field for future colonization by the countries of Europe, and that any attempt to interfere with the independence of any American country would be looked upon by the United States as an unfriendly act. He declared that we had no intention of interfering with any existing colonies and that we would take no part in Europe's quarrels.[5]

1970

Kenneth Bailey, Elizabeth Brooke, and John J. Farrell, *The American Adventure*

When the United States won its independence and the French had their revolution, the people in Latin American countries wanted to gain their independence from Spain. The people in these countries wanted to govern themselves.

In Haiti the people overthrew their French rulers, and by 1804 that country was independent. This was just the beginning. Revolutions took place in Peru, Colombia, Argentina, and Venezuela, and the Spanish were driven out.

Meanwhile, Russia had claimed a large territory on the Pacific coast south of Alaska, which was already in Russian hands. The United States government was uneasy about this, as well as about possible European interference in Latin America.

In a famous message to Congress in December, 1823, President Monroe proclaimed three important principles of American foreign policy. These principles were contained in widely separated passages of his address and came to be known as the Monroe Doctrine.

Great Britain supported the American policy because she did not want Spain to regain control of her empire. The British, who enjoyed profitable trade with the new Latin American countries, were ready to help the United States enforce the new doctrine. The Russians soon gave up their claims to the territory south of Alaska, and Portugal recognized the independence of Brazil.

The Monroe Doctrine became a foundation for United States foreign policy, and has been used by many American Presidents.[6]

1991

Clarence L. Ver Steeg and Carol Ann Skinner, *Exploring America's Heritage*

The American people were filled with a restless desire to find new opportunities and grow to the limit.

This desire was expressed in a belief known as Manifest Destiny. Countless Americans felt they had a mission to spread the nation and its citizens' democratic ideas across the whole continent. By the 1890's, this goal was nearly met.

In keeping with the needs of a young nation, President Washington (1789–1797) urged that America be friendly to all nations but avoid ties and agreements with them. Other citizens and leaders supported his wish to keep the new country separate. These people valued the nation's newly gained independence.

Then, in the 1820's, President Monroe (1817–1825) issued a warning later called the Monroe Doctrine. He told all nations to stay out of countries in North and South America. In turn, Monroe promised that the United States would stay out of conflicts in the rest of the world.[7]

DISCUSSION QUESTIONS

1. Explain the role that the United States had in the world from 1800 to the 1860s. Does this help explain why most U.S. history textbooks rarely mentioned the Monroe Doctrine or discussed U.S. foreign policy during this period?

2. What do these textbooks say were the reasons the United States introduced the Monroe Doctrine? Can you find any consistent themes?

3. Between 1945 and 1991 the United States and what was then the Soviet Union were in the middle of the Cold War. Looking at how

U.S. history textbooks in this section portray the Soviet Union (Russia) in the twentieth century, do you think the textbooks have a positive or negative view of this nation? Explain.

4. Do the textbooks in this section view the Monroe Doctrine in a positive or negative way? Research what nations in Central and South America feel (or have felt) about the Monroe Doctrine. What view do they have of this policy? Does their historical perspective help create this view?

5. On a map locate all the regions in which the United States wanted to stop European colonization. Was it realistic for the U.S. government in the 1820s to stop all European colonization in this area? Explain.

At a time of much unrest and numerous independence movements against Spain, many Latin American leaders greeted the Monroe Doctrine with great enthusiasm, even though most of them assumed the fledgling United States did not have enough military power to enforce it.

17

The Alamo

The Alamo today is a major historical site in San Antonio, Texas, visited by thousands of Americans each year. Despite the complicated—and contested— history surrounding the battle that took place there, the events still fire the imagination of many Americans. Yet for decades following the actual event, it was not given much attention in U.S. history textbooks

1888

John J. Anderson, *New Grammar School History of the United States*

Texas was once a part of Mexico, and Mexico belonged to Spain. A revolt took place, and Mexico became independent (1822). Settlers from the Southern part of the United States flocked to Texas, the most noted among them being General Houston.

A large number, being slaveholders, took their slaves with them. Hence Texas, which, as a part of Mexico, did not contain a single slave, soon came to have many. Presently the people of Texas set up a government of their own (1835). After hard fighting their success was assured, though Mexico, without continuing the contest, still refused to give up its claim to the territory.[1]

1922

James A. Woodburn, *The Makers of America*

Texas, at one time, was a part of Mexico but the Texans were not happy under Mexican rule. Most of the Texas people were Americans and did not like the Mexican government. Finally, in 1835, they revolted and declared their independence of the Mexican government, just as our Revolutionary forefathers did in the case of England in 1776.

They had a hard struggle but they had brave leaders in Sam Houston, Crockett, Bowie, and others. They fought as bravely as any men could possibly fight. They also suffered terribly when, as prisoners, they fell into the hands of the Mexicans. In one case more than 350 of them who had surrendered were marched out in line and shot.

At the Alamo, a fort in southern Texas, one thousand Mexicans laid siege to one hundred and eighty-three Texans. The Texans sent out word that they would neither surrender nor retreat. The Mexicans made an attack from three sides and all of the Texans with the exception of five or six died fighting. It would have been better for them if they had all died in battle as they were massacred soon after, "not a man being left alive to tell the tale." The Texas people to this day have not forgotten the Alamo.

A short time later (April, 1836) the two armies met at San Jacinto, near Galveston. The Texans shouted their battle cry "Remember the Alamo" and charged on the Mexicans. The Texans killed, captured, or routed the entire Mexican Army. Santa Anna, the Mexican ruler, was among the prisoners.[2]

1923

Wilbur F. Gordy, *Stories of Later American History*

At that time Texas was a part of Mexico. Already before [General Sam] Houston went down to that far-away land many people from the United States had begun to settle there. At first they were welcomed. But when the Mexicans saw the Americans rapidly growing in numbers they began to oppress them. The Mexican Government went so far as to require them to give up their private arms, which would leave them defenseless against the Indians as well as bad men. Then it passed a law which said, in effect, that no more settlers should come to Texas from the United States, so that the few thousand Americans could not be strengthened in numbers.

Of course, the Texans were indignant, and they rebelled against Mexico, declaring Texas to be an independent republic. At the same time they elected Houston commander-in-chief of all the Texan troops. This began a bitter war.

The Mexican dictator, Santa Anna, with an army four or five thousand strong, marched into Texas to force the people to submit to the government.

The first important event of this struggle was the capture of the Alamo, an old Texan fortress at San Antonio. Although the garrison numbered only one hundred and forty, they were men of reckless daring, without fear, and they determined to fight to the last.

The Mexican army, upon reaching San Antonio, began firing upon the Alamo. Their cannon riddled the fort, making wide breaches in the weak outer walls through which from every side thousands of Mexicans thronged into it. The Americans emptied their muskets and then fought with knives and revolvers. They fought with desperate bravery until only five of the soldiers were left.[3]

1955

Glenn W. Moon and John H. MacGowan, *Story of Our Land and People*

In the meantime Santa Anna's army reached the mission town of San Antonio. There were only 187 Texans in the town. Under command of Colonel William Travis, they tried to defend the settlement. But they were driven back to the Alamo, the mission chapel which had been turned into a fort.

Inside the Alamo's thick walls the handful of Texans held off 3000 Mexican soldiers for 11 days! They killed more than 500 of the enemy. When the hopeless fight was over, the defenders were dead or dying to the last man. Among the dead were two famous scouts, Davy Crockett and James Bowie.

Next, Santa Anna marched southeast to the mission town of Goliad.

There he surrounded a group of 300 Texans. They were soon forced to surrender. Then they were lined up and shot.

Santa Anna thought the slaughter at the Alamo and at Goliad would frighten Texans. He expected them to give up the fight. No man ever made a worse mistake.

Thousands who had paid little attention to the trouble in Texas now became fighting mad. "Remember the Alamo! Remember Goliad!" they shouted. All over Texas, men seized their guns and rode away to join Houston's army. When news of the Alamo reached the United States many Americans hurried to join in the fight.

Within a week Sam Houston and his army were on the march. He had only about 900 men, but every one had used a rifle since boyhood. On April 21, 1836, the Texans caught up with the Mexican army. A battle took place on the bank of the San Jacinto River.

Santa Anna was taken by surprise. The general was asleep; his men were eating and drinking. The battle lasted 20 minutes. Santa Anna's army was cut to pieces. Only two Texans were killed and 23 wounded.[4]

1966

Harold H. Eibling, Fred M. King, and James Harlow, *History of Our United States*

"Remember the Alamo!" Santa Anna's army approached San Antonio. The 8 Mexican-Texans and 179 American-Texans who held the town gathered together behind the walls of a mission church called the Alamo. Santa Anna sent a messenger to the Texans' commander, Colonel William Travis, saying that unless the Texans agreed to immediate and unconditional surrender, he would kill every last one of them. In reply, the Texans tried to singe his beard with a cannon shot from the walls of the Alamo. The battle was on!

For twenty-four hours the artillery of Santa Anna blasted away at the thick adobe walls. When the Mexican army advanced again, the Texans drove them back with deadly fire. Instead of retreating, as he might have done that day, Travis sent out a letter he hoped would bring assistance:

To the People of Texas and All Americans in the World . . . I am besieged by a thousand or more of the Mexicans under Santa Anna. I have sustained a continual bombardment for 24 hours and have not lost a man. The enemy has demanded surrender at discretion, otherwise, the garrison is to be put to the sword if the fort is taken. I have answered the demand with a cannon shot and our flag still waves proudly from the walls. I shall never surrender or retreat. Then, I call upon you in the name of Liberty, of Patriotism and everything dear to the American character, to come to our aid with all dispatch. The enemy is receiving reinforcements daily and will no doubt increase to three or four thousand in four or five days. If this call is neglected, I am determined to sustain myself as long as possible and die like a soldier who never forgets what is due to his own honor and that of his country. VICTORY OR DEATH.

W. Barret Travis
Lt. Col. Comdt.

Santa Anna's army continued its attack on the Alamo. Gallant Colonel Travis sent another urgent message requesting help and supplies:

The spirits of my men are still high, although they have had much to depress them. We have contended for ten days against an enemy whose numbers are variously estimated at from fifteen hundred to six thousand men . . . I will, however, do the best I can under the circumstances; and I feel confident that the determined valor and desperate courage . . . [of] my men will not fail them in the last struggle. . . .

Unfortunately for the Texans, the needed reinforcements and supplies never arrived. The "rebels" were not yet organized enough to respond to the call for help. The Mexican cannons slowly but surely battered the walls to pieces. Then, on March 6, 1836, Santa Anna's men rushed forward.

The Mexican army was beaten back twice. The third and last attack was a terrible thing. Many of Santa Anna's men got through and over the walls into the Alamo. The Texan defenders ran out of powder; then they fought with empty guns as clubs, and finally with their bare fists! When the battle was over and the fort had been taken, not a defender remained alive. Santa Anna had lost more than 1,500 men. The names of the 187 Texan heroes were inscribed on a monument at the Alamo.

Had you been the commander at the Alamo, would you have surrendered? Why, or why not?[5] [Original question from textbook]

1970

Kenneth Bailey, Elizabeth Brooke, and John J. Farrell, *The American Adventure*

Santa Anna arrived in Texas from Mexico City in March, 1836. He led an army of six to seven thousand men. He was anxious to crush the Texas rebellion before it got any larger.

Lieutenant Colonel William B. Travis and 187 men took over the Alamo, a mission in San Antonio, and waited for Santa Anna and his men to arrive. Among those waiting were David Crockett, a famous Tennessee frontiersman, and Jim Bowie, noted for his hunting knife.

When Santa Anna sent word to the Texans to surrender the Alamo, Colonel Travis replied, "I am determined to sustain myself as long as possible, and die like a soldier who never forgets what is due to his own honor and that of his country. Victory or death!" What country was Travis talking about when he said this? Do you think his stand was foolish—187 men against several thousand?

For three days the Mexicans besieged the Alamo, until the weary men in the mission could resist no longer. Every American there was killed. This needless massacre gave rise later on to a famous Texas battle cry, "Remember the Alamo!"[6]

1999

Beverly J. Armento, Jacqueline M. Cordova, J. Jorge Klor de Alva, Gary B. Nash, Franklin Ng, Christopher L. Salter, Louis E. Wilson, and Karen K. Wixson, *America Will Be*

In response to the settlers, Santa Anna sent several thousand soldiers to the Alamo, an old mission in San Antonio. About 200 Americans, including Davy Crockett and Jim Bowie, were holding the Alamo.

The Battle of the Alamo began on February 23, 1836. Mexican cannon pounded the Alamo walls for days. Each night the guns moved closer. By March 5, they were 200 yards away.

Early in the morning on March 6, Santa Anna directed the final attack. The Texans fought fearlessly. They threw back first one attack, then another. The Mexican troops kept coming, however, and they finally succeeded. They stormed the wall, opened the gates, and overran the Alamo's defenders. They killed almost everyone, including Bowie, Crockett, and the commander, William Travis.

The defeat at the Alamo aroused the feelings of the American settlers. "Remember the Alamo!" became a battle cry. The Texas army, growing stronger every day, never stopped hoping for revenge.[7]

DISCUSSION QUESTIONS

1. Investigate the story of the Alamo. Why do you think this story did not get much attention in U.S. history textbooks until the twentieth century? If this story was not always mentioned in earlier textbooks, does that mean it is not an important historical event? Explain.

2. The 1922 textbook compares the Texans with the men who fought the American Revolutionary War. After doing your research, explain if you think this is a good or bad comparison. Explain why you think this author might have made that comparison.

3. On a map show where the borders of Mexico were prior to 1836. Then show how these borders changed in 1836 and again in 1848. What impact do you think this had on both Mexico and the United States politically and economically?

4. According to these textbooks, exactly how many men were inside the Alamo?

5. The men inside the Alamo lost this battle, yet it is considered a great American story. Explain how this defeat in battle could be considered such a great moment in American history. Are there other examples in U.S. history in which Americans were not victorious but were still seen as heroes?

6. Some of the textbooks in this section call the people inside the Alamo Americans, while other textbooks call them Texans. After researching

this story, explain which term best describes the defenders of the Alamo.

After losing the Battle of Coleto (March 19–20, 1836), the Texan soldiers were sent to Goliad (in modern southeastern Texas) and originally given clemency. Unfortunately, the Mexican president, Santa Anna, did not agree with this proposal and on March 27, 1836, ordered all the Texan prisoners to be shot. In the end approximately 340 Texans were killed in what became known as the Goliad Massacre. Therefore, throughout the Texas Revolution it was not uncommon to hear Texan soldiers exclaim, "Remember Goliad! Remember the Alamo!"

18

The Trail of Tears

In 1838, during the presidential administration of Andrew Jackson, Native American tribes (most notably the Cherokee) were forced from their territories in the southeastern part of the United States to Indian Territory (officially Oklahoma today). The terrible journey is often referred to as the Trail of Tears, referring to the death and suffering that took place along the route.

1860

Benson J. Lossing, *A Primary History of the United States*

Finally, in 1836, the Creek joined the Seminoles, and in coaches, steamboats, and villages in Georgia and Alabama, many [white settlers were] attacked by them. General Scott, of whom I shall soon tell you more, went there, and beat the Creeks. During the summer of 1830, several thousands of them went to their new home beyond the Mississippi.[1]

1951

Clyde B. Moore, Fred B. Painter, Helen M. Carpenter, and Gertrude M. Lewis, *Building Our America*

The Indians were forced to give up their lands in the East for the new lands in the West. Each tribe was given a piece of land of its own. Settlers were not to cross the line into Indian lands. The United States built forts in the Indian lands. Soldiers were kept in the forts to see that Indians and settlers did not cross the line. The soldiers were also supposed to keep the Indians from fighting each other.

Many people thought all of this was a good plan. No more would the Indians be pushed out of their hunting grounds by land-hungry settlers. No more would settlers live in fear of being scalped by Indian warriors. As we shall see, the plan did not work for long. No sooner had the Indians been moved than American settlers began to cross the boundary line into the Indian lands. They not only went into Indian lands, but they also crossed the Sabine River into Mexico.[2]

1966

Harold H. Eibling, Fred M. King, and James Harlow, *History of Our United States*

Early in his term of office Jackson decided to clear the frontier of Indians once and for all. He was supported in this decision by people in the West. He sent the Army to tell the various Indian tribes to pack up and move beyond the Mississippi. Some tribes objected to being forced from their homes. They pointed out that their nations had signed treaties with the United States that guaranteed them the land they possessed. The Cherokee Nation took its fight to the Supreme Court, where eventually the Cherokees' rights were recognized. Jackson refused to honor the ruling of the Court, and in one way or another continued his policy of moving the red men.[3]

1977

Lewis Paul Todd and Merle Curti, *Rise of the American Nation*

But white settlers in Georgia were determined to crush the Cherokees, especially after gold was discovered there. Using all sorts of harassments they tried to force the Cherokees to sign a removal treaty. The Georgia legislature passed a law stating that Cherokee laws and treaty rights were null and void—that is, of no effect. The United States Supreme Court, with Chief Justice John Marshall presiding, declared the Georgia law unconstitutional and held that forcible removal of the Cherokees from their lands violated their treaties with the federal government. President Jackson is reported to have said, "John Marshall has made his decision; now let him enforce it."

The removal of Indians, including the Cherokees, went forward. Little or no preparation was made for the resettlement of the Indians. Tragic stories are told of how Indians, especially the Cherokees, were driven during the bitter cold of winter—thinly clad, without moccasins, sometimes in chains, often without food—into what was for them a strange and barren wilderness across the Mississippi River.

Andrew Jackson showed some personal concern for the plight of the Indians, but in his role as President he was responsible for the removal of a great many. His official position remained one of uncompromising support for Indian resettlement. He refused to listen to missionary groups who wanted to help the Indians achieve orderly, settled lives. He ignored not only the Supreme Court but also political critics, including Henry Clay, who opposed his Indian policy. When Jackson left the White House, the first major Indian removals had been largely carried out.[4]

1990

Roger LaRaus, Harry P. Morris, and Robert Sobel, *Challenge of Freedom*

Most of today's historians agree, however, that a second Jackson policy—that of Indian removal—was cruel and unfair. Under President Jackson, our government forced thousands of American Indians to leave their homelands to make room for white settlers. The Indian Removal Law of 1830 allowed Jackson to take the lands of several major Indian tribes. In return, these tribes were given new land farther west. But the lands given to the Indians were generally poor and ill suited for farming or for hunting. Thus, many thousands of Indians had to leave their homes, their farms, and their businesses for a life of hardship in the Southwest.[5]

DISCUSSION QUESTIONS

1. Discuss the overall theme that these textbooks adopt when discussing this topic. Have textbook authors generally portrayed the "Indian removal" as being a good or bad thing? Explain.
2. Do the textbooks in this section portray Andrew Jackson as being a good or bad leader? Research Andrew Jackson and see if historians agree with these textbook selections.
3. Research the Trail of Tears and explain what it would have been like for a Native American to have gone through this. Explain if you agree with the Supreme Court's decision or Andrew Jackson's in terms of removing the Native Americans. Do you consider this historical event "cruel and unfair," as the 1990 textbook does?
4. On a map of the United States show all the different routes the various Native American tribes had to take in order to get to their "Indian lands." Research where the U.S. government sent them and explain if you think the geography of this area had an impact on why the Native Americans were sent there.

Unlike the stereotypical images usually found in history textbooks of all Native Americans being nomadic savages, the Cherokee had actually assimilated a number of European customs and styles. It was not uncommon to see members of this nation wearing European-style clothing, working as farmers and ranchers, going to Christian churches, and attending schools.

19

The Mexican-American War, 1846–1848

From the very beginning, U.S. history textbooks have spent a great deal of time covering America's wars. While most can agree on when these wars started and ended, it is the question of what started them that causes much debate among historians. The outbreak of the Mexican-American War, in 1846, is a prime example. In the selections below, students are presented with multiple causes: from a misunderstanding over borders and money to aggression by an American president who wanted more territory.

1860

Benson J. Lossing, *A Primary History of the United States*

The coming in of Texas was the most important event at the beginning of Mr. Polk's administration. The government of Mexico had never acknowledged the independence of that State, but continued to claim it as a part of that republic. Of course the act of Congress in admitting it was very offensive.

This offense and an old quarrel about debts due from Mexico to people of the United States soon caused a war. Expecting this, the President ordered General Taylor and fifteen hundred soldiers to go to Texas in July.

They encamped at Corpus Christi, not far from the Rio Grande, or Grand River. At the same time some American war-vessels went into the Gulf of Mexico.

A large number of Mexican troops collected at Matamoras, near the mouth of the Rio Grande, at the close of 1845. Early in January following, General Taylor with most of his troops formed a camp and commenced building a fort on the opposite side of the river. General Ampudia . . . who commanded the Mexicans, ordered him to leave in twenty-four hours, but he refused to do so.

General Arista . . . now became the Mexican commander. He was a better soldier than Ampudia, and Taylor's situation became a dangerous one. Soon, armed Mexicans crossed the river, and late in April some Americans were killed by them. This was the first blood shed in THE WAR WITH MEXICO.[1]

1875

John J. Anderson, *A Grammar School History of the United States*

War with Mexico

Tyler's successor in office was James K. Polk, who was inaugurated on the 4th of March, 1845. His administration continued during only one term, but it was an eventful one. On the 4th of July, 1845, the Legislature of Texas approved the "annexation bill" passed by the United States Congress, and, by this act of approval, Texas became one of the United States.

Texas had been a province of Mexico, but, in consequence of the arbitrary policy of the Mexican rulers, the Texans revolted, and, in 1836, set up a government of their own. The annexation of Texas to the United States led to a war with Mexico; for Mexico still claimed Texas as a part of her own territory, and considered the act of annexation a sufficient cause of war.

Events of 1846

For the protection of the new state, Gen. Taylor proceeded, by order of President Polk, to the Rio Grande, opposite Matamoras, where he erected a fort, which was afterward named Fort Brown. Learning that the Mexicans were assembling troops at a point higher up the river, Taylor asked Capt. Thornton, with sixty-three dragoons, to reconnoiter. This little force was attacked on the 26th of April, 1846, and, after a loss of sixteen men, was compelled to surrender.

The Mexicans, in large force, having crossed the Rio Grande, for the purpose, as was supposed, of moving against Point Isabel, where the Americans had established a depot of supplies, Taylor marched to the relief of that place. After putting the Point in a good state of defence, he set out on his return to the river.

His progress was disputed at Palo Alto and Resaca de la Palma by Gen. Arista but, in both battles, the Mexicans were defeated with severe loss. In the first battle, fought on the 8th of May, the Mexicans numbered six thousand men, while the Americans consisted of but twenty-three hundred. The loss of the former exceeded five hundred.[2]

1885

Thomas Wentworth Higginson, *Young Folks' History of the United States*

But the other great event of Mr. Polk's administration was something about which people were not at all agreed, and which many, especially in the Northern States, regarded as a great calamity, the Mexican War. When the United States had annexed Texas, the nation found that it had still another question of boundary on its hands. Texas claimed that its western boundary was the Rio Grande, and Mexico claimed that it was the River Nueces; and, as these rivers were a hundred miles apart, there was a wide range of disputed territory between. The United States took up the cause of Texas, and General Taylor was sent to the disputed ground with a small army. The Mexicans, also, sent troops thither; and fighting soon began, first in a small way, then in some larger battles, at Palo Alto and Resaca de la Palma, in which the Americans were successful. Then General Taylor crossed the Rio Grande, and took Matamoras, which was within undisputed Mexican territory.

There was much excitement in Washington on hearing this news. Congress voted thus, May, 1846: "By the act of the Republic of Mexico, war exists between that government and the United States," though the Whig members declared that the war was not really begun by Mexico, but by General Taylor. Congress also voted ten million dollars for the war, and resolved to raise fifty thousand volunteers. There was not much sympathy for the war in the Eastern States; but the South-western States, which were nearest the scene of excitement, sent many volunteers to the aid of General Taylor. At last his army reached nearly seven thousand men, and with this he took, in three days, the fortified town of Montery, garrisoned by ten thousand Mexicans. Then General Santa Anna, who had formerly been President of Mexico, and was regarded as the best soldier of that re-public, took command of the Mexican army but was beaten by General Taylor, with a much smaller force, at Buena Vista.[3]

1922

James A. Woodburn, *The Makers of America*

The annexation of Texas led to a war with Mexico. Mexico had never really acknowledged the independence of Texas. She still claimed that Texas was a part of Mexico and was very angry when the United States an-nexed that territory.

There was also another cause for the war. The United States claimed that the Rio Grande was the southern boundary of Texas. Mexico claimed that Texas didn't extend that far south. The President sent a part of the United States army to take possession of the disputed strip of land. The Mexicans made an attack upon the American troops and the war was on. This was in the spring of 1846—only a year after Congress had voted to annex Texas.[4]

1930

William Backus Guitteau, *Our United States: A History for Upper Grammar Grades and Junior High School*

Causes of the War

The annexation of Texas alone might not have brought on war with Mexico, but there were other causes of friction between that country and the United States. In the first place, Mexico's repeated refusal to sell Texas was exasperating to the southern statesmen in control of our government. Bent on securing more slave territory, these leaders felt aggrieved because Mexico stood in their way. Then too, Mexico refused to pay the claims of our citizens whose property had been seized during the frequent Mexican revolutions. It is true that the Mexican government was bankrupt, and unable to pay these or any other claims; but this fact seemed to President Polk only another reason why Mexico ought to accept our offer to purchase California and New Mexico. On her part, Mexico resented the aid given by our citizens to the Texan revolutionists. The final grievance, so far as Mexico was concerned, was our annexation of Texas, even though this event came nine years after the "Lone Star State" had won her independence.

President Polk came into office determined to secure California and New Mexico, in addition to Texas, from our resentful neighbor. California was already on the point of declaring her independence; and President Polk believed that in spite of our Monroe Doctrine, Great Britain meant to possess that country if she could. Accordingly, Polk sent a commissioner to Mexico with an offer of forty million dollars for California and New Mexico. Popular feeling compelled the Mexican government to decline to receive our commissioner. Apparently the differences between the two countries could be settled only by an appeal to arms.

Outbreak of War

Besides her resentment over the annexation itself, Mexico had another grievance. Texas claimed that her southwestern boundary was the Rio Grande; Mexico insisted that it was the Nueces River. Adopting the Texan claim, President Polk ordered General Zachary Taylor to advance to the Rio Grande. Taylor's advance meant war. On April 24, 1846, a party of American dragoons was ambushed by a large force of Mexicans who had crossed to the east side of the Rio Grande. When this news reached Washington, President Polk sent a war message to Congress declaring: "Mexico has passed the boundary of the United States, has invaded our territory, and shed American blood upon the American soil." Congress promptly voted to enlist fifty thousand men for "the war which exists by the act of the Republic of Mexico."[5]

1951

Clyde B. Moore, Fred B. Painter, Helen M. Carpenter, and Gertrude M. Lewis, *Building Our America*

Trouble with Mexico arose soon after Texas came into the Union. Texans claimed the territory to the Rio Grande River. Mexico claimed the land between the Rio Grande and the Nueces rivers. President Polk sent an army to the Rio Grande. Mexico also sent an army to the Rio Grande.

War started in 1846. General Zachary Taylor led the American army across the Rio Grande. He won two or three small battles and then defeated a large Mexican army at Buena Vista. General Winfield Scott was sent by sea with another army. He landed at Vera Cruz, where Cortez had landed his army more than three hundred years before. Like Cortez, Scott marched on Mexico City. General Scott surprised the Mexicans by taking his army over steep mountain passes. The Mexicans thought only a mountain goat could climb them. Scott's army won two battles and captured Mexico City.[6]

1966

Harold H. Eibling, Fred M. King, and James Harlow, *History of Our United States*

Trouble over Texas

Mexico had been displeased when we recognized Texas as a republic in 1837. After we annexed Texas in 1845, Mexico showed outright hatred toward the United States. It looked as though the United States had plotted to take Texas away from her, Mexico said. She called home her minister to the United States. This meant that she was breaking off diplomatic relations with us, and our minister to Mexico must come home. Relations between Mexico and the United States were tense, and the situation grave.

About this time an old dispute flared up over the boundary between Mexico and Texas. Mexico said the boundary was the Nueces River; Texas said it was the Rio Grande fifty miles away.

President Polk sent an army under General Zachary Taylor to patrol the border south of the Nueces. At the same time he sent a group of diplomats to Mexico to try to buy California and New Mexico. The Mexican government refused to see the diplomats. In May of 1846, Polk ordered American troops to move south to the Rio Grande, which was patrolled by Mexicans. The Mexicans, taking this to be an act of war, attacked a group of Taylor's scouts and killed several.

War with Mexico

President Polk asked for a declaration of war saying: "Mexico has passed the boundary of the United States, has invaded our territory and shed American blood upon the American soil . . . war exists, and notwithstanding all our efforts to avoid it, exists by the act of Mexico herself." General Taylor did not wait for war to be declared. He marched at once into Mexico, capturing the cities of Matamoras and Monterrey. Then, going inland, he took the town of Buena Vista the next year, handing a bitter defeat to the much larger Mexican army under Santa Anna.[7]

1977

JoAnne Buggey, *America! America!*

Relations between the United States and Mexico reached a breaking point. Mexico had long threatened war with the United States if it should annex Texas. In addition, the United States government claimed that Mexico had not fulfilled its three-million-dollar debt to Americans who had suffered damages and lost property in Mexico. Another problem was a disagreement over the southern boundary of Texas. Mexico said the boundary was the Nueces River; the United States claimed it was the Rio Grande, which is 150 miles further south.

President Polk appointed John Slidell to work out a settlement of the many differences between the two neighboring countries. When the Mexican government refused to receive Slidell, Polk ordered General Zachary Taylor to cross the Nueces River and occupy the territory on the left bank of the Rio Grande. Polk's orders were considered an act of war by some people, who claimed that the Nueces River had been the southern boundary of Texas for over 100 years.

The commander of the Mexican forces also considered Taylor's occupation an act of war. The Mexican forces attacked and won this skirmish. On April 25, 1846, General Taylor sent word that the Mexican cavalry had crossed the Rio Grande and had killed, wounded, or captured sixty-three of the United States force.

Polk had what he needed and had little difficulty getting Congress to declare that "by act of the Republic of Mexico, a state of war exists between that government and the United States."

Forty-nine thousand men from Texas and the states along the Mississippi quickly responded to the call for volunteers. Only 13,000 volunteers came forward from the eastern states.

Feeling about the Mexican War was mixed. Southerners felt Texas was fine just the way it was. Abolitionists opposed the war because they felt it was just a war to get more slave territory. Former President John Quincy Adams claimed the war was an expedition by the South to look for "bigger pens to cram with slaves."[8]

1999

Beverly J. Armento, Jacqueline M. Cordova, J. Jorge Klor de Alva, Gary B. Nash, Franklin Ng, Christopher L. Salter, Louis E. Wilson, and Karen K. Wixson, *America Will Be*

As expected, Mexico reacted angrily to the news of statehood for Texas, with its southern border on the Rio Grande. Mexico felt threatened by having the land hungry United States across the Rio Grande. This triggered a war. In November 1845, President Polk sent an ambassador to Mexico City to try to negotiate a settlement. Mexican officials, however, refused to talk.

Next, President Polk, in order to start a war, commanded American forces in Texas to move down to the Rio Grande. They were now in territory that the Mexican government said was theirs. In April 1846, Mexican troops fought with an American scouting party, leaving 16 dead or wounded. With these casualties the conflict intensified immediately. The United States and Mexico were now at war.

American generals Winfield Scott and Zachary Taylor believed they needed to invade Mexico to win. General Taylor invaded Mexico from the north, crossed the Rio Grande, won a few quick victories, and took some important Mexican towns.[9]

DISCUSSION QUESTIONS

1. After reading all the textbooks in this section and doing your own research, explain who or what caused the Mexican-American War, 1846–1848.

2. On a map show where the Mexicans and Americans disagreed over borders. Explain why you think the two different borders were important to both sides in this conflict. Using the 1966 and 1977 textbooks in this section, explain if the Rio Grande is fifty or one hundred and fifty miles away from the Nueces.

3. The 1885 textbook claims that the eastern states did not support this war. Investigate this story and see how accurate it is. Cite reasons these states would have opposed the war.

4. Find President Polk's war address to Congress in 1848. What exactly did he say to Congress? Was he completely correct in everything he said?

On December 22, 1847, a young Whig member of the House of Representatives from Illinois offered up his "Spot Resolution," which asked the president of the United States to inform the American people of the exact spot in which the Mexican-American War had started. This rather forward representative wanted to challenge the validity of President Polk's claim that Mexico had started the war against the United States. This young upstart was none other than future president Abraham Lincoln.

20

The Mormons

Freedom of religion has been considered one of the cornerstones of American freedom, enshrined in the First Amendment to the U.S. Constitution. From the early religious colonies to the present day, religion has shaped much of America's history. But some religious groups have encountered hostility when they tried to practice their own religious beliefs in the United States. This section looks at one of these groups, the Church of Jesus Christ of Latter-day Saints (also known as the Mormons).

1860

Benson J. Lossing, *A Primary History of the United States*

Utah was settled by a people called Mormons. I have not time to tell you much about them. It would be a long story. They are a people with a very queer kind of religion; and they all do as their head man, or *Prophet*, as he is called, tell them to do. There are now a great many thousands of them in Utah, and I expect there will be much trouble yet, on their account, because they allow things to be done which the people of the United States do not like.[1]

1869

G.P. Quackenbos, *Elementary History of the United States*

Difficulties with the Mormons obliged Mr. Buchanan to send an army into their territory. The Mormons lived in Utah, far away from the settled portions of the United States. Here they defied the general government, claiming the right of naming their own rulers. When the army, however, arrived in the neighborhood of their chief city, the Mormons changed their tone and agreed to recognize the laws and authority of the United States.[2]

1885

Thomas Wentworth Higginson, *Young Folks' History of the United States*

There was also much disturbance in Illinois, where the religious sect called the "Mormons," or "Latter-Day Saints," who had built a city called Nauvoo, were assailed repeatedly by mobs. The Mormon sect had been founded fourteen years before, by a man named Joseph Smith, who claimed to have discovered a book called "The Book of Mormon," written on gold plates that were found buried in the earth. The Mormons first established themselves in Missouri, were driven thence by mob violence to Illinois, and thence to the Territory of Utah, where they made for themselves a settlement in the wilderness, and still remain.[3]

1923

Henry Eldridge Bourne and Elbert Jay Benton, *Story of America and Great Americans*

Another way to change the "desert" into fertile farm land is to carry water in ditches from mountain streams or lakes. This is called irrigation. The first settlers to irrigate their farms were the Mormons who were led by Brigham Young into the region about the Great Salt Lake in Utah. They started from Illinois and Iowa and had followed the Oregon Trail as far as South Pass. The owner of a trading post which they passed on the route, learning that they planned to raise crops in the valley of the Great Salt Lake, declared he would give them a thousand dollars for the first ear of corn. Their leader replied, "Wait and see!" The first glimpse of the land led some of them to wonder if the trader was not right, for the soil glistened with salt and seemed so powdery that it could not be plowed without being wet.

The farmers in Utah were always sure of water, for the valley is bordered by high mountains whose tops are covered with snow nearly the whole year. As the snow melts it feeds streams with an endless supply of water. All that was necessary was to save as much as possible and carry it by ditches and flumes to the fields.[4]

1955

Glenn W. Moon and John H. MacGowan, *Story of Our Land and People*

The Mormons settled in Utah. During the Mexican War some Americans started a settlement in the Rocky Mountain region. The settlers belonged to a religious group called the Mormons or, more correctly, the Church of Jesus Christ of Latter Day Saints. The Mormon religion was founded by Joseph Smith.

Smith was born in Vermont in 1805. When he was 14 he moved with his family to Palmyra, New York. Smith was intensely interested in religion, and he had many visions.

Smith told later how an angel appeared to him one day, led him to a hill near his father's farm, and told him to dig in the ground. Smith reported that he found golden plates containing sacred writings. These writings he translated; they were the source of a book Smith later published called The Book of Mormon.

Many people laughed at Joseph Smith. But some believed him and helped him found a new religion. The Mormons moved westward, hoping to find a friendly locality.

In Illinois, Smith and his followers founded a settlement. But they had trouble with neighbors who did not like the new religion. Smith was murdered by a mob. A new leader, Brigham Young, took charge. The Mormons decided to move to the Far West and find a new home, far from any other settlements.

From Illinois, Brigham Young led a pioneer group of 140 men and three women. They followed the Oregon Trail to South Pass in the Rocky Mountains. There they turned southwest on what later became the trail to California.

They reached a valley, encircled by mountains, on the shore of Great Salt Lake. Brigham Young declared, "This is the place." The Mormons cleared the sage-brush and made their first permanent camp. The loneliness of the hidden valley was one reason the Mormons chose it. Here, in Utah, they thought, they could live in peace.

The first work of the advance party was to dig canals. In this way, water could be brought from the mountains to irrigate, or to make fertile by watering, a few acres of desert soil. Food crops were planted, and riders carried back word that everything was ready for the great journey. Then from distant Illinois 1000 wagons set forth to cross 1500 miles of prairie and mountain.

At the end of the dangerous journey, the whole Mormon company went promptly to work. They dug more canals, planted more acres, and built mills and workshops. They intended to make the land support them, and to make whatever clothing, furniture, and tools they needed. They soon established a thriving settlement and "made the desert bloom."

At the end of the Mexican War, the United States took possession of the whole Southwest. The land where the Mormons had settled became Utah Territory. In 1896 Utah entered the Union as a state.[5]

1986

James West Davidson and John E. Batchelor, *The American Nation*

Mormons Move West

Among the early pioneers to settle in the Mexican Cession were the Mormons. The Mormons belonged to the Church of Jesus Christ of Latter Day Saints. The church was founded in the 1820s by Joseph Smith. Smith, a farmer who lived in upstate New York, won many followers.

Early Years

Smith was an energetic and well-liked man. But some of his teachings angered non-Mormons. For example, at first Mormons believed in owning property in common. Smith also said that a man could have more than one wife. The Mormons were forced to move from New York to Ohio, then to Missouri, and later to Illinois.

In the 1840s, the Mormons built the town of Nauvoo, Illinois, on the banks of the Mississippi River. The Mormons worked together for the good of their community. They ran successful farms and industries. By 1844, Nauvoo was the largest town in Illinois. Its clean streets were lined with neat brick houses.

However, the Mormons again had trouble with their neighbors. In 1844, a mob attacked Nauvoo and killed Joseph Smith. The Mormons quickly chose Brigham Young as their new leader. Young realized that the Mormons needed a home where they would be safe. He had read about a valley between the Rocky Mountains and the Great Salt Lake in Utah. Young decided that the isolated valley would make a safe home for the Mormons.

An Impossible Task

To move 15,000 men, women, and children from Illinois to Utah seemed an impossible task. Young relied on faith and careful planning to achieve his goal. In 1847, he led an advance party into the Great Salt Lake valley. For two years, Mormon wagon trains struggled across the plains and over the steep Rockies.

Once they reached Utah, the Mormons had to survive in the desert climate of the valley. Once again, Young proved to be a gifted leader. He planned an irrigation system to bring water to farms. Young also drew up plans for a large city, called Salt Lake City, to be built in the desert.

The Mormon settlement in Utah grew quickly. Like other white settlers, Mormons took over thousands of acres of Indian land, usually without paying anything for it. Congress recognized Brigham Young as governor of the Utah Territory in 1850. Trouble broke out when non-Mormons moved to the area. In the end, peace was restored, and Utah became a state in 1896.[6]

DISCUSSION QUESTIONS

1. Research the relations between the Mormons in Utah and the U.S. government prior to the Civil War. Does your information help you understand the story the authors of the 1860 textbook told students?

2. On a map of the United States trace the route the Mormons took to get to Utah. See what other major routes you can find that people took westward in the 1800s and trace those on the map as well. Explain what role geography played in helping or hurting these settlers move into and settle the western United States.

3. Read your current history textbook and investigate other American religions that were not welcomed by some people in the United States. Compare their story to that of the Mormons and explain if you think they are similar or not.

4. Do you think textbooks written in the twentieth century were more tolerant of the Mormons than those in the nineteenth century? Explain.

5. Why do you think so many textbook authors in this section seemed to be impressed with how this group of people irrigated and maintained their crops in this part of the United States?

Historians today refer to the period in which Joseph Smith founded his new religion as the "Second Great Awakening." It was a time of religious revivalism in the United States and a backlash against secularism.

PART V

The Civil War and Reconstruction

21

Dred Scott

Historians have argued for decades over what exactly caused the Civil War. In the sequence of causes, the case of Dred Scott v. Sanford *has always figured prominently. Born a slave in Missouri, Dred Scott was taken by his master north to a territory that did not allow slavery (modern-day Minnesota). Scott's lawyers argued that since he was living in free territory he was automatically a free man. The U.S. Supreme Court did not see it that way and helped spark a new wave of dissension between North and South.*

1885

Thomas Wentworth Higginson, *Young Folks' History of the United States*

Mr. Buchanan's inauguration took place on March 4, 1857, and that very year the Supreme Court pronounced a decision called the "Dred Scott Decision," declaring the right of slaveholders to take their slaves with them into any part of the country.

This made a great excitement throughout the free States; and something else soon happened, which excited the slave States almost as much. This was what is commonly called "John Brown's Raid." Capt. John Brown's name has been already mentioned in describing the resistance of the "Free State" settlers of Kansas to the "Border Ruffians" of Missouri.[1]

1888

John J. Anderson, *New Grammar School History of the United States*

Two days after the inauguration an important decision comes from the Supreme Court in relation to a slave named Dred Scott. This decision is the opinion of a majority of the judges. Scott is declared to be in law not a person, but a thing. No colored man can become a citizen of the United States, and Congress has no more right to stop the carrying of slaves from one State to another or into a Territory than it has to stop the carrying of horses or any other property. So, in substance, says the decision. Speaking for a majority of the Court, the Chief Justice asserts that when the Constitution was adopted, colored men "had no rights which the white man was bound to respect." This decision, so at variance with the convictions and feelings of the great body of people at the North, comes with startling effect. It sends men into the Republican party, for there and only there, it seems to them, can the stride of slavery be arrested. It unites the Republicans in a more compact body, and makes them more resolute. It is one of the agents working to divide the Democratic party into two factions, and thus making a Republican victory possible in the next presidential election.[2]

1905

Thomas B. Lawler, *A Primary History of the United States*

Two days after President Buchanan had taken his seat the United States Supreme Court gave a decision of the utmost importance on the question of slavery.

Dred Scott, a slave, had been taken by his owner to the free states of Illinois and Minnesota, and after some years he was brought back to live in Missouri, a slave state. Scott now claimed his freedom, saying he had lived on free soil and was therefore free.

His case came before the Supreme Court of the United States. This court decided that Scott could not bring a suit in a court because he was a slave, in other words, merely property. The court declared that a man could take slaves anywhere, as he would a horse or a cow or other property. The court also declared that the Missouri Compromise Act was of no value, as Congress had no right to make a law that would prevent a man from moving property anywhere.

This famous decision opened all the territories of the United States to slavery. It created an intense feeling in the North. In the South equally intense feelings were aroused by the John Brown raid. Ten years had brought about a wonderful change for the negro. Before the law he was now the equal of any one. From being merely property he had become a citizen with the great right to cast his vote in all elections.[3]

1930

William Backus Guitteau, *Our United States: A History for Upper Grammar Grades and Junior High School*

Two days after President Buchanan was inaugurated, the Supreme Court of the United States gave its famous decision in the Dred Scott case. Dred Scott was a Missouri slave whose master, an army surgeon, had taken him first into Illinois, then to Minnesota Territory. In Illinois, slavery was prohibited by the Northwest Ordinance and by the state constitution; while Minnesota was in the northern part of the Louisiana Territory, from which slavery was excluded by the Missouri Compromise. After two years' residence in Minnesota, Scott was taken back to Missouri. Many years afterwards, he brought suit in the Missouri courts to recover his freedom on the ground that his residence in free territory had made him a free man. Defeated in the Missouri court, Scott carried his case to the Supreme Court of the United States for final decision.

Two important questions were passed upon by that tribunal. First, could a negro whose ancestors had been sold as slaves become a citizen of Missouri? To this question, the answer of the court was "no." The negro, said Chief Justice Taney, could not possibly become a citizen, for the Constitution was not intended to apply to any but the white race. When the Constitution was adopted, negroes were considered "so far inferior that they had no rights which the white man was bound to respect." Since Dred Scott was not a citizen, he could not bring suit in the United States Court.[4]

1977

JoAnne Buggey, *America! America!*

Dred Scott had been a slave. He was taken by his master, an army surgeon, to the free Wisconsin Territory for five years.

After his owner died, Scott returned to Missouri where abolitionists persuaded him to sue for his freedom based on his stay in free territory. Scott was sold to an owner in New York. He then sued the owner as a citizen of another state. The case was reviewed by the Supreme Court. (Under the Constitution, the Supreme Court has the authority to consider a case in which a citizen of one state sues a citizen of another.)

Chief Justice Taney delivered the Supreme Court's opinion. He said that Scott could not sue because he was not a citizen under Missouri law. Furthermore, he could not be a citizen of the United States. Taney also said that the Missouri Compromise was illegal because it deprived slaveholders of their property. According to the Court, since slaves were considered property, slavery could not be banned in any part of the country.[5]

1990

Roger LaRaus, Harry P. Morris, and Robert Sobel, *Challenge of Freedom*

During the 1830's, the owner of Dred Scott, a slave, had moved from the slave state of Missouri to the Wisconsin Territory. Scott had gone with his owner. But the Wisconsin Territory had outlawed slave owning within its lands. In 1846, Dred Scott brought a lawsuit to win his freedom. Because he had lived in a free territory, Scott said, he was no longer a slave. But when the case reached the Supreme Court, Justice Roger Taney felt that Scott was still a slave. The Court, influenced by Taney, ruled that a slave remained the owner's property even in a free territory.

The Dred Scott case struck a blow against the antislavery cause. The Supreme Court's ruling meant that the Missouri Compromise was un-constitutional. Territorial governments did not have the power to outlaw slave owning in their lands. Slave owning was legal in any territory. The outcome of the Dred Scott case caused an angry public outcry across the North. Many northerners believed that Chief Justice Taney, a southerner, had used the law to help the South. The South, on the other hand, was delighted with the Dred Scott case. Southerners held that the ruling meant that slave owning was a right. And many southerners hoped that slavery would now be spread throughout the country.

The Supreme Court's ruling made little real difference in terms of slave owning in the western territories. But it added greatly to sectional bitterness in our country. After the Dred Scott case, a growing number of Americans no longer believed that the slave question could be settled in a peaceful manner.[6]

DISCUSSION QUESTIONS

1. In the 1885 textbook the author spends just as much time discussing John Brown's raid at Harpers Ferry as he does the case of Dred Scott. After researching both of these events, explain which you think was more of a factor in causing the Civil War.

2. Explain why the Dred Scott case was usually not considered an important cause of the Civil War in textbooks published in the 1800s.

3. Investigate Dred Scott's life history. Did he have a typical life for an average slave in the years before the Civil War? Explain.

4. You will notice that many textbooks in this section refer to "colored people" and "negroes," while today the term most often used is "African Americans." Research and discuss why the same group of people has been referred to by three (or more) different names over the past hundred years. By using these different names, were textbooks reflecting the attitudes in society at that time? Explain.

Of the nine Supreme Court justices sitting on the bench in 1856, seven of them had been appointed by pro-slavery presidents and five actually came from families that owned slaves.

22

Slavery

The issue of slavery has been a difficult one for many U.S. history textbooks to deal with over the years. Before the Civil War it was a rare textbook indeed that even mentioned that there were African slaves in the United States. From the end of the Civil War until the mid-twentieth century, textbooks began to deal with the topic of slavery more often, but in many instances these books may have done more to deepen racial stereotypes rather than dispel them. It is arguably not until the 1960s, after the civil rights movement had begun, that U.S. history textbooks really began to grapple with slavery as a historical issue of major importance to the United States.

1888

John J. Anderson, *New Grammar School History of the United States*

How many inhabitants are now here we do not know. If we say upward of two millions, we are supposed to be near the truth. Of these, not fewer than four hundred thousand are negro slaves, all Africans or descendants of Africans. The negroes did not come here of their own accord. They were kidnapped, and brought by force. At first they were brought in Dutch ships, one of these beginning the cruel business by landing twenty negroes at Jamestown in 1619.

A few years later English ships were engaged in this monstrous traffic. Though the Quakers of Pennsylvania and New Jersey, as well as most of the other colonists, were decidedly opposed to slavery, there did not seem to be sufficient power, if there had been sufficient will, to stop the importation. Said Oglethorpe: "Slavery is opposed to the Gospel," and yet seven years after his first coming to Georgia, slave ships were discharging their cargoes at Savannah. Negro slavery, law or no law, found its way into every one of the thirteen colonies. It was forced upon them by English kings, queens, dukes, and lords. These dictated laws which gave to them the monopoly of the slave-trade with British provinces, and thus filled their pockets with the ill-gotten gain. In twenty years they took from Africa about three hundred thousand negroes. Six thousand were taken to South Carolina in one year. Says Bancroft: "The sovereigns of England and Spain were the greatest slave-merchants in the world."

In New England most of the slaves were house servants. In New York they were employed on the farms as well as in the house. In Pennsylvania there were not many slaves, owing to the large supply of "indented servants." These were white persons, mostly from England and Ireland, who, not being able to pay their passage money, were sold, with their consent, to land owners for a term of years. Such persons were also numerous in the colonies south of Pennsylvania. "Like negroes, they were purchased on shipboard as men buy horses at a fair." If one ran away, he was pursued. If captured, he was whipped. In 1670, there were as many as six thousand indented servants in Virginia alone.

In Maryland, after five years' service, the servant, according to custom, became a free man. His former master then gave him two suits of clothing, a gun, some tools, and a hog or two. Where tobacco was cultivated, in Maryland, Virginia, and North Carolina, negro slaves were numerous. In South Carolina, where large crops of rice were raised, there were more slaves than free persons.[1]

1906

Oscar Gerson, *History Primer*

When we were studying the story of Jamestown, we learned that about 300 years ago a number of negroes were brought to Virginia.

They were not hired as servants, but were sold to the white settlers as slaves.

Slaves were owned by their masters just as a horse or dog was. The slaves did not get wages for their work. They were fed and clothed by their masters, and were given rough cabins or huts to live in. They were bought and sold, or exchanged by their owners just as horses are today.

Many of the slaves had kind owners, but some had cruel masters, who beat them and made them work too hard.[2]

1923

Wilber F. Gordy, *Stories of Later American History*

The cotton-gin brought about great changes. Before its invention it took a slave a whole day to separate the seed from five or six pounds of cotton fiber. But by the use of the cotton-gin he could separate the seed from a thousand pounds in a single day.

This, of course, meant that cotton could be sold for very much less than before, and hence there arose a much greater demand for it. It meant, also, that the labor of slaves was of more value than before, and hence there was a greater demand for slaves.

As slavery now became such an important feature of southern life, let us pause for a glimpse of a southern plantation where slaves are at work. If we are to see such life in its pleasantest aspects, we may well go back to Virginia in the old days before the Civil War. There the slaves led a freer and easier life than they did farther south among the rice-fields of South Carolina or the cotton-fields of Georgia.

If we could visit one of these old Virginia plantations as it used to be, where wheat and tobacco were grown, we should see first a family mansion, often situated on a hilltop amid a grove of oaks. The mansion is a two-story house, perhaps made of wood, and painted white. With its vine-clad porch in front, and its wide hallway inside, it has a very comfortable look.

Not far away is a group of small log cabins. This cluster of simple dwellings, known as "the quarters," is the home of the slaves, who do the work in the house and fields.

On the large plantations of the far south, there were sometimes several slave settlements on one plantation, each being a little village, with the cabins set in rows on each side of a wide street. Each cabin housed two families; belonging to each was a small garden.

The log cabins contained large fireplaces, and it was not unusual for the master's children to gather about them when the weather was cold enough for fires, to hear the negroes tell quaint tales and sing weird songs. The old colored "mammies" were very fond of "Massa's chillun" and liked to pet them and tell them stories.

Sometimes the cooking for the master's family was done in the kitchen of the "big house," but more often in a cabin outside, from which a negro waitress carried the food to the dining-room. The slaves had regular allowances of food, most of which they preferred to cook in their own cabins. Their common food was corn bread and ham or bacon.

Some of the slaves were employed as servants in the master's house, but the greater part of them worked in the fields. They went out to work very early in the morning. It often happened that their breakfast and dinner were carried to them in the fields, and during the short rest which they had while eating their meals they would often sing together. The slaves had their holidays, one of them being at the time of hog-killing, which was an annual festival. In some parts of the south, in November or December, corn-husking bees were held, just as the white people held them on the frontier. When the corn was harvested, it was piled up in mounds fifty or sixty feet high.[3]

1934

Rolla M. Tryon, *The American Nation: Yesterday and Today*

Classes of Slaves

There were two classes of slaves: the house servants and the field hands. The house servants took care of the master's children, did the housework, and performed such work as carpentry and blacksmithing. They were generally devoted to their masters and were much liked by the master and his family. The field hands did the hard work in the cotton or rice fields. Their hours of work were long, from sunrise to sunset, like the hours of Northern factory hands of that time. Some Negroes served as "drivers" and waked the slaves in the morning or drove them to the fields when they were late. Once in the fields, the slaves were directed by white men called overseers, who told them what work to do and saw that they did it.

Plantation work was relieved now and then by amusements. There were dances, and trips once in a while to some neighboring town to see a circus. Possum and coon hunts were common. The Negroes had a natural genius for music, and at their camp meetings and church services sang the beautiful "spirituals," which everyone still enjoys. They played the banjo and the fiddle. Christmas lasted at least a week and was a great holiday.

Discipline on a plantation was usually strict, but punishments depended on the master and overseers. Some were cruel, and their slaves were severely whipped for laziness or disobedience; some were very kind, and their slaves had gentle treatment. Some owners even burned marks on their slaves when the latter committed some crime. On the other hand, some white people lived all their lives on plantations without seeing a slave so much as whipped. Some slave owners were almost as fond of their slaves as of their families.

Slaves were bought and sold at auction like any other property. As the demand increased, the price grew higher. In 1800 a strong young man who could work in the cotton fields was worth $200; in 1860 a similar slave would sell at about $1300. The best Southerners did not like to sell their slaves, and especially did not like to break up a family by selling father, mother, and children to different owners. This was sometimes done, however.

Southern Opinion of Slavery

Before the invention of the cotton gin many Southerners wished to end slavery. Men like Washington gave freedom to their slaves. As late as 1820 many leading Southerners admitted the evils of the system, but by about 1830 they had changed their minds. They now said that slavery was the best labor system for Negroes, and that it must be right because some of the heroes of the Bible were slaveholders. Whipping was done only when necessary, they said, and slaves were better cared for in sickness and old age than the working classes in the industrial cities and towns of the North.

Moreover, the South felt that freeing the slaves would be a very dangerous thing. Who would feed, clothe, and take care of the slaves if they were freed? Where would they live? Who would work on the plantations?[4]

1977

JoAnne Buggey, *America! America!*

"It is a pity," a southern planter wrote his brother in 1802, "that . . . Slavery and Tyranny must go together and that there is no such thing as having an obedient and useful slave, without the painful exercise of undue and tyrannical authority."

The way a slave lived was not up to the slave. It was the slaveholder who determined how a slave would live. And sometimes even the slaveholder's power was limited. Bad times, for example, could force the master or mistress to sell slaves and break up families. No matter what, the slaves had little control over their future.

Two factors encouraged whites to act with brutality. One was the fear of slave rebellions. Although there were slaves who planned rebellions to free themselves and other slaves, very few uprisings were carried out. Always white southerners' fear of slave uprisings was much greater than the actual threat.

The other factor that led to brutality was the knowledge that the law was always on the side of whites. The following article is an example.

Tuscaloosa, Alabama, August 3, 1827—Mr. McNeily having lost some clothing, the slave of a neighboring planter was charged with theft. McNeily, with his brother, found the Negro driving his master's wagon and seized him. McNeily and his brother either did beat or were about to beat the Negro when the Negro resisted and stabbed McNeily, so that he died in an hour.

The Negro was taken before a justice of the Peace, who, after serious thought, gave up his authority—perhaps through fear of the crowd that had formed. The Justice acted as president of the mob when it was decided the Negro should be immediately executed by being burnt to death—the black man was led to a tree and tied to it and a large quantity of pine knots collected and placed around him; and the fatal torch was applied to the pile against the protest of several gentlemen. . . . This is the second Negro who has been thus put to death in that county.

Slave marriages had no legal status. Kind masters and mistresses might let the enslaved people dress for the occasion, and often the ceremony would be carefully arranged by the white family. But the fact was the marriage meant nothing legally. No matter how hard slave men and women tried to maintain family relationships, husbands, wives, and children were often separated through sales.

Slaves often expressed creative imagination in their music as well as in their religion. Songs used for worship often had a double meaning. Many appeared to talk of the road to heaven, but were also used as a signal to run away to the North.

Songs were also used to work by.

Massa in the great house counting out his money, Oh, shuck that corn and throw it in the barn; Mistis in the parlor eating bread and honey,

Oh, shuck that corn and throw it in the barn. Sheep shell corn by the rattle of his horn, Oh, shuck that corn and throw it in the barn; Sent it to the mill by the whippoorwill, Oh, shuck that corn and throw it in the barn.

For the slaves, music became an important means of communicating with the world and challenged their imagination. Out of this challenge came the basis for much modern rock music and jazz, as well as much jive or hip talk. Often substituting the word *darling* or *love* for *Jesus* or *God* was the basis of changing a religious song into a love song. Try the reverse on some modern love songs you know and see.[5]

1990

Roger LaRaus, Harry P. Morris, and Robert Sobel, *Challenge of Freedom*

Most slaves hated slavery. They often felt anger and bitterness toward their masters, and almost all slaves longed for freedom. A leading American historian noted that even after more than 200 years of slavery, most slaves were eager for freedom. "Though the history of southern bondage," he wrote, "reveals that men can be enslaved under certain conditions, it also demonstrates that their love of freedom is hard to crush."

In general, slaves had good reasons for hating slavery and for dreaming of liberty. Slaves' time and skills belonged not to themselves but to their masters. But perhaps worst of all was the fact that slaves had little or no control over their own lives. Slave families could be broken up through the sale of family members. Moreover, slaves could not own property. The slave codes—the laws that governed slaves—stated that slaves could not own property because they were themselves property. And how could one form of property own another?

The slave codes that grew over the years in the antebellum South were most often cruel and unfair toward slaves. This was because such laws were based upon the idea that slaves were the chattel—the private property—of their owners. Thus, slaves had no more legal rights than did livestock or other personal belongings. Because of this, slaves had no way to protect themselves through the law. Moreover, slaves were not allowed to travel without passes from their masters. Slave codes also prohibited slaves from learning to read and to write. And there were many other laws that greatly limited the rights of slaves. Thus, slave codes worked to restrict slaves in every way possible.[6]

DISCUSSION QUESTIONS

1. In the 1888 textbook the author mentions both slaves and indentured (here called "indented") servants. Investigate the differences between these two groups and explain why indentured servitude disappeared and slavery continued. This textbook also discusses the fact that at one time people in the North owned slaves as well. Find out when this practice came to an end and why.

2. Explain why you think textbooks written before the Civil War rarely mentioned African slavery.

3. Many of the textbooks in this section seem to go out of their way to explain that while there were some "bad" slave owners, there were also some "good" slave owners. Explain why you think textbooks often made that distinction.

4. The 1934 textbook describes two types of field hands: house servants

and field servants. Research and explain what the differences were between these groups. Was the author of this textbook correct when he said that house servants were "generally devoted to their masters" and were much like family?

5. The 1934 textbook makes a few claims about southerners using the Bible to prove that slavery was a legitimate system and that slaves in the South were actually treated better than industrial workers in the North. Research both of these claims and see if they are accurate.

6. The 1977 textbook discusses the penalty that one slave received as punishment for a supposed crime. Investigate other laws that white plantation owners had for slaves in the South.

It has been estimated that in 1860 there were approximately four million African slaves living in the United States.

23

African American Soldiers

Although rarely mentioned in textbooks prior to the 1980s, the story of African American soldiers during the Civil War is crucial to understanding that conflict, in which more than two hundred thousand black men fought on the Union side.

1890

Mara L. Pratt, *American History Stories, Vol. 1*

You have not forgotten how short a time ago it was that the anti-slavery men in Boston had been mobbed; you have not forgotten how bitter many Northerners felt towards black men and women, and towards anti-slavery men and women; you have not forgotten the Run-away Slave Law, which allowed a slave owner to pursue his slaves into the Northern States and take them wherever they were found.

All these feelings had been changing little by little during these two years of war. Nowhere was there quite such bitter feeling, and in Boston it seemed to have died away entirely.

Early in this year, after the Proclamation had been sent forth, there began to be much talk of raising a negro army. "Why not let these slaves fight for their own freedom?" the people began to say.

"Niggers can't fight! Niggers don't know enough to fight!" cried some, who did not quite believe in them yet.

"Whoever saw a nigger soldier?" cried another.

"Fancy a nigger trying to Forward, march! Right wheel! Left wheel! Right about Face!" laughed some of the soldiers.

But for all this the "nigger" regiments were formed; and they proved as well-behaved and as brave as those who laughed at them, I have no doubt.

The first regiment of colored men was the Fifty-fourth, Massachusetts, Robert G. Shaw its colonel.

This regiment was to have been sent to the capital by way of New York; but it was found that the feeling against negroes was still strong in that city, so strong that there began to be signs of mobs ready to attack this regiment if it passed through that city.

These troops, therefore, were sent by way of water from Boston.

To show you how rapidly the feeling against these black people died out, I must tell you that in only a few months from this time, all New York turned out to cheer a colored regiment that marched down Broadway on its way to the war. Yes, indeed, they were cheered as long, and with as much noise and hearty good-will as had Ellsworth's troops been cheered two years before, when they marched down this same street.[1]

2003

James West Davidson and Michael B. Stoff, *The American Nation*

African American Contributions

When the war began, thousands of free blacks volunteered to fight for the union. At first, federal law forbade African Americans to serve as soldiers. When Congress repealed that law in 1862, however, both free African Americans and escaped slaves enlisted in the Union army.

In the Union Army

The army assigned African American volunteers to all-black units, commanded by white officers. At first, the black troops served only as laborers. They performed noncombat duties such as building roads and guarding supplies. Black troops received only half the pay of white soldiers.

African American soldiers protested against this policy of discrimination that denied them the same treatment as other soldiers. Gradually, conditions changed. By 1863, African American troops were fighting in major battles against the Confederates. In 1864, the United States War Department announced that all soldiers would receive equal pay. By the end of the war, about 200,000 African Americans had fought for the Union. Nearly 40,000 lost their lives.

Acts of Bravery

One of the most famous African American units in the Union army was the 54th Massachusetts Regiment. The 54th accepted African Americans from all across the North. Frederick Douglass helped recruit troops for the regiment, and two of his sons served in it.

On July 18th, 1863, the 54th Massachusetts Regiment led an attack on Fort Wagner near Charleston, South Carolina. Under heavy fire, troops fought their way into the fort before being forced to withdraw. In the desperate fighting, almost half the regiment was killed.

The courage of the 54th Massachusetts and other regiments helped to win respect for African American soldiers. Sergeant William Carney of the 54th Massachusetts was the first of 16 African American soldiers to win the Medal of Honor. Such soldiers had "proved themselves among the bravest of the brave," Secretary of War Edwin Stanton told Lincoln.[2]

DISCUSSION QUESTIONS

1. What is your reaction after reading this section? Are you surprised that textbooks once used words that are now considered offensive? Why do you think it was all right to use this language in the 1890s but it is not acceptable today?

2. Research the role of African Americans during the Civil War. Explain what role this group actually played during the war.

24

African Americans During Reconstruction

Following the Civil War, the question of how the South would be "reconstructed"—in terms of its racial, social, political, and economic ways of life—was hotly debated. How the victorious North went about this process has been a very difficult historical topic to approach ever since.

1869

G.P. Quackenbos, *Elementary History of the United States*

During 1866 and 1867, there were much excitement and bitter feeling on the question of Reconstruction, that is, of restoring the seceded states to their former position in the Union. The President and Congress differed widely in opinion, the latter insisting, among other things, on further guarantees of the rights of the freedmen. It was only after a long struggle that most of the seceded states were, in July, 1868, restored to their former relations in the Union.[1]

1875

John J. Anderson, *A Grammar School History of the United States*

In March, 1865, Congress passed an act known as the Freedmen's Bureau Bill. By the term freedmen were meant all the colored people of the South, who, at the breaking out of the late war, were slaves; but who had afterward been declared free by proclamation of the president. The bill had for its object the supervision and relief of freedmen and loyal refugees. A second bill, amending and continuing in force the first, although vetoed by the president, was passed in July, 1866.[2]

1923

Henry Eldridge Courne and Elbert Jay Benton, *Story of America and Great Americans*

President Lincoln long before the Civil War ended thought of ways by which the North and the South could forget the hatreds of that terrible struggle and unite in common tasks for the welfare of the Republic. After he was dead the Northern leaders declared that the Southerners were plotting to enslave the negroes again. Many Northern politicians went to the Southern states and persuaded the negroes, to whom votes had been given, to choose them for the offices and keep the Southern leaders out of power. Such men were called "carpet-baggers," because they carried a carpetbag, the suit-case of that time, and did not mean to live permanently in the South.

The Southerners would have ended this "carpet-bag" rule if the Government under President Grant had not kept soldiers in the South to support the "carpet-baggers." As soon as he became President General Hayes declared that the Southerners must be allowed to govern themselves. He withdrew the soldiers and "Carpet-bag" government came to an end. By this means the Southern states were restored to an equal place in the Republic and Lincoln's dream of a reunited country could be made true.[3]

1930

William Backus Guitteau, *Our United States: A History for Upper Grammar Grades and Junior High School*

The Carpet-Bag Governments and Negro Rule

The close of the Civil War found the South almost ruined. The opposing armies had destroyed an immense amount of property, while the planters suffered enormous losses from the freeing of their slaves. The southern people had invested millions of dollars in Confederate bonds, and their soldiers were paid in paper money, all of which was now worthless. But a still greater hardship was in store for the impoverished and defeated South. The new "carpet-bag" governments, supported by federal troops, began a rule of plunder and corruption which made the reconstruction period more unbearable than the war itself.

The experience of South Carolina was typical of what was going on all over the South. The legislature of that state during the years 1868–1872 consisted of one hundred and fifty-five members, two thirds of whom were negroes. Only twenty-two of the members could read and write; thirty members together paid $83 in taxes, while ninety-one members paid no taxes whatever. These patriots openly announced that they intended "to squeeze the state as dry as a sucked orange"; and one of the colored members gave it as his opinion that "South Carolina ought not to be a state unless she can support her statesmen." The statesmen promptly voted themselves large salaries, let contracts at enormous profits, and divided the proceeds with corrupt contractors. Millions of dollars were wasted and millions were stolen, while the taxpayers had to pay the bills. In a single year, the legislature spent $200,000 in equipping the capitol building with costly armchairs, lounges, and other furniture, including a free bar for the use of the members. When the term of this infamous body came to a close, South Carolina's debt had been increased by twenty-five million dollars.

Conditions were almost as bad in the other southern states, several of which became bankrupt as the rule of plunder continued. In some cases it was impossible to discover the amount of the state debt, because no record was kept of the bond issues. It was estimated in 1872 that the carpet-bag governments in the eleven reconstructed states had increased the state debts by at least $131,000,000.

The Ku Klux Klan

Denied the ballot, southern white men had no legal means of checking this corruption; so they organized a secret society known as the Ku Klux Klan, or Invisible Empire. The object of this society was to secure white rule at the South; to accomplish this, it was determined to intimidate the negroes, and drive out the carpet-baggers and scalawags. Members of the Klan rode about at night, both horses and riders covered with white sheets, each horse with muffled hoofs so that it walked noiselessly over the ground. To the superstitious negroes, these midnight visitors seemed to be the ghosts of the dead Confederates, returning to rebuke their former slaves. Drawing up before the hut of some negro politician, the horseman, who carried a tank concealed beneath his long white robes, would demand a drink of water, then drink three or four bucketful with the remark: "That's good; the first I've had since Shiloh." Another would ask some frightened negro to hold his horse, then, taking off what appeared to be his head, would ask him to hold that also. The carpet-baggers and scalawags could not be frightened so easily as the superstitious blacks; but grotesque notices were posted at night on trees or fences, warning them to leave the country. If they failed to heed the warning, the terrible Ku Klux riders would pay them a midnight visit, and perhaps flog them to death.

All over the South the negroes were becoming terrorized, while the carpet-baggers appealed to the federal government for protection. Congress replied by passing the severe "Force Acts" of 1871, which finally broke up the Ku Klux organization. But it was evident that the southern whites would no longer tolerate the rule of the corrupt and ignorant men who were plundering their section; and at last Congress passed a law which permitted southern white men to vote, even though they had supported the Confederacy. The natural leaders of the South then regained control of the government, and the dark days of reconstruction came to an end. The South frankly accepted her defeat in the war, but she has never forgotten the evil days of her carpet-bag governments. Not Appomattox, but the humiliation suffered during her reconstruction, created a bitterness toward the North which only the lapse of half a century could efface.[4]

1934

Rolla M. Tryon, *The American Nation: Yesterday and Today*

Remaking Social Life

Besides having to make their living in a new way, the Southern people had to learn new ways of thinking. Before the war there had been three great classes: the white slaveholders, who were at the top of social life; the white people that had no slaves, who were called "poor whites" and who did not mix socially with the slaveholders; and the slaves themselves. Now there were no slaves: all were free together, and all were very poor together. This meant that the South had to make a new kind of society based on an equal chance to make a living. Now the old ideas lasted a long time. People thought as they always had, but they had to live in a different way. This caused confusion and made it harder for the South to create its new life. The hardest part of all was that so many people in the North did not understand the problem and blamed the South for making slow progress. They thought the South was trying to make trouble, when it was really trying to get out of trouble.

The Freedmen

Besides facing the question of earning a living, the South was faced with the question of the Negroes. The Negroes were made free by the Thirteenth Amendment to the Constitution, December 18, 1865. This amendment made every slave free in every part of the Union. Some of the Negroes were very happy at this and wandered forth from their old homes to see what freedom was like, but others did not want to leave their masters and stayed with them just as they always had.

Very few Negroes indeed had any idea of what to do. Under slavery they had had no responsibility for doing anything except what they were ordered to do, but after the war they were suddenly forced to look out for themselves. Of course they made mistakes. Some of them refused to work and got their living by stealing. A false rumor went round that the government was going to give every Negro forty acres of land and a mule. Many Negroes waited about until these gifts should be made. The Southern whites were greatly annoyed by so many thefts and so much loafing when workmen were needed. For these reasons some states passed laws compelling the Negroes to work under a plan like the indentured-servant system of colonial times. The states also fined the Negroes or put them into jail if they became tramps, in order to make them settle down somewhere and work. These laws were called Black Codes, and to people in the North who knew nothing of Southern conditions they seemed very oppressive.

Negro Rule

The Northern politicians and the Negro voters made plans to rebuild the railroads, improve the schools, and start industry once more. But neither the Negroes, nor the ignorant, untrained politicians knew how to do these excellent things. Worse than that, many of the politicians and Negroes were dishonest. They put themselves into offices and voted themselves big salaries. Once a member of the House of Representatives in South Carolina sold his vote for $15,000. Judges could be bribed to make decisions in court. In this same state, where conditions were worst, the members of the legislature (four fifths of them were Negroes) voted themselves a restaurant at state expense. There the members ate and drank at their leisure; and when they left to go home they stuffed their pockets with free cigars, and even had food, clothing, and furniture sent to their homes at the state's expense. As a result the debts of the Southern states and their taxes mounted higher and higher. During this period the white men were not allowed to vote unless they had fulfilled many difficult conditions. Even if they voted, the carpetbaggers who reported the elections said that they were outvoted by the Negroes. In this way the Southern white people were kept from having a voice in the government of their own states.

Taking the Negro's Vote Away

Not all these evils were due to dishonest men; some were due to ignorance. Some of the Northerners who went into the South were honest men who really wished to do the South a good turn, but who were so ignorant about life in the South that they had no idea how little they knew. But whether they were dishonest or ignorant, the evils resulted just the same.

Southern white men became angry and then desperate. For a time they refused to have anything to do with government. But this exactly suited the carpetbaggers, and things became worse than ever. So the Southern white men became Democrats, because the Northern politicians steered the new Negro voters into the Republican party. They began to prevent the Negroes from voting by standing near the voting places and threatening them with injuries. Finally the whites formed a secret society called the Ku-Klux Klan, and went about at night dressed in long white robes and told the Negroes they must stop voting or get hurt. The Northern politicians were forced to go back home. It took years to bring this about, but by 1880 the process was complete. Never since that time have the Southern Negroes had any considerable political power.[5]

1955

Glenn W. Moon and John H. MacGowan, *Story of Our Land and People*

Since many southern white leaders had lost the right to vote, a new group of men ran southern state governments. Some were "poor whites" and Negroes. Southerners called white men who rose to power during Reconstruction scalawags and carpetbaggers. Scalawags were southerners who had taken no part in the war or who tried to win northern favor. Carpetbaggers were northerners who went south after the war. The name came from the fact that they packed their belongings in cheap luggage called "carpetbags." Some were teachers or ministers who came to help the Negroes, but many were adventurers looking for money and power.

Most southerners hated the carpetbaggers and scalawags. They blamed them for raising taxes and running the states into debt. There were plenty of scandals. A story was told about one scalawag who had never had more than a few dollars before the war. During Reconstruction he got a state job that paid $8000 a year. In three years he deposited $100,000 in savings banks. When asked how he could save so much, he replied, "I did it, sir, by the practice of the most rigid economy."

The Reconstruction Period had a dark and a bright side. Southern white men who could not vote grew angry at the way the new state governments were run. They had no lawful way to interfere so they took an unlawful way. They formed the Ku Klux Klan. This was a secret society of young men. Under cover of night they rode about the country in white sheets that made them look like ghosts. They tried to frighten Negroes and keep them from voting. Later, they began whipping and even killing Negroes and scalawags.

Decent southerners got out of the Klan when they saw it was going too far. Congress passed a law in 1871 to break up the Klan. But the idea lingered on. The Ku Klux Klan still exists in some sections of the United States, but has no connection with the Klan of earlier days.

There was a brighter side to Reconstruction. In the North people raised money to build schools and train teachers for Negroes. Many southerners also helped to educate former slaves. Slowly and painfully Negroes adjusted to new conditions. Some were lucky enough to get a little land of their own; certain southerners gave small tracts of land to former slaves. However, most Negroes had to work as farm laborers. An increasing number moved to towns where they worked at jobs no one else wanted.

Every year the number of Negro college graduates increased. Others learned a trade. A few were able to save enough money to start small businesses. Progress was slow; even today the average Negro does not have as much money or education as the average white person. But remember that less than a hundred years ago most Negroes were completely ignorant and without money. They were turned loose to earn a living without much help from anyone. Negroes have made great progress during and since Reconstruction.[6]

1966

Harold H. Eibling, Fred M. King, and James Harlow, *History of Our United States*

New State Governments

Some of the new state governments set up under the Reconstruction Act were inefficient. Two groups of men took advantage of the fact that the South's former leaders could not vote or hold office. Hundreds of men hurried down from the North, many of them intending to enrich themselves in Southern politics. People called them carpetbaggers because many of them carried their possessions in traveling bags made of carpet cloth.

The carpetbaggers were aided by many of those Southerners who qualified for public office by swearing that they had not borne arms against the United States. For the most part these men, called scalawags, were dishonest politicians also out to enrich themselves.

Besides the carpetbaggers and scalawags, the new legislatures had many Negroes. Some of these were educated freemen; some were ex-slaves who had never had an opportunity to learn to read or to write or to study government. Some of the carpetbaggers and scalawags influenced their fellow legislators to spend state money unwisely, and in some cases fraudulently, piling up huge state debts. Some of the new state governments passed good laws. The legislators voted to build hospitals, roads, and railroads and to found orphan asylums. They voted for schools. By 1878 the constitutions of nearly all Southern states required tax-supported free public schools for all children.

Getting Back to Home Rule

Southerners soon looked for a way to rid themselves of corrupt politicians and of Republican control. It seemed to them that the first step was to keep the Negroes from voting. White men, who wished to regain control in their states, thought they could do so by restoring the Democratic party to power. To promote these ends, secret societies were formed, such as the Ku Klux Klan and Knights of the White Camelia. The Klan was the most powerful. Dressed in sheets and hoods, Klansmen appeared at Negroes' homes by night and warned the occupants not to vote.

As the Klan grew in numbers, it grew bolder. Threats against Negroes turned into violence. Members of the Klan, and other secret societies, did terrible things to their opponents, especially to the Negroes. Northerners demanded that Congress step in and protect the Negroes' right to vote. The Fifteenth Amendment was added to the Constitution. It stated that no citizen shall be denied the right to vote "on account of race, color, or previous condition of servitude." Laws were passed that placed Southern elections under national control. President Grant, who followed Johnson, used military force to prevent violence by the Klan.[7]

1977

Lewis Paul Todd and Merle Curti, *Rise of the American Nation*

Negroes were elected to the southern "carpetbag" governments, and they played an important role in some of them. In recent years, however, some historians have pointed out that the Negro's role in these governments has often been exaggerated. Only one black American served briefly as a southern governor. In only one southern state—South Carolina—did black members for a time hold a majority in the state legislature. Only Mississippi sent black Senators, two of them, to Washington. One was Hiram Revels, a native of North Carolina who, after studying at Knox College in Illinois, had been a teacher and minister. The other was Blanche K. Bruce, who had escaped from slavery in Virginia and who had also been a teacher.

The record of black citizens in reconstruction politics also has often been misrepresented, according to recent historians. Many Negroes, to be sure, who had been denied an education and experience in public life through no fault of their own, were victimized by clever carpetbaggers and scalawags, whose leadership they followed. Others showed independence and political skill, among them Robert Brown Elliott of South Carolina, a brilliant lawyer and scholar, and P.B.S. Pinchback of Louisiana, son of a Mississippi planter and a black mother.

The Negroes in public life during reconstruction did not demand revenge upon white southerners. In fact, most black leaders favored returning the right to vote to their former white masters. The records of those elected to the United States Congress compared well with the records of many of their white colleagues.[8]

1991

Carlton L. Jackson and Vito Perrone, *Two Centuries of Progress*

Republican Rule

The Reconstruction Act of 1867 put the South under military control. With the power of Union troops backing them, Republicans took over the new state governments in the South. The leadership for these new Republican governments came from three groups. First, there were the scalawags. Scalawags were Southerners who cooperated with the Reconstruction governments. Then there were the carpetbaggers. Carpetbaggers were Northerners who went to the South after the Civil War in search of new opportunities. Some carpetbaggers wanted only money and power for themselves. Others went south because they honestly wanted to be helpful. Finally, there were the blacks. The votes of blacks helped Republicans gain power. Blacks played an important role in all levels of government during Reconstruction.

The Republican governments during Reconstruction had a mixed record. On the one hand there was corruption, waste, and poor leadership. On the other hand much progress was made in some important ways. War-damaged areas were re-built. Work in education had been begun by the Freedmen's Bureau, which had started thousands of schools in the South. This work was continued by most of the new state governments. They set up free public schools. Other public services were improved. Welfare programs were begun to care for the poor and the insane. Prisons and hospitals were improved. Women were given more rights. Progress was also made in reforming the judicial system.

But even though progress was made under Republican rule, the ex-Confederates in the South did not like the new state governments. Ex-Confederates viewed scalawags as traitors. Carpetbaggers were outsiders. But perhaps worst of all for most ex-Confederates was the fact that blacks could vote and take part in government.

The Role of Blacks

There was a time when the period of Republican rule in the South was called "Black Reconstruction." This term, however, is not correct. It suggests that blacks controlled the Reconstruction governments. This is not true. Blacks in office depended on white support. Only in South Carolina did blacks have a legislative majority—and then only in the lower house.

Some of the blacks that held office were poorly educated. At times they were easily used by others. Other black leaders, however, were well educated. They held high office on both the state and national levels. They served well and had successful careers. The names of many of these leaders—Hiram R. Revels, Blanche K. Bruce, John R. Lynch, Joseph H. Rainey, and others—are among those of outstanding blacks in the history of the United States.

The Problem of Corruption

Under Republican rule, state governments in the South let their debts grow rapidly. For example, Louisiana's debt rose from about $17,350,000 to more than $29,000,000 in four years. In five years Alabama's debt grew from $8,355,000 to $25,000,000. Debts in other states also grew very quickly.

State debts grew partly because it cost money to rebuild war-torn areas and to set up new public services. But state debts also grew because of corruption in government—getting money in ways that are not honest. For example, Arkansas paid a workman $9,000 to repair a bridge which had cost $500 to build. Governor H.C. Warmoth of Louisiana was paid a salary of $8,000 a year. But he left office after four years with $800,000 in his pocket.

There are many other examples of such corruption. But it should be noted that there had been corruption before blacks, scalawags, and carpetbaggers took office. There was corruption after these people left office. Moreover, corruption in the South was part of a national wave of corruption which was sweeping the nation.[9]

DISCUSSION QUESTIONS

1. The 1869 and 1875 textbooks both discuss Reconstruction very briefly. Look at the final pages of your history textbook and see what historical events the final few pages discuss. How well do you think your current textbook does at "historically" telling these recent stories? Explain.

2. Many of the textbooks in this section argue that the carpetbaggers and African American politicians were very corrupt and were ruining the South's state governments. Investigate this claim and explain whether or not it is true. Looking at the textbooks in this section, explain how the stories of African American politicians change over time.

3. How is the Ku Klux Klan portrayed over the years in these textbooks? Has its image improved or gotten worse over time? Explain why you think that is.

4. Define what a stereotype is. Then read through the textbooks in this section and see if you can find passages that might be perceived as stereotyping African Americans.

5. The 1966 textbook mentions other white supremacist groups in the South after the Civil War. Investigate what other groups existed and explain what happened to them.

After the Civil War, South Carolina was the only former Confederate state in which African Americans held a majority of seats in the state legislature.

PART VI

---

*The Old West and
Industrialization*

25

Andrew Carnegie and the Homestead Strike

One of the most serious labor disputes in American history pitted industrialists Andrew Carnegie and Henry Clay Frick against the striking workers at Carnegie's Homestead, Pennsylvania, steel plant. Armed conflict broke out between the two camps. In the end the union was crushed, and it took years before labor unions were reestablished in some parts of the United States.

1955

Glenn W. Moon and John H. MacGowan, *Story of Our Land and People*

Early machines and railroads were built of iron, which was heavy and broke easily. Steel was too expensive to use until a new method of making it was discovered. This was the Bessemer process. In this process, a blast of air was blown through melted iron to remove impurities. The oxygen in the air absorbs the impurities. An Englishman, Henry Bessemer, discovered the method in 1855. At about the same time an American named William Kelly also discovered it. A young railroad official named Andrew Carnegie saw its possibilities.

As a child, Carnegie had come to America from a Scotch village. His family was so poor he had to go to work when he was thirteen. Step by step, he rose to become a high official of the Pennsylvania Railroad when he was only twenty-five. Then he suddenly gave up his job and went into another business.

The Civil War had just ended. Carnegie saw that new industrial developments were starting. He realized the nation would need much iron and steel. He had already saved his money and invested it so carefully that he had several thousand dollars. This was his capital—money saved out of income to use in producing new goods.

With his capital, Carnegie built a steel mill near Pittsburgh, Pennsylvania. He was the first to try the Bessemer process in America. Thanks to Carnegie's leadership, the United States forged ahead in steel production. Steel became and has remained a great source of America's strength. And Carnegie gave away most of the money he made. His great fortune was used to found libraries and colleges.[1]

1961

Edna McGuire and Thomas B. Portwood, *Our Free Nation*

Later years brought other violent contests. In 1892 the iron and steel workers in the Carnegie plant at Homestead, Pennsylvania, went out on strike. A fierce battle was fought, in which ten men were killed and many were wounded. In the end the workers lost the contest.

Violent contests between business and labor led to bitter feeling on both sides. Leaders of industry were not inclined to make rapid changes in their methods of dealing with labor. On the other hand, workmen, having learned that it might be possible to secure better conditions of living through united effort, were determined to press their advantage.

The laborers held it to be their right, as citizens in a democratic nation, to share in the profits of industry which they had helped to create. They wanted to receive their share through higher wages and better working conditions. In spite of a difference of opinion between capital (owners of business) and labor, some progress was made in securing better relations between them. Much remained to be done, however, in the twentieth century.[2]

1977

JoAnne Buggey, America! America!

Between 1880 and 1890 there were over one thousand strikes each year. Many of them involved bloodshed and the destruction of property.

In 1892, the Carnegie Steel Corporation locked out its workers to break the union at its Homestead Plant, outside of Pittsburgh. Battles soon broke out between the workers and the guards hired by the company.

In 1894 workers struck the Pullman factory in Chicago. The American Railway Union, led by Eugene V. Debs, refused to run trains that had Pullman cars on them. In the violence that followed, President Cleveland sent in troops to bring back order.[3]

1990

Roger LaRaus, Harry P. Morris, and Robert Sobel, Challenge of Freedom

Another incident that hurt the labor movement took place in 1892 at the Homestead plant of the Carnegie Steel Company. The steelworkers' union had called a strike. But the manager of the Homestead plant, Henry Clay Frick, wanted to break the union. He brought in strikebreakers and hired Pinkerton detectives to protect them. In one clash seven detectives were killed by the strikers. But Frick would not back down. Alexander Berkman, a radical, tried to kill Frick. But Frick survived the attack. Public sympathy was with Frick and the Carnegie Steel Company. Both the strike and the steelworkers' union were soon broken.[4]

DISCUSSION QUESTIONS

1. Why do you think that most textbooks liked to focus on Carnegie's rags-to-riches story rather than the events of the Homestead strike?
2. Investigate and see if you can find other examples of labor strikes in the history of the United States. Was the violence during the Homestead Strike a common or uncommon experience? Explain.
3. The textbooks that do mention the Homestead Strike also usually

mention how violent it was. By doing your own research, explain why this event became so violent.

In his autobiography Andrew Carnegie noted, "Nothing I have ever had to meet in all my life, before or since, wounded me so deeply. No pangs remain of any wound received in my business career save that of Homestead. It was so unnecessary."

26

Wounded Knee Massacre

In December 1890, the U.S. Army was ordered to South Dakota to help finish rounding up the last of the Lakota and move them to Nebraska. The final major battle between the U.S. Army and Native Americans saw twenty-five U.S. soldiers killed with thirty-nine wounded, and more than three hundred Lakota killed. It was an event seared into the memory of the Lakota, but one that was not included in U.S. history textbooks until the end of the twentieth century.

1986

Lewis Paul Todd and Merle Curti, *Triumph of the American Nation*

The End of the Fighting

It was on the northern plains, however, that the United States cavalry wrote the final bloody chapter in the long and tragic history of Indian-white warfare.

The events leading up to this final tragedy had their roots in 1889 with a religious revival that swept through the Indian tribes. The revival was celebrated in what the whites called the "Ghost Dance." It was based on the belief that an Indian Messiah was about to appear. With his arrival dead Indians would rise from their graves to join the living, the buffalo would again roam the plains, and the white intruders would vanish from the Indian lands like mist under the morning sun.

The Ghost Dance was not a call to war. It was, on the contrary, the celebration of a vision—the restoration of the old and treasured Indian way of life. As such, it awakened new hope in the hearts of a broken, despairing people. The Ghost Dance cult quickly gained followers, including many Sioux on the northern plains. White miners and settlers, alarmed at what they feared might be another outbreak of warfare, demanded that the army put an end to the activity.

At Wounded Knee in South Dakota in December 1890, a unit of the 7th Cavalry responded to this demand. The cavalry arrested a band of Sioux men, women, and children who were traveling to the Pine Ridge Reservation in search of food and protection. The troops surrounded the Indians and disarmed them. During the process a disturbance broke out, and someone fired a shot. Immediately, without warning, the troops opened fire with rifles and with Gatling guns, the earliest type of machine guns. They poured a deadly hail of lead into the band of unprotected Sioux, killing or mortally wounding 90 men and 200 women and children.

Many Americans expressed their horror at such brutality. Others rejoiced that at last General Custer had been "avenged." The brutal massacre at Wounded Knee brought an end to all organized armed resistance from Indians.[1]

2001

Wayne E. King and John L. Napp, *United States History*

A religious movement known as the Ghost Dance developed in 1890. Some American Indians believed that performing this dance would protect them from soldiers' bullets, bring back the buffalo herds, remove settlers from their lands, and bring back their former way of life.

The Ghost Dance frightened the settlers. An army was sent to prevent violence. The Seventh Cavalry arrived to arrest and disarm several hundred Ghost Dance followers from different tribes at Wounded Knee, South Dakota, on December 28, 1890.

The next day the cavalry tried to disarm the Ghost Dance followers. Someone fired a shot. It is not known who fired. The soldiers turned their guns on the followers and killed or wounded about 290 men, women, and children. Twenty-five soldiers were also killed. This massacre at Wounded Knee ended the fighting between the United States government and the American Indians of the western plains.[2]

DISCUSSION QUESTIONS

1. Why does the 1986 textbook refer to the history of Native Americans' dealings with white Americans as "long and tragic"?
2. On a map, show where the Dakota called home in the 1880s and 1890s.
3. The 1986 textbook makes a reference to General George A. Custer. Research General Custer's life and explain what the connection is between him and the massacre at Wounded Knee.

Twenty U.S. soldiers received Medals of Honor, the military's highest award, for their actions at Wounded Knee on December 29, 1890.

27

Immigration

Between 1870 and 1920 approximately twenty million new immigrants came to the United States, a process that forever altered our national identity and made Ellis Island an icon of our national folklore. No less than today, the arrival of so many newcomers stirred debates and tensions.

1885

Thomas Wentworth Higginson, *Young Folks' History of the United States*

The census of 1880 showed an enormous increase of population in the United States, and there was no State or Territory which did not share this increase in a greater or less degree. Between 1870 and 1880 the whole population increased from about thirty-eight and a half millions (38,558,371) to more than fifty millions (50,155,783), this being a gain of more than a million a year. This estimate includes all persons residing within the limits of the United States, except the Indians within the Indian Territory, or supported elsewhere by the general government, and the inhabitants of Alaska. These are omitted because they are not regarded as being legally "citizens" of the United States.

Great as this increase has been, it is probable that the rapid increase in results of the next census in 1890 will be yet more surprising. The facts as to immigration alone are enough to show that the population of the United States is now increasing faster than ever before. During the five years preceding 1880, the number of foreign immigrants into this country never reached half a million a year. In 1880 it rose to 593,703; and in 1881, to 720,045. These immigrants now come more largely from Germany than from anywhere else. In 1881 there were 249,572 from Germany, 95,188 from Canada, 91,810 from Scandinavia (Norway, Sweden, and Denmark), 76,547 from England, and 70,990 from Ireland. These immigrants now go most largely to the States west of the Mississippi; some to Kansas and Colorado, there to engage in mining or cattle-raising; some to Texas, where there is an immense extent of fertile country, under a mild climate; and some to the new States of the North-west, where the wheat crop is found to be very abundant in spite of cold weather. Railways are being rapidly extended in all these directions, and there are already several of these great lines across the continent, instead of one, as at first.[1]

1912

Henry William Elson, *A Guide to United States History for Young Readers*

The Pacific Coast and the Chinese

The great railroad strike had scarcely subsided when a commotion arose in San Francisco, the fame of which soon spread from one ocean to the other. On a vacant place known as the sand lots in the edge of the city a large crowd of men gathered night after night to listen to the impassioned oratory of a man who wore a workingman's garb, but who seemed born for the public rostrum. His name was Dennis Kearney. Born in Ireland, he had spent his early manhood on the sea as a common sailor, but for some years had been a laborer in San Francisco. His fiery speeches usually ended with the same passionate edict, "The Chinese must go."

This was one of the first serious anti-Chinese outbursts on the Western coast. But the feeling against the Orientals had been growing for some years, and it now broke forth and grew in intensity till it enlisted the attention of the whole nation. Kearney became so violent that he was arrested and sent to jail; but the agitation did not subside.

The Chinese had begun coming to the coast about 1851, at first only a few at a time, then more and more until the white population became alarmed. The cry against the Chinese first arose from the laboring classes. They complained that a Chinaman would work for wages on which an American would starve. He would work any number of hours, live on the cheapest food, and dwell in the meanest hovel or in a hole in the ground, and withal he would maintain a smiling countenance.

All this was exasperating to the American workingman, who found himself underbidden in every field of labor. Nor was there any end in sight to the coming of the Chinese. China with her four hundred millions of inhabitants could furnish an inexhaustible supply of cheap labor, especially since no Chinaman made any pretense of remaining in America. They would come and work a few years, hoarding their few hundred dollars of earnings, and then go back to their native country, whence thousands of others would come to repeat the process. So it might continue indefinitely and the American laborer would simply be crowded out by the Chinese coolies.

"Gold Hills" was the name by which America was known in China. And indeed, when viewed from the standpoint of the Chinese, it seemed like a land of gold, for their wages, low as they were in America, were said to be ten times as great as in their own country. The value of money was so much greater in China than in America that when a Chinaman went back with three or four hundred dollars he was looked upon by his countrymen as a rich man. The bait was therefore an alluring one. It was like the attraction of the Klondike a few years ago, when gold was discovered there.

The laboring men took the lead in opposing the coming of the Orientals, but they were not long alone, nor was the labor question the chief one. The Chinese are pagans and they refused to give up one jot of their superstition. With all their industry they are addicted to low and degrading vices.

When European immigrants come to our shores they come to stay; they expect to become American citizens, to grow up with the country. They intend America to be the future home of their children and grandchildren; they adopt our laws and customs and become a part of us. But not so with the Chinese. They do not wish to become citizens. They care nothing for our customs, our religion, or our institutions. You can make a good American out of a German, a Frenchman, an Englishman, or a Russian Jew; but a Chinaman is a Chinaman all the time, and can no more be an American than a leopard can change his spots.

Here then was a great question. Shall we permit this undesirable class to come in vast numbers until they drag down American life to their own level? Two race problems we have already had to solve: the Indian problem, which began with the landing of the Virginians and the Pilgrims; and the negro question, which brought about the dreadful tragedy of the Civil War. Should another race problem now be permitted when it was in our power to nip it in the bud?

Such was the reasoning of the American people, and especially of the Californians. But some reasoned that we had no right to bar the Chinese or any other people from the country; that the earth is the Lord's and no people have an exclusive right to occupy particular portions of it. Let the Chinese come, argued these; we can do them good by teaching them the true religion. While sending missionaries to the far-off heathen, let us not neglect the opportunity that comes to our doors.

But those who took this position were few in comparison with the class who demanded that the Chinese must go. Frequently the feeling against the Chinese resulted in mob violence. One uprising at Los Angeles caused the death of twenty-one Chinamen. In 1885 twenty-eight Chinamen were murdered by miners in Wyoming for refusing to join a strike.

Attempts were made to hamper and annoy the undesirable class by State or city laws. In Oregon a law forbade the employment of Chinese on State contract work; but the Federal Court threw the law overboard on the ground that it violated our treaty with China, and because "the right to reside in a country implies the right to earn a living."

San Francisco passed an ordinance requiring the hair of all prisoners to be cut short. This would have been a dreadful blow to the Chinese had it stood test of the courts, for they value their queue as life itself. One day while a Chinaman was asleep some practical jokers cut off his queue. When he awoke and saw what was done, he screamed and instantly committed suicide by dashing his head against a stone wall. This ordinance was very properly pronounced null and void by the courts, because cruel, and because it was class legislation.

It was not long until the Chinese question became a strong factor in National politics. Both great parties were ready to make a bid for the electoral votes of the coast States and in the campaign of 1880 both pronounced against Chinese immigration. The same year a new treaty was made with China, by which the United States was permitted to "regulate, limit, or suspend" the coming of Chinese laborers.

This opened the way and Congress soon took the matter up in earnest. The first anti-Chinese measure passed by Congress met with a veto by the President, but another, in May, 1882, received his signature and became a law. By this law Chinese laborers were forbidden to come to the United States, for a period of ten years. But the law was evaded in this way: A Chinaman already here could, on returning to his own country, take out a certificate that would readmit him to this country, if he chose to come back. Many of them would sell these certificates in China and others would use them in getting across our borders, because to the inspectors all Chinese looked alike. Many also were smuggled across the Canadian border. These abuses were corrected by an additional law passed in 1888, forbidding the return to the United States of all Chinese who went back to their own land.

Last came the Geary law of 1892, the most sweeping of its kind ever enacted by any country. This law was to continue for ten years, but was extended at the end of that time. It is so effective that Chinese laborers are almost wholly debarred from the United States, and thus we are relieved of a race problem that might have become a serious menace to our institutions.[2]

1930

William Backus Guitteau, *Our United States: A History for Upper Grammar Grades and Junior High School*

The Immigration Problem

Since the founding of our government, more than twenty-five million immigrants have come to the United States, and today it is estimated that there are thirteen million persons of foreign birth living here. In the single year of 1905, one million immigrants landed on our shores, or more than all the colonists who came to America from the first landing at Jamestown until the Declaration of Independence. Our traditional policy has always been to welcome the honest men and women of other lands who wish to come here; and our country's wonderful development would have been impossible without the brain and muscle of the millions of immigrants who have turned to America as the land of opportunity.

At times our hospitality has been abused; and European governments have been known to use the United States as a dumping ground for convicts, paupers, anarchists, and other undesirable citizens. Hence in 1882 Congress passed a law excluding from this country the pauper, criminal, and insane classes of aliens, also anarchists, persons suffering from contagious disease, and Chinese laborers. A treaty was made with Japan in 1907, by which Japanese laborers were also excluded.

Immigrants from Southern Europe

Beginning about 1880 there has been a marked change in the source of our immigration. Before that time the great majority of immigrants came from Great Britain, Germany, and the Scandinavian countries; while only a small proportion came from the peoples of southern and eastern Europe. But since 1880 the immigration from southeastern Europe has greatly increased, while that from northern Europe has relatively declined.

With this change in the source of our immigration, there has been a corresponding change in the character of the immigrants themselves. The immigrants from northern Europe were better educated, more familiar with representative government, and in many cases were skilled artisans and mechanics. In contrast with them, a large proportion of the immigrants from southeastern Europe are illiterate, or unable to read and write their own language; and nearly all are unskilled workers. The demand for the exclusion of illiterate immigrants led Congress on three occasions to pass bills debarring immigrants who could not read, but each time the measure was vetoed by the President. At last in 1916, it was possible to secure the necessary votes in Congress to pass this measure over the President's veto; so that immigrants who are unable to read their own language are now excluded from the United States.[3]

1955

Glenn W. Moon and John H. MacGowan, *Story of Our Land and People*

Immigrants settled in cities. Many, though by no means all, of the people who settled in the slums were newcomers to America. After 1865, factories and mines needed an ever increasing number of workers. From faraway lands came masses of eager immigrants or people who moved to America from foreign lands. They were attracted by stories of good jobs and high wages. Many of the "greenhorns," as the new immigrants were called, had a hard time learning American ways.

But most of them soon became hardworking citizens. They wanted more than anything else to belong, to become part of America, the land of their dreams. But it was not easy. They did not understand American methods and traditions. Some had a hard time learning English. And they often were cheated and exploited when they first arrived.

Immigrants who came to America before 1890 had an easier time than those who have come in more recent years. Earlier immigrants usually went to work on farms. Most of them saved enough to buy a farm, or they obtained some free land under the Homestead Act.

Before 1890 most immigrants came from the British Isles and western Europe. The potato famine of the 1840's caused thousands of Irish to come to the United States. And the failure of the Revolution of 1848 made many freedom-loving Germans flee their "Fatherland" for America. A little later, bad times and business failures in Scandinavia encouraged many Swedes and Norwegians to seek a new start in America. All these groups adjusted to American life without great difficulty.

"New" immigrants met new problems. The story was different for workers from southern and eastern Europe who came after 1890. These groups—the Italians, Poles, and various Slavic nationalities—made up what was called the "New Immigration." (Those who came from northern and western Europe before 1890 made up the "Old Immigration.")

When the "new" immigrants arrived, after 1890, almost all the good land had been claimed. Because of the new machines, farm workers were not needed. So Italians, Poles, and Slavic groups had to find jobs in factories or mines. Because most of the new immigrants had had little chance to attend school in their old homes, they found it hard to learn to read and write English.

Many citizens feared that the new "wave" of immigrants was a danger to American democracy. They said the newcomers lacked knowledge and experience to vote intelligently. American workers complained that foreigners took their jobs and pulled down the scale of wages because they would work for low pay. Labor leaders asked the government to reduce the number of immigrants coming into the country.

Congress began to restrict immigration. Ever since colonial days there had existed a certain amount of distrust of immigrants. Why, you may ask, should any American feel prejudice against immigrants? After all, the United States is a nation of immigrants. All Americans, even the Indians, are either immigrants or descendants of immigrants.

Nevertheless, many people born in America tended to be critical of newcomers. One reason was the fact that a number of criminals and half-witted people had been coming to America. This situation caused Congress in 1882 to pass a law that forbade idiots, beggars, and criminals to enter the United States. However, the total number of immigrants who came to America continued to increase each year until World War I.

In the early 1880's, the public became excited about the immigration of Chinese workers or "coolies." Contractors had brought in thousands of Chinese to work on western railroads. The Chinese accepted low wages and lived in a way that cost very little. For this reason, other workers feared and hated them. There were riots and killings. Public opinion forced Congress to pass a law in 1882 that forbade immigration of Chinese laborers.

Thus began a long series of laws to regulate immigration. In 1917 a new law required foreigners to pass a literacy test to prove they could read and write.[4]

1970

Kenneth Bailey, Elizabeth Brooke, and John J. Farrell, *The American Adventure*

As America's business world grew, the need for workers grew. New machines and electrical power made it possible to produce huge quantities of goods in very little time. Factories expanded into gigantic industries.

Hundreds of people were needed to produce enough goods to meet worldwide demands. The population of the United States was not growing fast enough to provide the labor force for so much production. Where would American businesses find new workers? In other countries, of course. Many poor Europeans were anxious to come to America to work and build a better future for themselves.

The United States had always been a nation made up of people who came from other lands. New arrivals to America wrote to their families and friends about their jobs and their good life. The letters encouraged relatives and families to leave their homes in Europe to travel to America.

Before 1880, almost all immigrants to America came from Britain, Germany, Ireland, and the Scandinavian countries. In the 1880's, Russians, Czechs, Serbs, Poles, Ukranians, and Italians came in great numbers. Some people called these years "the flood time" of immigration. These new citizens brought new foods, new music, new entertainments, and many other cultural gifts to America.

Most of the immigrants stayed to work in the big cities, such as New York, Providence, Boston, Cincinnati, Chicago, and Philadelphia. Unfortunately, most cities were not prepared to house and care for these millions of new Americans. Too few homes, overcrowded schools, and poor sanitation were major problems. Immigrant neighborhoods became centers of disease and poverty. The immigrants worked long hours in factories, in coal mines, and on farms to better their situations. Some became discouraged and returned to Europe. But most stayed and gradually found a place in American life.[5]

1985

Ernest R. May, *A Proud Nation*

Changing Character of Immigration

Most of the 3.5 million immigrants who came to America between 1820 and 1850 were from the British Isles or northern Europe. Most were Protestant. Then the Irish, fleeing from famine and harsh British laws at home, began to arrive in the 1840's. Most of these immigrants were Roman Catholic.

After 1850 many people came from Italy, Austria-Hungary, Greece, and the other Balkans, Poland, and Russia. These non-English-speaking peoples with varied cultural backgrounds added entirely new elements to American society.

Newcomers from Eastern Europe

People's reasons for leaving Europe after 1850 were as varied as their cultures. Poland at the time was divided between Russia, Prussia, and Austria-Hungary. Many Poles wished to escape foreign rule. Thousands of Jews fled persecution in Russia. Armenians wanted to escape Turkish persecution. Italians and Greeks left their countries because many could live there only in poverty.

The United States offered more political and economic freedom than many Europeans could hope to experience in their countries. In addition, unskilled immigrants could earn five times more in the United States than in some parts of Europe. Many immigrants planned to earn money and then to return home. While some achieved that goal, others stayed, and sent money so that their families could join them.

Immigrants sailed from many European ports. The passage to the United States took at least six weeks. During that time immigrants lived in crowded holds of ships not designed to carry passengers. They were jammed back near the rudder in an area that became known as steerage.

Although the majority of the new immigrants came from farms or small towns, hardly 20 percent farmed after reaching the United States. Most lacked the money to buy land, so many newcomers settled in cities. There, skilled workers set up their own shops. The unskilled found jobs as porters, peddlers, dock workers, or heavy construction laborers. Others worked in the textile, iron and steel, and meat-packing industries. Some went to coal-mining towns.

Newcomers from China

As never before, immigrants also came from Asia. Thousands of Chinese crossed the Pacific during the 1860's to work in gangs on the Central Pacific Railroad. After the transcontinental railroad was completed, most settled in California. Some missed railroad work and left California in the

1870's to work on the construction of the Alabama and Chattanooga Railroad in Mississippi.

The first Chinese immigrants were welcomed in California when they came in the 1850's. The governor, John McDougal, even suggested a land grant program to encourage more Chinese to come to California. The economy, however, changed when railroad construction was over and mines gave out. Jobs were harder to get and many Americans resented Chinese workers willing to accept low wages. As the economic depression settled across the country, the Chinese and other newcomers were blamed for it.

More and more Chinese suffered discrimination, even violence. The Workingmen's Party in California urged the government to pass laws discriminating against the Chinese. The Sidewalk Ordinance, for instance, prohibited people who used poles to carry merchandise from walking on the sidewalk. Since only the Chinese were used to carrying goods in this manner, the law was specifically against them.

Some Americans demanded that Chinese immigration be stopped. In 1882 Congress passed the Chinese Exclusion Act, which prohibited Chinese laborers from entering the country for ten years. When this act was renewed a second time in 1902, Congress deleted the terminal date.

Strangers in Another Land

Between 1860 and 1900, more than fourteen million Europeans left their homelands to come to the United States. Many felt caught between cultures, identifying with the words of the Norwegian Ole Rolway, "We have become strangers, strangers to the people we forsook, and strangers to the people we came to." Such an upheaval of persons brought significant changes to American cities and industries.

Americans of longer standing witnessed these changes and reacted, sometimes with fear, sometimes with anger. Newcomers and established citizens alike struggled to adjust to the changing times.

Most of the immigrants settled in cities and soon found a kind of comfort and support in ghettos within the city. A ghetto is a section of a city where many members of some minority or ethnic group live. Areas called "Little Italy," "Greektown," and "Chinatown" became communities within the larger city, where immigrants could maintain the cultures they cherished. Early in the 1900's, more Italians lived in New York City's "Little Italy" than in Rome.

In the city many immigrants struggled with unfamiliar language and customs. Most found work in factories, sweatshops, or mines. Many Germans, Irish, and Swedes worked in steel plants.[6]

DISCUSSION QUESTIONS

1. Research what life was like for a Chinese immigrant to America in the late 1800s and early 1900s. Then read the textbook from 1912 and explain whether this book's rhetoric about Chinese immigrants would have shocked students at that time or not.

2. The 1930 textbook refers to the "immigration problem." Why would a textbook written during this time call this large number of incoming new Americans a "problem"?

3. Looking at the textbooks in this section, explain whether or not the image of the immigrant in this country has changed over the past one hundred years. Cite examples from the textbooks to prove your point.

4. Look at the arguments some of these textbooks gave for why Americans did not want immigrants coming to this country. Discuss whether or not these same arguments are similar to the ones used today against the newest wave of immigrants?

5. Both the 1970 and 1985 textbooks claim that it was American businesses that helped bring so many new, poor immigrants to the United States. Investigate the economic reasons immigrants came to the United States and see if these textbooks are correct.

Throughout the 1800s and into the early 1900s, topics such as U.S. history, civics, and English were offered in American schools in order to help transform the children of new immigrants, helping them learn how to speak the language and what it means to be an American citizen.

28

McKinley Assassination

On September 5, 1901, citizens of the United States found themselves mourn-
ing, for the third time in their history, the assassination of one of their presidents.
On that day in Buffalo, New York, President William McKinley was attending
the World's Fair when an assassin, Leon Czolgosz, shot him in a reception line.
Upon McKinley's death the vice president, Theodore Roosevelt, took over and
became the twenty-sixth president of the United States.

I922

James A. Woodburn, *The Makers of America*

The story of Theodore Roosevelt's life will always be interesting to young and old. He was Vice-President when McKinley was shot. When he heard that the President was dying he was in the Adirondack Mountains, more than twenty miles from a railroad station. At midnight, in darkness and rain, he made a perilous ride by horse and wagon, down the steep mountainside. When he reached the station at daybreak he learned that McKinley was dead.[1]

1946

George Earl Freeland and James Truslow Adams, *America's Progress in Civilization*

In September, 1901, occurred the tragic death of President McKinley. He had been elected over William Jennings Bryan in 1896, and again in 1900. Six months after the inauguration, while attending the Pan-American Exposition at Buffalo, he was shot by an insane anarchist, who approached him with a pistol concealed in a handkerchief wrapped about his hand. For several days the life of the President hung in the balance, and on the fourteenth of September he died. Vice-President Theodore Roosevelt at once succeeded him as President of the United States.

Theodore Roosevelt was one of the most dynamic and popular leaders that the United States has known. A frail child, he had developed into a vigorous, driving type of man. Early in life he had chosen politics as a career. He had held the offices of United States Civil Service Commissioner, Police Commissioner of New York City, Assistant-Secretary of the Navy, Governor of New York, and Vice-President of the United States before succeeding to the Presidency. He had served with distinction in the Spanish-American War, and so colorful were his actions that they were recounted in detail in American newspapers to increase his popularity with the public.[2]

1961

Edna McGuire and Thomas B. Portwood, *Our Free Nation*

In 1901, while President McKinley was attending an exposition, or fair, at Buffalo, New York, he was shot. The man who shot the President was opposed to any form of government. Eight days later President McKinley died. On September 14, 1901, Theodore Roosevelt became President of the United States. The new President supported a program which pleased those people who believed that government should go forward in step with the needs of the times.[3]

2001

Wayne E. King and John L. Napp, *United States History*

Less than one year after being re-elected, McKinley was assassinated. Theodore Roosevelt, at age forty-two, became the youngest President of the United States when he took office in 1901. He became a very powerful President.[4]

DISCUSSION QUESTIONS

1. Using a current history textbook, compare the story of the McKinley assassination to the stories of other American presidents who have been killed while in office. Is the coverage always the same? Do some leaders receive more attention than others? Explain why you think this is.
2. The story of McKinley's assassination seems to have virtually disappeared in the past few decades. Explain why students today rarely hear anything about McKinley's death.

Vice President Theodore Roosevelt was mountain climbing in northern New York when a park ranger brought him the news that McKinley had been gravely wounded by an assassin.

29

The Philippine-American War

The Philippine-American War officially lasted from 1899 to 1902 (although some historians argue it lasted until 1917). A nearly forgotten conflict, it was a brutal guerilla war that foreshadowed many of America's overseas ventures in the century to come.

1905

Thomas B. Lawler, *A Primary History of the United States*

American Rule in the Philippines

The Philippines were discovered by Magellan in 1521. Under many brave leaders, like Legaspi and Salcedo, the flag of Spain was firmly planted there, and the great city of Manila was founded (1571) at the mouth of the Pasig river.

On the arrival of the Spaniards the population numbered about half a million barbaric people. They were for the most part Malays.

Under the direction of the Augustinians, the Jesuits, and other religious orders, the natives were converted to Christianity and were civilized. So successful was this work that the population at the beginning of the twentieth century numbered about eight millions, and the Filipinos were the only Christian people in the Orient.

After the victory of Dewey at Manila the Filipinos met in convention at Malolos and organized a republic. When the treaty with Spain ceded the Islands to the United States, the natives under Aguinaldo rose (February 4, 1899) in rebellion. A bitter warfare followed, until Aguinaldo was captured and his armed bands scattered.

A Civil Commission was now appointed to rule the Islands, schools were everywhere opened, a new coinage was introduced, and roads were improved. It is hoped that through these measures an era of peace, prosperity, and happiness now awaits the Filipino people.[1]

1916

Charles Morris, *Primary History of the United States: The Story of Our Country for Young Folks*

Fighting Near Manila

A few words more will tell all I need say about the war. Many of the people of the Philippines wanted to be free from the United States as well as from Spain, and a strong army of them began to fight for their freedom. There were fierce battles near Manila and many were killed and wounded on both sides, and for a time the United States had another war on its hands. Our country lost more soldiers in this war than in the war with Spain.

Peace in the Philippines

The war in the Philippines ended in 1901, after it had lasted more than two years. The people went back to their work, and the United States gave them so good a government that they were well satisfied. They were allowed to vote and elect their own people to many of the offices, and all was soon going on so well that they were glad to belong to the United States.[2]

1930

William Backus Guitteau, *Our United States: A History for Upper Grammar Grades and Junior High School*

Our Government of the Philippines

The inhabitants of the Philippines, like the Cubans, had taken up arms against Spanish tyranny. They wanted independence, and at first refused to recognize our authority over the islands. Under a native chief, Aguinaldo, the Filipinos waged a guerrilla warfare for nearly two years, but the capture of their leader ended the insurrection.

The vast Philippine archipelago is peopled by numerous tribes, many of which are but slightly civilized. Self-government was out of the question when Spain surrendered the islands, but the United States is educating the people so that they may become prepared to govern themselves. Meantime, executive authority is vested in a governor and other officers appointed by the President, while the Filipinos elect their own legislature. Our country has spent large sums for schools, libraries, sanitation, and public works on the islands, and much progress has been made. Independence has been promised to the Philippines as soon as their people show a capacity for self-government.[3]

1946

George Earl Freeland and James Truslow Adams, *America's Progress in Civilization*

The close of the Spanish-American War and the years immediately following saw a great expansion of American interests in the Caribbean Sea and in the Pacific Ocean. Cuba came under the protection of the United States, and remained so until her people had established a stable government of their own. The Philippine Islands were at once placed under American control, and have remained there since. They have recently been given a conditional independence to be worked out in a definite term of years. Hawaii had requested annexation by the United States and in 1898 this step was taken.[4]

1955

Glenn W. Moon and John H. MacGowan, *Story of Our Land and People*

War always brings far-reaching changes. While it may settle a few questions, it almost always raises new and more difficult ones. The Spanish-American War of 1898 was no exception. It involved the United States in problems no one had foreseen.

For one thing, Americans found they had to fight a long bloody war in the Philippines. Like most other people, the Filipinos wanted to govern themselves. They expected to become independent when Spain was defeated. But President McKinley and his advisers felt the Filipinos lacked education and experience; so the United States decided to keep control for a while.

The Filipinos had a capable, determined leader named Aguinaldo. He had been fighting Spaniards for years. Now he organized resistance against the United States.

The Filipinos knew they had no chance of winning a regular battle so they split up into small groups of guerillas. They hid in the mountains or the jungle and struck suddenly when least expected. The guerillas were savage fighters.

The warfare dragged on for two years; it was an ugly struggle, much like the Indian wars of colonial days. Aguinaldo was finally captured and his followers surrendered. But it took years to win the friendship and respect of the Filipinos.

Americans built schools and roads, fought disease and developed industries, but still the Filipinos were dissatisfied. They admitted a government of their own probably would not be so efficient as American rule; but they preferred an inefficient government of their own to foreign control.

American leaders promised the Filipinos they would become independent as soon as they proved able to govern themselves. Step by step, the Filipinos were allowed to take more power in running the islands.

At last in 1934, Congress passed a law providing for the Philippines to become independent in 12 years. That seemed a long delay to Filipino leaders. Then came World War II. The islands put up a strong resistance to the Japanese but they were quickly conquered. Most Filipinos remained loyal to the United States; they did their best to help defeat Japan. Thus they earned the right to be a partner in the struggle for a better world.

Soon after the War ended the American government officially withdrew. The Philippine Islands became independent on July 4, 1946—one hundred seventy years after the 13 American colonies declared their independence. Thus each year the United States and the Republic of the Philippines celebrate their birthday or Independence Day on July 4.

The Filipinos have not forgotten how easily Japan conquered their islands in World War II. They realize they would need help to fight off a future attack. On the other hand, the United States wanted to keep bases in the Philippines. So in 1947 the American and Filipino governments made a 99-year treaty. It provides that United States may have certain military and naval bases in the Islands and it assures the Philippines of American protection.[5]

1966

Harold H. Eibling, Fred M. King, and James Harlow, *History of Our United States*

The Treaty of Paris

By signing the Treaty of Paris, Spain agreed to give up Puerto Rico, Guam, and the Philippines to the United States and to grant independence to Cuba. The United States also agreed to pay Spain $20,000,000 for the Philippines. This suited everybody except the Filipinos. They resented American control as much as they had Spanish.

Independence for the Philippines

The American government was undecided as to what to do about the Philippines. Many Americans felt that the islands should be granted the independence for which they had been fighting so long. Others argued that a weak new country would be the natural prey of a strong nation, such as Germany, which was frantically searching for island bases in the Pacific.

President McKinley finally decided that it was the duty of our country to take over the Philippines, guide them, and prepare the people for independence. Business interests wanted this done because it would help to expand our trade in the Far East.

Meanwhile, the Filipinos had set up an independent government. They resisted our efforts to take control of their country until their leader was captured. We set up a government, with William H. Taft as governor. We promised that our government would interfere very little and that the Filipinos would be allowed wide freedom to run their own affairs.

The people of the Philippines did not believe this promise, but they wisely decided to wait and see what would happen. The United States upheld its promise to the letter. Modern schools and hospitals were established. Roads were built and streets paved. Communication and transportation were improved. Sewers were built and water-supply systems installed. In time, most of the bad feeling for the United States disappeared.

Filipino leaders kept demanding independence. As a result, the islanders were given more and more voice in their own government. A Filipino legislative assembly was set up. Public schools were opened in the principal cities and later in outlying districts. Normal schools were opened for the training of Filipino teachers. In 1934 the American government promised complete independence by 1946.

In what ways was the American plan for helping the Philippines a good one?[6] [*Original question from textbook*]

1991

Carlton L. Jackson and Vito Perrone, *Two Centuries of Progress*

The United States had gained more colonies as a result of the Spanish American War. The anti-imperialists wanted to give up all the lands won during the war. This became an important issue in the election of 1900. McKinley was reelected by a large majority. The people had spoken. They seemed to want an empire.[7]

DISCUSSION QUESTIONS

1. The 1905 textbook discusses the war while there was still fighting taking place in the Philippines. Why do you think this textbook barely

mentions the war, even though it was probably a popular topic at that time? How does your current textbook portray events that happened more recently?

2. None of the textbooks in this section discusses any battles or leaders during the Philippine-American War. Look at how your current history textbook covers the Vietnam War or World War II. Do textbooks do a better of portraying these other wars as compared to the Philippine-American War?

3. The 1916 textbook claims that the Filipinos at first were against the United States taking over but later were happy with U.S. rule. Research this war and explain whether both of these statements are correct or not.

4. Most of the textbooks in this section describe the positive things that the United States did for the Filipinos but rarely, if ever, discuss the actual fighting that took place between the two sides during the war. After investigating how this war was fought and what U.S. rule was like after the war, explain why you think these textbooks focus on these positive events.

5. Explain why the story of the Philippine-American War is basically ignored in U.S. history textbooks. In your opinion, should this war receive more attention, less attention, or does it get enough attention in history textbooks? Explain.

From 1565 to 1898 the Philippines had been a colony of Spain. After the Spanish-American War it then became an American colony until July 4, 1946.

NOTES

A NOTE ON U.S. HISTORY TEXTBOOKS

1. It should be noted that the first junior high school was founded in 1909 in Columbus, Ohio.

1. IMAGES OF NATIVE AMERICANS

1. Noah Webster, *History of the United States: To Which is Prefixed a Brief Historical Account of our [English] Ancestors, from the dispersal at Babel to their Migration to America and of the Conquest of South America by the Spaniards* (New Haven: Durrie & Peck, 1832), 69–72.
2. Benson J. Lossing, *A Primary History of the United States* (New York: Mason Brothers, 1860), 8–10.
3. Thomas Wentworth Higginson, *Young Folks' History of the United States* (Boston: Lee and Shepard, 1885), 20–24.
4. Oscar Gerson, *History Primer* (New York: Hinds, Heydon & Eldridge, 1906), 18–26.
5. Wilbur F. Gordy, *Stories of Early American History* (New York: Charles Scribner's Sons, 1913), 22–29.
6. William Backus Guitteau, *Our United States: A History for Upper Grammar Grades and Junior High School* (New York: Silver, Burdett, 1930), 45–46, 50–55.
7. George Earl Freeland and James Truslow Adams, *America's Progress in Civilization* (New York: Charles Scribner's Sons, 1946), 104–12.
8. JoAnne Buggey, *America! America!* (Glenview, IL: Scott Foresman, 1977), 42–43.
9. Clarence L. Ver Steeg and Carol Ann Skinner, *Exploring America's Heritage* (Lexington, MA: D.C. Heath, 1991), 65–69.

2. COLUMBUS'S FIRST VOYAGE

1. Noah Webster, *History of the United States: To Which is Prefixed a Brief Historical Account of our [English] Ancestors, from the dispersal at Babel, to their Migration to America, and of the Conquest of South America by the Spaniards* (New Haven: Durrie & Peck, 1832), 73–75.
2. G.P. Quackenbos, *Elementary History of the United States* (New York: D. Appleton, 1869), 7–10.
3. Thomas Wentworth Higginson, *Young Folks' History of the United States* (Boston: Lee and Shepard, 1885), 32–35.
4. Wilbur F. Gordy, *Stories of Early American History* (New York: Charles Scribner's Sons, 1913), 5–9.
5. Roman Coffman, *The Story of America: The Age of Discovery, Book I* (Dansville, NY: F.A. Owen, 1927), 38–42.
6. Irving Robert Melbo, *Our America: A Textbook for Elementary School History and Social Studies* (Indianapolis, IN: Bobbs-Merrill, 1948), 15–21.
7. Ernest R. May, *A Proud Nation* (Evanston, IL: McDougal, Littell, 1985), 35–36.

3. POCAHONTAS AND CAPTAIN JOHN SMITH

1. Benson J. Lossing, *A Primary History of the United States* (New York: Mason Brothers, 1860), 35–36.
2. G.P. Quackenbos, *Elementary History of the United States* (New York: D. Appleton, 1869), 30–32.
3. Edward Ellis, *The Eclectic Primary History of the United States* (New York: American Book Company, 1884), 30–33.
4. Thomas Wentworth Higginson, *Young Folks' History of the United States* (Boston: Lee and Shepard, 1885), 115–16.
5. William H. Mace, *A Primary History: Stories of Heroism* (Chicago: Rand McNally, 1909), 57–63.
6. Henry Eldridge Bourne and Elbert Jay Benton, *Story of America and Great Americans* (Boston: D.C. Heath, 1923), 65–66.
7. George Earl Freeland and James Truslow Adams, *America's Progress in Civilization* (New York: Charles Scribner's Sons, 1946), 60.
8. JoAnne Buggey, *America! America!* (Glenview, IL: Scott Foresman, 1977), 86–89.
9. Lewis Paul Todd and Merle Curti, *Triumph of the American Nation* (Chicago: Harcourt Brace Jovanovich, 1986), 23–24.

4. ANNE HUTCHINSON

1. Benson J. Lossing, *A Primary History of the United States* (New York: Mason Brothers, 1860), 63.
2. Thomas Wentworth Higginson, *Young Folks' History of the United States* (Boston: Lee and Shepard, 1885), 69–71.
3. William Backus Guitteau, *Our United States: A History for Upper Grammar Grades and Junior High School* (New York: Silver, Burdett, 1930), 89.
4. George Earl Freeland and James Truslow Adams, *America's Progress in Civilization* (New York: Charles Scribner's Sons, 1946), 66.
5. JoAnne Buggey, *America! America!* (Glenview, IL: Scott Foresman and Company, 1977), 93–94.

6. James West Davidson and John E. Batchelor, *The American Nation* (Englewood Cliffs, NJ: Prentice-Hall, 1986), 103.

5. THE PEQUOT WAR

1. Noah Webster, *History of the United States: To Which is Prefixed a Brief Historical Account of our [English] Ancesters, from the dispersal at Babel, to their Migration to America, and of the Conquest of South America by the Spaniards* (New Haven: Durrie & Peck, 1832), 125–26.
2. Benson J. Lossing, *A Primary History of the United States* (New York: Mason Brothers, 1860), 48–49.
3. G.P. Quackenbos, *Elementary History of the United States* (New York: D. Appleton, 1869), 46–49.
4. Thomas Wentworth Higginson, *Young Folks' History of the United States* (Boston: Lee and Shepard, 1885), 134–6.
5. John J. Anderson, *New Grammar School History of the United States* (New York: Clark and Maynard, 1888), 76–77.
6. Thomas B. Lawler, *A Primary History of the United States* (Boston: Ginn, 1905), 81–82.
7. Wilbur F. Gordy, *Stories of Early American History* (New York: Charles Scribner's Sons, 1913), 178–81.
8. Clyde B. Moore, Fred B. Painter, Helen M. Carpenter, and Gertrude M. Lewis, *Building Our America* (New York: Charles Scribner's Sons, 1955), 173–74.
9. Lewis Paul Todd and Merle Curti, *Rise of the American Nation* (New York: Harcourt Brace Jovanovich, 1977), 30.
10. James West Davidson and John E. Batchelor, *The American Nation* (Englewood Cliffs, NJ: Prentice-Hall, 1986), 104–5.

6. THE SALEM WITCH TRIALS

1. John J. Anderson, *A Grammar School History of the United States* (New York: Clark and Maynard, 1875), 35.
2. Edward Ellis, *The Eclectic Primary History of the United States* (New York: American Book Company, 1884), 54–55.
3. William Backus Guitteau, *Our United States: A History for Upper Grammar Grades and Junior High School* (New York: Silver, Burdett, 1930), 138.
4. JoAnne Buggey, *America! America!* (Glenview, IL: Scott Foresman, 1977), 125.
5. Beverly J. Armento, Jacqueline M. Cordova, J. Jorge Klor de Alva, Gary B. Nash, Franklin Ng, Christopher L. Salter, Louis E. Wilson, and Karen K. Wixson, *America Will Be* (Boston: Houghton Mifflin, 1999), 194.

7. THE BOSTON MASSACRE

1. Noah Webster, *History of the United States: To Which is Prefixed a Brief Historical Account of our [English] Ancestors, from the dispersal at Babel, to their Migration to America, and of the Conquest of South America by the Spaniards* (New Haven: Durrie & Peck, 1832), 224.
2. Benson J. Lossing, *A Primary History of the United States* (New York: Mason Brothers, 1860), 112–14.
3. John J. Anderson, *A Grammar School History of the United States* (New York: Clark and Maynard, 1873), 66–67.
4. Thomas Wentworth Higginson, *Young Folks' History of the United States* (Boston: Lee and Shepard, 1885), 166–69.

5. William H. Mace, *A Primary History: Stories of Heroism* (Chicago: Rand McNally, 1909), 152–53.
6. Glenn W. Moon and John H. MacGowan, *Story of Our Land and People* (New York: Henry Holt, 1955), 133.
7. Harold H. Eibling, Fred M. King, and James Harlow, *History of Our United States* (River Forest, IL: Laidlaw Brothers, 1966), 118–19.
8. Wayne E. King and John L. Napp, *United States History* (Circle Pines, MN: American Guidance Service, 2001), 101.

8. LEXINGTON AND CONCORD

1. Noah Webster, *History of the United States: To Which is Prefixed a Brief Historical Account of our [English] Ancestors, from the dispersal at Babel, to their Migration to America, and of the Conquest of South America by the Spaniards* (New Haven: Durrie & Peck, 1832), 231–32.
2. Benson J. Lossing, *A Primary History of the United States* (New York: Mason Brothers, 1860), 119.
3. G.P. Quackenbos, *Elementary History of the United States* (New York: D. Appleton, 1869), 83–85.
4. Edward Ellis, *The Eclectic Primary History of the United States* (New York: American Book Company, 1884), 97–98.
5. Henry William Elson, *A Guide to the United States History for Young Readers* (New York: Doubleday, Page, 1912), 73–74.
6. William Backus Guitteau, *Our United States: A History for Upper Grammar Grades and Junior High School* (New York: Silver, Burdett, 1930), 163–64.
7. George Earl Freeland and James Truslow Adams, *America's Progress in Civilization* (New York: Charles Scribner's Sons, 1946), 168–71.
8. Kenneth Bailey, Elizabeth Brooke, and John J. Farrell, *The American Adventure* (San Francisco: Field Educational Publications, 1970), 113–14.
9. Carlton L. Jackson and Vito Perrone, *Two Centuries of Progress* (Mission Hills, CA: Glencoe/McGraw-Hill, 1991), 97–98.

9. THE BATTLE OF TRENTON

1. Noah Webster, *History of the United States: To Which is Prefixed a Brief Historical Account of our [English] Ancestors, from the dispersal at Babel, to their Migration to America, and of the Conquest of South America by the Spaniards* (New Haven: Durrie & Peck, 1832), 221–22.
2. Edward Ellis, *The Eclectic Primary History of the United States* (New York: American Book Company, 1884), 108–9.
3. William H. Mace, *A Primary History: Stories of Heroism* (Chicago: Rand McNally, 1909), 177–79.
4. Henry Eldridge Bourne and Elbert Jay Benton, *Story of America and Great Americans* (Boston: D.C. Heath, 1923), 159–60.
5. Glenn W. Moon and John H. MacGowan, *Story of Our Land and People* (New York: Henry Holt, 1955), 148.
6. Edna McGuire and Thomas B. Portwood, *Our Free Nation* (New York: Macmillan, 1961), 164–65.
7. Clarence L. Ver Steeg and Carol Ann Skinner, *Exploring America's Heritage* (Lexington, MA: D.C. Heath, 1991), 256.

10. GEORGE ROGERS CLARK

1. John J. Anderson, *New Grammar School History of the United States* (New York: Clark and Maynard, 1888), 183–85.
2. Thomas B. Lawler, *A Primary History of the United States* (Boston: Ginn, 1905), 112–14.
3. Henry Eldridge Bourne and Elbert Jay Benton, *Story of America and Great Americans* (Boston: D.C. Heath, 1923), 165.
4. Clyde B. Moore, Fred B. Painter, Helen M. Carpenter, and Gertrude M. Lewis, *Building Our America* (New York: Charles Scribner's Sons, 1951), 249–50.
5. Kenneth Bailey, Elizabeth Brooke, and John J. Farrell, *The American Adventure* (San Francisco: Field Educational Publications, 1970), 126–27.
6. Clarence L. Ver Steeg and Carol Ann Skinner, *Exploring America's Heritage* (Lexington, MA: D.C. Heath, 1991), 259.

11. WOMEN IN THE AMERICAN REVOLUTION

1. G.P. Quackenbos, *Elementary History of the United States* (New York: D. Appleton, 1869), 111.
2. Ibid., 112–13.
3. Oscar Gerson, *History Primer* (New York: Hinds, Heydon and Eldridge, 1906), 91–93.
4. John W. Wayland, *History Stories for Primary Grades* (New York: Macmillan, 1922), 26–28.
5. Ibid., 29–30.
6. Ibid., 175–81.
7. Rolla M. Tryon, *The American Nation: Yesterday and Today* (Boston: Ginn, 1934), 120–21.
8. George Earl Freeland and James Truslow Adams, *America's Progress in Civilization* (New York: Charles Scribner's Sons, 1946), 204–5.
9. Lewis Paul Todd and Merle Curti, *Rise of the American Nation* (New York: Harcourt Brace Jovanovich, 1977), 118.
10. Beverly J. Armento, Jacqueline M. Cordova, J. Jorge Klor de Alva, Gary B. Nash, Franklin Ng, Christopher L. Salter, Louis E. Wilson, and Karen K. Wixson, *America Will Be* (Boston: Houghton Mifflin, 1999), 285–86.

12. SHAYS' REBELLION

1. G.P. Quackenbos, *Elementary History of the United States* (New York: D. Appleton, 1869), 128–29.
2. John J. Anderson, *New Grammar School History of the United States* (New York: Clark and Maynard, 1888), 203.
3. Rolla M. Tryon, *The American Nation: Yesterday and Today* (Boston: Ginn, 1934), 128–29.
4. Lewis Paul Todd and Merle Curti, *Rise of the American Nation* (New York: Harcourt Brace Jovanovich, 1977), 135.
5. Beverly J. Armento, Jacqueline M. Cordova, J. Jorge Klor de Alva, Gary B. Nash, Franklin Ng, Christopher L. Salter, Louis E. Wilson, and Karen K. Wixson, *America Will Be* (Boston: Houghton Mifflin, 1999), 295–96.

13. THE BARBARY PIRATES

1. Benson J. Lossing, *A Primary History of the United States* (New York: Mason Brothers, 1860), 178–79.
2. G.P. Quackenbos, *Elementary History of the United States* (New York: D. Appleton, 1869), 136–37.
3. Edward Ellis, *The Eclectic Primary History of the United States* (New York: American Book Company, 1884), 151.
4. William Backus Guitteau, *Our United States: A History for Upper Grammar Grades and Junior High School* (New York: Silver, Burdett, 1930), 262–63.
5. Edna McGuire and Thomas B. Portwood, *Our Free Nation* (New York: Macmillan, 1961), 226–27.
6. Kenneth Bailey, Elizabeth Brooke, and John J. Farrell, *The American Adventure* (San Francisco: Field Educational Publications, 1970), 154.
7. James West Davidson and John E. Batchelor, *The American Nation* (Englewood Cliffs, NJ: Prentice-Hall, 1986), 250.

14. SACAGAWEA

1. G.P. Quackenbos, *Elementary History of the United States* (New York: D. Appleton, 1869), 138.
2. William H. Mace, *A Primary History: Stories of Heroism* (Chicago: Rand McNally, 1909), 325–29.
3. William Backus Guitteau, *Our United States: A History for Upper Grammar Grades and Junior High School* (New York: Silver, Burdett, 1930), 260–61.
4. Clyde B. Moore, Fred B. Painter, Helen M. Carpenter, and Gertrude M. Lewis, *Building Our America* (New York: Charles Scribner's Sons, 1951), 296–301.
5. Harold H. Eibling, Fred M. King, and James Harlow, *History of Our United States* (River Forest, IL: Laidlaw Brothers, 1966), 224–25.
6. Ernest R. May, *A Proud Nation* (Evanston, IL: McDougal, Littell, 1985), 308–9.

15. TECUMSEH

1. Benson J. Lossing, *A Primary History of the United States* (New York: Mason Brothers, 1860), 183–84.
2. G.P. Quackenbos, *Elementary History of the United States* (New York: D. Appleton, 1869), 140–43.
3. John J. Anderson, *New Grammar School History of the United States* (New York: Clark and Maynard, 1888), 241–43.
4. Charles Morris, *Primary History of the United States: The Story of Our Country for Young Folks* (Philadelphia: J.B. Lippincott, 1916), 189–92.
5. William Backus Guitteau, *Our United States: A History for Upper Grammar Grades and Junior High School* (New York: Silver, Burdett, 1930), 271–72.
6. Harold H. Eibling, Fred M. King, and James Harlow, *History of Our United States* (River Forest, IL: Laidlaw Brothers, 1966), 215–16.
7. James West Davidson and John E. Batchelor, *The American Nation* (Englewood Cliffs, NJ: Prentice-Hall, 1986), 254–55.

16. THE MONROE DOCTRINE

1. John J. Anderson, *A Grammar School History of the United States* (New York: Clark & Maynard, 1873), 136.

2. Thomas Wentworth Higginson, *Young Folks' History of the United States* (Boston: Lee and Shepard, 1885), 258.
3. Thomas B. Lawler, *A Primary History of the United States* (Boston: Ginn, 1905), 156.
4. William Backus Guitteau, *Our United States: A History for Upper Grammar Grades and Junior High School* (New York: Silver, Burdett, 1930), 308–9.
5. George Earl Freeland and James Truslow Adams, *America's Progress in Civilization* (New York: Charles Scribner's Sons, 1946), 258.
6. Kenneth Bailey, Elizabeth Brooke, and John J. Farrell, *The American Adventure* (San Francisco: Field Educational Publications, 1970), 166.
7. Clarence L. Ver Steeg and Carol Ann Skinner, *Exploring America's Heritage* (Lexington, MA: D.C. Heath, 1991), 428.

17. THE ALAMO

1. John J. Anderson, *New Grammar School History of the United States* (New York: Clark and Maynard, 1888), 274.
2. James A. Woodburn, *The Makers of America* (New York: Longmans, Green, 1922), 231–34.
3. Wilbur F. Gordy, *Stories of Later American History* (New York: Charles Scribner's Sons, 1923), 208–11.
4. Glenn W. Moon and John H. MacGowan, *Story of Our Land and People* (New York: Henry Holt, 1955), 282–83.
5. Harold H. Eibling, Fred M. King, and James Harlow, *History of Our United States* (River Forest, IL: Laidlaw Brothers, 1966), 296–97.
6. Kenneth Bailey, Elizabeth Brooke, and John J. Farrell, *The American Adventure* (San Francisco: Field Educational Publications, 1970), 174.
7. Beverly J. Armento, Jacqueline M. Cordova, J. Jorge Klor de Alva, Gary B. Nash, Franklin Ng, Christopher L. Salter, Louis E. Wilson, and Karen K. Wixson, *America Will Be* (Boston: Houghton Mifflin, 1999), 372–73.

18. THE TRAIL OF TEARS

1. Benson J. Lossing, *A Primary History of the United States* (New York: Mason Brothers, 1860), 206.
2. Clyde B. Moore, Fred B. Painter, Helen M. Carpenter, and Gertrude M. Lewis, *Building Our America* (New York: Charles Scribner's Sons, 1951), 332–33.
3. Harold H. Eibling, Fred M. King, and James Harlow, *History of Our United States* (River Forest, IL: Laidlaw Brothers, 1966), 281.
4. Lewis Paul Todd and Merle Curti, *Rise of the American Nation* (New York: Harcourt Brace Jovanovich, 1977), 239–40.
5. Roger LaRaus, Harry P. Morris, and Robert Sobel, *Challenge of Freedom* (Mission Hills, CA: Glencoe, 1990), 192–93.

19. THE MEXICAN-AMERICAN WAR, 1846–1848

1. Benson J. Lossing, *A Primary History of the United States* (New York: Mason Brothers, 1860), 212–13.
2. John J. Anderson, *A Grammar School History of the United States* (New York: Clark and Maynard, 1875), 143–44.
3. Thomas Wentworth Higginson, *Young Folks' History of the United States* (Boston: Lee and Shepard, 1885), 274–75.

4. James A. Woodburn, *The Makers of America* (New York: Longmans, Green, 1922), 235–37.

5. William Backus Guitteau, *Our United States: A History for Upper Grammar Grades and Junior High School* (New York: Silver, Burdett, 1930), 362–63.

6. Clyde B. Moore, Fred B. Painter, Helen M. Carpenter, and Gertrude M. Lewis, *Building Our America* (New York: Charles Scribner's Sons, 1951), 336–37.

7. Harold H. Eibling, Fred M. King, and James Harlow, *History of Our United States* (River Forest, IL: Laidlaw Brothers, 1966), 299.

8. JoAnne Buggey, *America! America!* (Glenview, IL: Scott Foresman, 1977), 340–41.

9. Beverly J. Armento, Jacqueline M. Cordova, J. Jorge Klor de Alva, Gary B. Nash, Franklin Ng, Christopher L. Salter, Louis E. Wilson, and Karen K. Wixson, *America Will Be* (Boston: Houghton Mifflin, 1999), 374.

20. THE MORMONS

1. Benson J. Lossing, *A Primary History of the United States* (New York: Mason Brothers, 1860), 218–19.

2. G.P. Quackenbos, *Elementary History of the United States* (New York: D. Appleton, 1869), 174.

3. Thomas Wentworth Higginson, *Young Folks' History of the United States* (Boston: Lee and Shepard, 1885), 270–71.

4. Henry Eldridge Bourne and Elbert Jay Benton, *Story of America and Great Americans* (Boston: D.C. Heath, 1923), 225–26.

5. Glenn W. Moon and John H. MacGowan, *Story of Our Land and People* (New York: Henry Holt, 1955), 291–93.

6. James West Davidson and John E. Batchelor, *The American Nation* (Englewood Cliffs, NJ: Prentice-Hall, 1986), 325–27.

21. DRED SCOTT

1. Thomas Wentworth Higginson, *Young Folks' History of the United States* (Boston: Lee and Shepard, 1885), 286.

2. John J. Anderson, *New Grammar School History of the United States* (New York: Clark and Maynard, 1888), 296.

3. Thomas B. Lawler, *A Primary History of the United States* (Boston: Ginn, 1905), 187–88.

4. William Backus Guitteau, *Our United States: A History for Upper Grammar Grades and Junior High School* (New York: Silver, Burdett, 1930), 391–92.

5. JoAnne Buggey, *America! America!* (Glenview, IL: Scott Foresman, 1977), 367–68.

6. Roger LaRaus, Harry P. Morris, and Robert Sobel, *Challenge of Freedom* (Mission Hills, CA: Glencoe, 1990), 276–77.

22. SLAVERY

1. John J. Anderson, *New Grammar School History of the United States* (New York: Clark and Maynard, 1888), 120–22.

2. Oscar Gerson, *History Primer* (New York: Hinds, Heydon & Eldridge, 1906), 104.

3. Wilber F. Gordy, *Stories of Later American History* (New York: Charles Scribner's Sons, 1923), 159–63.

4. Rolla M. Tryon, *The American Nation: Yesterday and Today* (Boston: Ginn, 1934), 283–87.
5. JoAnne Buggey, *America! America!* (Glenview, IL: Scott Foresman, 1977), 354–58.
6. Roger LaRaus, Harry P. Morris, and Robert Sobel, *Challenge of Freedom* (Mission Hills, CA: Glencoe, 1990), 212–13.

23. AFRICAN AMERICAN SOLDIERS

1. Mara L. Pratt, *American History Stories, Vol. 1* (Boston: Educational Publishing Co., 1890), 116–17.
2. James West Davidson and Michael B. Stoff, *The American Nation* (Upper Saddle River, NJ: Pearson Education, 2003), 498–99.

24. AFRICAN AMERICANS DURING RECONSTRUCTION

1. G.P. Quackenbos, *Elementary History of the United States* (New York: D. Appleton, 1869), 198.
2. John J. Anderson, *A Grammar School History of the United States* (New York: Clark and Maynard, 1875), 183.
3. Henry Eldridge Courne and Elbert Jay Benton, *Story of America and Great Americans* (Boston: D.C. Heath, 1923), 276.
4. William Backus Guitteau, *Our United States: A History for Upper Grammar Grades and Junior High School* (New York: Silver, Burdett, 1930), 470–72.
5. Rolla M. Tryon, *The American Nation: Yesterday and Today* (Boston: Ginn, 1934), 341–44.
6. Glenn W. Moon and John H. MacGowan, *Story of Our Land and People* (New York: Henry Holt, 1955), 387–91.
7. Harold H. Eibling, Fred M. King, and James Harlow, *History of Our United States* (River Forest, IL: Laidlaw Brothers, 1966), 356–59.
8. Lewis Paul Todd and Merle Curti, *Rise of the American Nation* (New York: Harcourt Brace Jovanovich, 1977), 367–68.
9. Carlton L. Jackson and Vito Perrone, *Two Centuries of Progress* (Mission Hills, CA: Glencoe/McGraw-Hill, 1991), 324–26.

25. ANDREW CARNEGIE AND THE HOMESTEAD STRIKE

1. Glenn W. Moon and John H. MacGowan, *Story of Our Land and People* (New York: Henry Holt, 1955), 423–25.
2. Edna McGuire and Thomas B. Portwood, *Our Free Nation* (New York: Macmillan, 1961), 443.
3. JoAnne Buggey, *America! America!* (Glenview, IL: Scott Foresman, 1977), 445.
4. Roger LaRaus, Harry P. Morris, and Robert Sobel, *Challenge of Freedom* (Mission Hills, CA: Glencoe, 1990), 403–4.

26. WOUNDED KNEE MASSACRE

1. Lewis Paul Todd and Merle Curti, *Triumph of the American Nation* (Chicago: Harcourt Brace Jovanovich, 1986), 493–94.
2. Wayne E. King and John L. Napp, *United States History* (Circle Pines, MN: American Guidance Service, 2001), 360–61.

27. IMMIGRATION

1. Thomas Wentworth Higginson, *Young Folks' History of the United States* (Boston: Lee and Shepard, 1885), 336–38.
2. Henry William Elson, *A Guide to the United States History for Young Readers* (New York: Doubleday, Page, 1912), 322–27.
3. William Backus Guitteau, *Our United States: A History for Upper Grammar Grades and Junior High School* (New York: Silver, Burdett, 1930), 513–14.
4. Glenn W. Moon and John H. MacGowan, *Story of Our Land and People* (New York: Henry Holt, 1955), 496–99.
5. Kenneth Bailey, Elizabeth Brooke, and John J. Farrell, *The American Adventure* (San Francisco: Field Educational Publications, 1970), 227–28.
6. Ernest R. May, *A Proud Nation* (Evanston, IL: McDougal, Littell, 1985), 479–82.

28. McKINLEY ASSASSINATION

1. James A. Woodburn, *The Makers of America* (New York: Longmans, Green, 1922), 310.
2. George Earl Freeland and James Truslow Adams, *America's Progress in Civilization* (New York: Charles Scribner's Sons, 1946), 468.
3. Edna McGuire and Thomas B. Portwood, *Our Free Nation* (New York: Macmillan, 1961), 524.
4. Wayne E. King and John L. Napp, *United States History* (Circle Pines, MN: American Guidance Service, 2001), 433.

29. THE PHILIPPINE-AMERICAN WAR

1. Thomas B. Lawler, *A Primary History of the United States* (Boston: Ginn, 1905), 237–38.
2. Charles Morris, *Primary History of the United States: The Story of Our County for Young Folks* (Philadelphia: J.B. Lippincott, 1916), 246.
3. William Backus Guitteau, *Our United States: A History for Upper Grammar Grades and Junior High School* (New York: Silver, Burdett, 1930), 533.
4. George Earl Freeland and James Truslow Adams, *America's Progress in Civilization* (New York: Charles Scribner's Sons, 1946), 466.
5. Glenn W. Moon and John H. MacGowan, *Story of Our Land and People* (New York: Henry Holt, 1955), 523–25.
6. Harold H. Eibling, Fred M. King, and James Harlow, *History of Our United States* (River Forest, IL: Laidlaw Brothers, 1966), 487–88.
7. Carlton L. Jackson and Vito Perrone, *Two Centuries of Progress* (Mission Hills, CA: Glencoe/McGraw-Hill, 1991), 389–90.

INDEX